report
2000:
a man's guide
to women

report
2000:
a man's guide
to women

wild nights

hot days

perfect relationships

great sex

RODALE

edited by Larry Keller

Sex and Values at Rodale

We believe that an active and healthy sex life, based on mutual consent and respect between partners, is an important component of physical and mental well-being. We also respect that sex is a private matter and that each person has a different opinion of what sexual practices or levels of discourse are appropriate. Rodale is committed to offering responsible, practical advice about sexual matters, supported by accredited professionals and legitimate scientific research. Our goal—for sex and all other topics—is to publish information that empowers people's lives.

Notice

This book is intended as a reference volume only, not as a medical manual. All health information given here is designed to help you make informed decisions about your sex life and health. It is not intended as a substitute for any treatment that may have been prescribed by your doctor. If you suspect that you have a medical problem, we urge you to seek competent medical help.

The credits for this book appear on page 261.

ISBN 1–57954–230–1 hardcover

Distributed to the book trade by St. Martin's Press

2   4   6   8   10   9   7   5   3   1   hardcover

Visit us on the Web at www.rodalebooks.com, or call us toll-free at (800) 848-4735.

RODALE

WE INSPIRE AND ENABLE PEOPLE TO IMPROVE
THEIR LIVES AND THE WORLD AROUND THEM

Report 2000: A Man's Guide to Women Staff

MANAGING EDITOR: Ken Winston Caine

EDITOR: Larry Keller

CONTRIBUTING WRITERS: Jeffrey Bouley, Ken Winston Caine, Brian Chichester, Stephanie Dolgoff, Matt Fitzgerald, Perry Garfinkel, Greg Gutfeld, Sarí Harrar, Bel Henderson, Larry Keller, Christian Millman, Donna Raskin, Kenton Robinson, Julia VanTine, Stephanie Williams

ASSOCIATE ART DIRECTOR: Charles Beasley

INTERIOR AND COVER DESIGNER: Tanja Lipinski Cole

ILLUSTRATOR: Christian Musselman

CARTOONIST: Leo Cullum

ASSOCIATE RESEARCH MANAGER: Jane Unger Hahn

BOOK PROJECT RESEARCHER: Deborah Pedron

COPY EDITOR: Kathryn A. Cressman

PRODUCTION EDITOR: Marilyn Hauptly

LAYOUT DESIGNER: Donna G. Rossi

STUDIO MANAGER: Leslie M. Keefe

MANUFACTURING COORDINATORS: Brenda Miller, Jodi Schaffer, Patrick Smith

Rodale Active Living Books

VICE PRESIDENT AND PUBLISHER: Neil Wertheimer

EXECUTIVE EDITOR: Susan Clarey

EDITORIAL DIRECTOR: Michael Ward

MARKETING DIRECTOR: Janine Slaughter

PRODUCT MARKETING MANAGER: Kris Siessmayer

BOOK MANUFACTURING DIRECTOR: Helen Clogston

MANUFACTURING MANAGERS: Eileen Bauder, Mark Krahforst

RESEARCH MANAGER: Ann Gossy Yermish

COPY MANAGER: Lisa D. Andruscavage

PRODUCTION MANAGER: Robert V. Anderson Jr.

OFFICE MANAGER: Jacqueline Dornblaser

OFFICE STAFF: Suzanne Lynch Holderman, Julie Kehs, Mary Lou Stephen, Catherine E. Strouse

contents

3 PROMOTE PERPETUAL PASSION

4 TUNE UP YOUR SEX MACHINE

5 ORCHESTRATE SIZZLING DATES

6 SEX IN THE PUBLIC EYE

7 SIDESTEP THE SEX POLICE

8 SPOT-CHECK CYBERSEX

introduction

Sex is as old and natural as breathing. Both seem simple enough at first blush: in/out, in/out. . . .

But sex is ever so much more pleasurable and oh-so-much more complicated.

Anything that hinges on the balance of the ever delightful and delicate male-female dynamic has incredible potential for passion, pleasure, and pain—and constant evolution.

We probably don't need to tell you that there's not much new about the act of breathing. But there is always something new in the art of sex. Hence, *Report 2000* (and *Report 2001, 2002, 2003*, and so on, to come). Stick with us, and you'll never be left behind.

We promise to keep you joyfully informed of all the latest talk, technique, and think so you may remain a healthy, happy, sophisticated, and wholesome explorer on the sexual frontier. So that you—and your partner(s)—can enjoy your sex lives *all* your lives. We'll tell you everything that's out there that works—and what doesn't work—to keep your relationships passionate.

What could possibly be new in the world of sex? Consider these recent developments that are covered in depth in this year's book.

● Womenspeak and womenthink

What women want and what they consider desirable in a man continue to shift. Sometimes for good reason. Sometimes for reasons that no man will ever understand. But with this book as your advisor, you'll know how to keep your relationships vibrant and exciting. You'll learn the latest theories on how to talk to women—and how to decode their words and actions.

● Sex appeal

Science is on the verge of busting baldness, and today men have more options than ever to deal with hair loss so they can enter the boardroom or bedroom with greater confidence than before. We give you the bald truth about the latest cures.

● The Internet

It brings us first-class sexual-health advice and low-class and no-class pornography. We tell you how to find the best of it all and how to talk sexy online.

● Science and medicine

With Viagra, they've miraculously pumped up the previously dormant sex lives of thousands of men—and more passion potions are on the horizon. Should you call your doc?

● Laws and mores

From the really needed to the ridiculous. We give you simple, straight advice on how to maneuver through the tricky minefield of sexual harassment laws and how to conduct an office romance—if you are so inclined.

● Life after divorce

Step by successful step, we lead you into the contemporary dating scene.

● The romantic meal

We tell you not where to buy it, but how to prepare it and serve it and utterly and seductively impress your woman.

● Passionate weekends

Managing the perfect getaway is an art form. You, now, can be an artist. (Women do tend to get excited by the artistic types.)

This edition is stuffed, packed, crammed, loaded, exploding with dynamite, expert guy-to-guy advice guaranteed to ignite your love life. Time for me to step aside so you can get down to the real nitty-gritty.

Carry on,

Ken Winston Caine
Managing Editor

SURVIVE
THE WAR
OF THE SEXES

Funny thing about clichés. As trite as they are, most ring true. Including this one: Can't live with 'em; can't live without 'em.

Men and women have forever been eyeing each other as suspiciously as matadors and bulls. Some recent books by women about men warn of 101 lies that men tell women and 187 types of men to avoid.

Men are equally wary. Most of us like women. We genuinely like them. We just don't get women. Yet we gamely forge onward into the darkness.

In this section, we attempt to shed some light on the gender wars. Maybe these words will provide solace or insight as you endure your own battles. But if you're still in the dark, there may be nothing else to say but this: Can't live with 'em; can't live without 'em.

TOP TEN

Turn-Ons

Ten things that women say are turn-ons, according to Extraordinary Togetherness *by Sarí Harrar and Julia VanTine.*

1 Jeans and a sport jacket

2 Work boots

3 Nice to her parents and to children

4 Witty banter

5 Gives small gifts for no reason at all

6 Good stereo system

7 Good music collection

8 A massage

9 Candlelight

10 Showering together

MUST READS

Eight Ways She Jerks Your Chain

Ever find yourself at a flower show with your partner rather than watching the televised Dallas Cowboys cheerleader tryouts you looked forward to all week? Ever wonder how the hell this happened? Stephanie Dolgoff tells us how. She may be tried as a traitor for this but, fortunately for us, she revealed to Men's Health *magazine precisely how wily women snooker us hapless men into these and other acts without our even knowing it. These are the secrets.*

Women are sneaky creatures. In fact, ever since Eve snookered Adam into eating that apple, women have had a long, glorious history of getting men to do exactly what they want, usually without the guys realizing they've been gotten at all. (Disagree? Then explain that long, expensive weekend you spent tossing back tea at the Lace House Victorian bed-and-breakfast.)

As a woman, I've long been sworn to secrecy about how my sex pulls this off. However, since *Men's Health* promised me a tidy sum to tell what I know about this subject—and since, for cash money, I'd rat out my grandmother for stealing packets of Sweet'N Low from the diner—the time has finally come to reveal all.

To follow: eight devious maneuvers we women use to get what we want, why you men fall for them, and how you can avoid heading down the path that put Adam in so much trouble.

Sneaky Trick #1: The Enthusiastic Endorsement

Even if you're a decent dresser, your mate probably wouldn't mind making alterations to your wardrobe. Though she didn't pick out that hideous tie you're wearing, she did pick you. Thus, she feels entitled to wardrobe input.

But how can she put her fashion stamp on you when direct criticism of your Charlie Daniels Band T-shirt collection usually just makes you defensive? This is where the following trick comes in: The minute you put on a piece of clothing your mate actually approves of, she'll suddenly become more breathless than Newt Gingrich doing wind sprints. "I loooove that shirt! It makes you look so . . . I don't know . . . broad across the shoulders." What she's trying to do is convince you that such fawning could come your way all the time, if only you'd wear more duds like this one. Before long, you're ordering everything in the J. Crew catalog.

● **What to do if your mate pulls this on you:**
Watch out—you can quickly start looking like a Ken doll dressed in the latest fashions. So signal Barbie to back off. "Just say, 'Thanks, I'm glad you like it. But for the record, you're not going to like all the shirts I buy,'" advises Jane Greer, Ph.D., a couples therapist in New York City.

Sneaky Trick #2:
The "Just Some Guy I Work With" Ploy

Every once in a while, your partner may feel like you're not paying enough attention to her—and that's when she'll resort to this trick. For no apparent reason, she'll casually mention a guy at her office. "I was having lunch today with Chris, this guy I work with, and he said the funniest thing." Pause. Smile. "You know, we should really fix him up with somebody."

She's trying to spark some jealousy. Since you've never met Chris, you have no clue if he's a mailroom dweeb or a studly UPS driver parading around in those hunky brown shorts. In fact, all you really know is your mate thinks Chris is funny—and a romantic match for someone. Presto! Just like that, you're feeling competitive and you're morphing into Super Mate.

● **What to do if your mate pulls this on you:**
Neutralize it by calling her bluff. "Say, 'Set Chris up? That's a great idea! Who'd you have in mind?'" advises Dr. Greer. Seeing that you're not threatened by Chris, she'll never mention him again.

perfect figures

Some 65 percent of women surveyed in a poll conducted for NBC News but only 43 percent of men surveyed said that efforts to promote equality for women have not gone far enough. In the same poll, 78 percent of men said sex roles in marriage today are more equal than traditional, compared to 61 percent of women.

Sneaky Trick #3:
The "You're So Smart" Strategy

Guys space out when it comes to gift-giving occasions. So how do we remind you about your mom's birthday? We take advantage of your shoddy memory and let you think one of our brilliant ideas was yours.

Us: Weren't you talking about what to give your mom for her birthday? I saw this scarf she'd like and I remembered what you said.

YOU (TAKING CREDIT WHERE NONE IS DUE): Oh, yeah, I guess I was saying we should buy her a scarf. Where'd you see it?

● **What to do if your mate pulls this on you:**

Most of the time, this is a win-win situation—your mom scores a new scarf; you look considerate. Just make sure your woman isn't using this trick for nefarious purposes. If you start hearing questions like, "Remember last week, when you said you wanted to stop being a professional juggler and go to medical school instead?" it's time to slam on your mate's brakes.

"A guy needs to say, 'Look, I don't remember the conversation, and I'm not sure that's what I want to do,'" says Dr. Greer.

Sneaky Trick #4: Volume Moderation

This is a sexy game of "you're getting warmer," only with moans and groans instead of words. When my friend Molly first started dating her husband, Rich, she, like most women, had a hard time explaining what she wanted him to do in bed. "When he'd get close to the right spot, I'd become incredibly, unnaturally vocal—like out of a porno video," explains Molly. "He became trained to see the connection."

● **What to do if your mate pulls this on you:**

Give the woman what she wants. The happier she is in bed, the happier you'll be. And if your neighbor complains about the noise? "Try saying, 'It sounds like you're really enjoying this. Does it feel all right?'" advises Ron Wynne, Ph.D., a clinical psychologist in Washington, D.C. "She'll know you're getting the message, and she might be less dramatic in the future."

Sneaky Trick #5: We Buy You Stuff We Want You to Have

Rachel is famous for this one. "I can't stand spending time in Dave's apartment because it's so gross," she explains. "But I'm not his mother, so I refuse to pester him about cleaning it." The alternative? Making it easy for him to clean it himself. "I'll say, 'Oh, I saw these dish towels. And since you were wiping your hands in your chest hair last week, I thought you might like them.'" Rachel comes off as giving, while Dave deduces he should keep his place more habitable.

● **What to do if your mate pulls this on you:**

Analyze what message she's trying to send when she brings you a Dustbuster, an Ab Roller, or any other odd gift. Then decide if that's a change you want to make. If so, say thanks and put the thing to use. If not, accept the gift, but let it lie fallow. "If she wants to spend her money on that stuff, that's cool," says Dr. Wynne. She'll go broke eventually.

Sneaky Trick #6:
The Prolonged Apology

From Clarissa's vast repertoire comes this move, designed to make you do the chores you should probably be doing anyway. As Clarissa is leaving for work, she says to Kyle, "Oh, sweetie, I'm sorry, but I left some dishes in the sink. I'm working until midnight and I have to get up tomorrow at 6:00 A.M. for a conference call, but I should be able to wash them between 1:00 A.M. and 2:00 A.M. Unless the bullet wound in my leg starts acting up." She goes on like this until Kyle says he'll do the dishes.

Women under the age of 40 are just as likely to cheat on their partners as men are.

○ What to do if your mate pulls this on you:

Assess whether you're doing your share of household chores. If so, this is just a ploy to prod you to do her work, too. Say, "You're the best, honey. And try a little Bactine on that bullet wound." But if you really have been slacking off, say, "Sounds like you want me to do the dishes—why don't you just ask?" She'll figure out that there are better ways of achieving what she wants.

Sneaky Trick #7:
The Best-Friend's–Husband Game

Sometimes, a woman has a gripe she's either too embarrassed or too ticked off about to bring up directly. So she invokes the straw man—her best friend's mate. "Jamie never asked me how I was doing when I came home from work," my friend Liza says of her husband. So over dinner one night, Liza told Jamie a story in a tone of sheer outrage: "My friend's husband is so self-involved he never—can you believe it?—asks her how her day was!" Jamie had to agree the guy was a clod. "Since then, he always asks me about my day," Liza reports.

○ What to do if your mate pulls this on you:
Figure out if she's gossiping or trying to tell you something. "If your hands feel clammy, or if you feel guilty, she's probably talking about you," suggests Dr. Wynne. "In that case, joke about it. Say, 'Hmm, he sounds a lot like me.'"

Sneaky Trick #8:
The Major Hair Scare

Nothing will stop a woman from getting a compliment if she wants one. The most effective way of pulling it off? Threatening to alter a part of her physical appearance that she knows you like. "What would you think if I cut my hair?" is one that I have used. (I have long, dark, curly hair, which I've been told is my best feature.) I pose this zinger while casually twisting my hair up and away from my face, as if I'd look equally gorgeous with a GI Jane 'do. The question is usually greeted by silence. Then alarm. Then an ode to the beauty of my lustrous locks.

◉ What to do if your mate pulls this on you:
Pay the woman a compliment. If that's all she wanted, she'll stop bugging you. And if she really was considering chopping off all her hair, you may have spared yourself sack time with Uncle Fester.

Talkin' the Talk

Perhaps nothing so epitomizes the gulf between men and women as the way we communicate—or don't communicate. Sometimes it seems like women are speaking an obtuse foreign language, and we don't have the benefit of a Berlitz course to learn it. Authors Donna Raskin and Larry Keller tackled the subject in these excerpts from Good Loving *and were still talking to each other afterward.*

You know the phrase "the gentle art of conversation"? It was *not* devised by a man.

Men tend to perceive conversation with a mate as a form of competition or challenge—like playing office politics or jockeying for position in the passing lane. When we're asked a question, we don't just answer—we want to give the right answer (or the right excuse). If talking turns into a debate or argument, naturally we want to win it. If the conversation revolves around our partners' problems, 9 times out of 10, we move into advice-giving mode, trying to come up with solutions to the puzzle laid out before us.

Our adversarial attitude toward conversation is not just mental; it's physical, too. Conversation can be as stressful as any physical challenge men face in life. It actually quickens our heart rates and causes our temperatures to rise. Left unchecked, our impulse to wrestle with conversation can also cause tempers to rise and very quickly lead a conversation into the not-so-gentle realm of a full-blown argument. But it doesn't have to be this way.

Top 10 Things Men Should Never Say to Women

She doesn't just talk differently, she listens differently. And some of your passing remarks just aren't as funny to her as they are to you, smart guy. To keep you out of the doghouse, here are 10 lines you shouldn't utter within earshot of your woman.

10 "It's different for guys."

9 "You're just like your mother."

8 "So this is PMS."

7 "What's gotten into you?" (Asked when she initiates sex.)

6 "You're not *that* fat."

5 "Why are you so angry? She didn't mean anything to me."

4 "What's that on your chin?"

3 "I forgot my wallet."

2 "I'll call you."

And the number one thing you should never say:

1 "Why do we need a piece of paper when we already know how we feel?"

Guy Talk

It's the basic nature of men to equate the rigors of conversation with more physical challenges. We don't talk about stuff; we do stuff. We're hands-on, proactive. "Men get their identities from their achievements, not from their relationships," explains Dan Jones, Ph.D., director of the Counseling and Psychological Center at Appalachian State University in Boone, North Carolina. Thus, we have a hard time simply having a talk, empathizing with a partner, commiserating with her. We need the talk to have a point or a goal, or to address a concrete issue that can be solved with advice and specific actions.

This is just the opposite of what women want. Usually, all that they want is to feel that you've heard them, regardless of whether your conversation comes to a specific resolution.

That's not the only way that we differ in conversational style. Just for your own edification, here are some other examples that reveal our competitive leanings when it comes to conversation, says Dr. Jones.

- Men issue commands; women make requests. For example, a man will say, "Close the door," while a woman will ask, "Will you please close the door?" This gives men power and makes women seem subservient.

- Believe it or not, men talk more than women. While women initiate conversations, men interrupt a lot more and thus gain control of the discussion.

- In conversation, men like to give information, not get it. This, by the way, is why we don't like to ask for directions.

Speaking Her Language

Unless you want every conversation to descend into a fight or heated debate, temper your world-conquering approach to conversation, says Dr. Jones. Not only will doing this ease stress in mind and body but it can also make you closer to your partner. To become a conversational man, steal a few pages from your partner's rule book. Follow these precepts and you should find yourself well on the way to becoming a guy who speaks her language. Here's how.

- **Listen up.**
The most obvious advice is the hardest to follow, isn't it? But it's a fact that women usually just want you to listen more than they want your advice. How can you tell when she really wants your advice? She'll ask for it, says Dr. Jones. Wait to hear if she says, "What do you think?" Until then, keep your mouth shut and your ears open.

- **Open up.**
"It takes bravery to make yourself vulnerable," says Dr. Jones. "Men should look at attempts to be intimate as acts of courage." Don't be afraid to make revealing statements about yourself. To a woman, that's what conversation is all about.

- **Calm down.**
Men get very agitated in the face of disagreement. That agitation often propels us to higher levels of anxiety—which explains the rising heart rate and body temperature. So if you feel yourself getting hot under the collar, take five. Explain to your partner that you're having trouble relaxing and that you need a few minutes to calm down so that you can communicate more effectively.

- **Don't get angry if you're sad.**
In conversation, as in life, men have been trained to think the best defense is a good offense. So when we're feeling hurt or sad, rather than express those feel-

ings in a conversation, we'll often repress them and show anger instead, says Dr. Jones. You don't necessarily have to show your hurt feelings if you don't want to, but if you're going to mask those feelings, mask them in a neutral way instead of covering them up with an angry outburst.

● **Practice patience.**

We guys are often impatient with women's conversational style. "When will she get to the point?" we wonder, as our conversational radar scans for opportunities to offer advice, give information, or share one of our own experiences.

Instead, try this experiment, suggested by Jonathan M. Kramer, Ph.D., a clinical psychologist and marriage and family therapist in La Jolla, California, and author of *Why Men Don't Get Enough Sex and Women Don't Get Enough Love*: "Turn off your male conversational radar, take slow, full breaths to relax, and just let yourself be with your woman in conversation. Draw her out. Listen to what she's trying to say. Let her know you understand by paraphrasing what she says. Add whatever seems relevant, but keep the focus on her."

How Women Communicate

In this second excerpt from Good Loving, *authors Donna Raskin and Larry Keller reveal the nuances of womenspeak.*

You knew women were a breed apart from us; you just had no idea to what extent that was true. It's not just breasts, soft skin, and quarts of estrogen that make the difference between the genders. For instance, language skills come more easily to women than men.

This explains why conversations with your woman may have left you in the dust on occasion.

If you're going to hold your own in the arena of verbal communication, it pays to study the tactics of the other side. One of the best ways to learn how to talk to women is to listen to them talk among themselves.

Talking Her Talk

We know you're not about to go and eavesdrop on your partner's next gabfest with her girlfriends. After all, your goal is to understand her better, not bore yourself to death. So, we did the eavesdropping for you. Here are a few key ways that women make conversation. Incorporate these ways into your communication arsenal, and you may find yourself that rarest breed of men—the guy who, according to his woman, "really listens, really understands me."

● **Show her you're still alive.**
At regular intervals, let her know (or at least, let her think) you're listening by nodding or saying "mm-hm." "Better yet," says Jonathan M. Kramer, Ph.D., a clinical psychologist and marriage and family therapist in La Jolla, California, and author of *Why Men Don't Get Enough Sex and Women Don't Get Enough Love*, "try paraphrasing what you think she said. Don't parrot. Rephrase what you heard with an 'Are you saying . . . ?'" If you got it right, she'll be amazed that you really heard her. And if you didn't, she'll clarify what she meant and will be glad that you're sincerely trying to listen and understand her.

● **Offer support.**
After she has vented, you have a choice of offering her two things: advice or sympathy. If she asks for advice, give it. If she doesn't—or you're not sure how she wants you to respond—choose support and sympathy. In conversation, women try hard to gauge what the speaker needs and then offer it to them. Women also ask questions; they don't search for the answer. This gets the other person to open up more.

● **Praise unconditionally.**
Women tend to hear criticism, not praise. So when you say,

Top 10 Things Women Should Never Say to Men

When it comes to conversation, there are a few choice sentences that should never be uttered in a man's presence. You don't have to clue her in; we'll tell her for you. Copy this page and leave it on her pillow. She'll get the hint.

10 "Here's how my last boyfriend did it."

9 "His car/boat/house is bigger than yours."

8 "At least after we're married, I won't have to worry about money."

7 "What are you looking at?"

6 "What are you thinking?"

5 "Deeper."

4 "Does this happen a lot?"

3 "Are you done yet?"

2 "Did you put on deodorant?"

And the number one thing a woman should never say to a man:

1 "Are you sure you know what you're doing?"

"You looked better in that green dress than in the blue dress," they hear, "He doesn't think I look good in the blue dress." When giving praise, leave out the "buts" and any other conditionals. "Look for something positive to say," advises Dr. Kramer. "The blue in that dress goes great with your eyes. The green one makes you look 21."

Controlling Conversation

It's all well and good to understand how women communicate. But what happens when you're in a certain conversational situation with your woman and she starts crying? Or nagging? Or criticizing? Or, worst of all, what if she's winning the argument? Relax. Whatever scenario you find yourself in, here's how you can talk your way out of it.

● **She wants to talk.**
The words men dread the most: "Honey, we have to talk." If your partner says this, your personal defenses may switch to red alert. But before that happens, take a deep breath and ask yourself, "Do I want to talk?" If the answer is yes, great. If it's no, there is no law against telling her you're not in the mood but that you'll be ready in a half-hour (or 2 hours, after the game). But you have to be prepared to keep your word and talk, says Dan Jones, Ph.D., director of the Counseling and Psychological Center at Appalachian State University in Boone, North Carolina.

● **She's babbling.**
One minute she's talking about the hard day she had at work; the next she's blathering about fat knees and wondering why her best friend hasn't sent her a birthday card. When that's the case, take the pressure off yourself. You don't have to solve a problem or offer advice. Just listen.

● **She's crying.**
Good rule of thumb: When she clearly shows an emotional response, respond to the emotion, not the words. "It would be ridiculous to walk away from someone who says she's fine if there are tears streaming down her face," says Dr. Jones. "Respond to the tears by holding her or saying something soothing. You don't necessarily have to force her to make sense of her feelings right in the moment."

● **She's nagging.**
Sorry to tell you this, but studies have shown that women "nag" more than men because we tend not to respond as readily to requests as our female counterparts. Get in the habit of stating specifically when you'll perform a task. For in-

stance, the first time she asks you to take out the garbage, say, "I'll do it right after dinner." And, of course, stick to your promise.

◉ She's winning.

As we mentioned earlier, women are better at conversation than men are. When you're fighting, that fact can be darn frustrating. Scary, too. Often, instances of violence in a home can be traced to moments where men feel frustrated at their inability to adequately defend themselves verbally in an argument, says Dr. Jones.

To make sure that you never even get close to that kind of breaking point, don't be afraid to tell her to slow down, right there in the middle of the fight. Tell her that she has lost you and you can't keep up. Or maybe you can tell her that you need time to think about what she said and figure out what you really think and feel, says Dr. Kramer.

In Praise of Nice Guys

Most of us think of ourselves as nice guys. And who among us hasn't been baffled by the inexplicable romance between an appealing woman and a horse's heinie. Daylle Deanna Schwartz explains the attraction and urges women not to rule out nice guys in her book All Men Are Jerks until Proven Otherwise.

I've gotten to the point of truly appreciating a nice man instead of a jerk. The jerks often seem more exciting, but I don't find getting taken for granted exciting anymore. The jerks are more of a challenge. But I no longer find it challenging to see how much pain I can take from a man before cracking up. The professional jerks have a wonderful facade that's nice to look at. But I no longer enjoy seeing a man who doesn't treat me with respect. Jerks say many wonderful things that I yearn to hear. But these days, my ears only want to hear what's for real. So in the long run, I'll personally take a nice guy over some gorgeous jerk any time. The one thing I've gotten out of being with too many jerks is an appreciation for nice guys. I can live without the excitement of wondering where the pain will come from next.

Men consistently ask me to tell women to give nice guys a chance. They complain women are too judgmental when they first meet men and don't give themselves a chance to get to know a nice guy. They feel that a lot of good guys get passed over because they don't pass the initial test. I agree. I used to be more look-oriented. A guy needed to have a perfect body if he wanted to date me. I attracted young, hot guys, but it didn't make me happy. The price of their egos was too high. That doesn't mean all good-looking guys are jerks. But when one is nice, too, we often wonder what's wrong. Why is he being so nice to us? What's the matter with him? We should wonder instead what's wrong with us for feeling this way. Don't we deserve to be given the best by a man, even if it comes easily? As Lea said in a support group, "I was going out with Jake and found him attractive. But he was very good to me. Listen to me! I say, 'But he was good to me' like it's a bad thing. When a man is very good to me, it puts me off, as it did with Jake. I'm more turned on by men who aren't as nice. It's sick. I dump the good men for ones I complain about constantly. Why can't I be happy with someone decent?"

Many of us don't want to be with a nice guy, even though the men we're attracted to may make us miserable. For years, I wrote off nice guys. They didn't seem sexy. They seemed too easy. I wanted to work hard to keep a guy's interest. I blew off nice guy after nice guy as I fell for the jerks. How I wish I could get some of those nice guys back now! More and more men are trying to be bastards in order to attract women. Do we really want to create more monsters? As Greg admitted, "Most of the time, when I treat a woman well, she dumps me. I'm a good guy. Why don't women appreciate that? These days my guard is up, and I'm hesitant to be nice. Sometimes I put on an attitude and don't do much for a woman I'm out with. But you know what? Then she wants me more. I'm working very hard to get myself to a point where I'm more of a bastard. If that's what women want, I'll give it to them!"

Nice Guys Mean More Responsibility

Sometimes we avoid nice men because it puts pressure on us to reciprocate. If we get involved with men who aren't jerks, we may have to deal with being in a relationship. Being with a jerk is safer: We know it won't last. We have excuses when it doesn't work out. It's less of a commitment. It demands less responsibility on our parts. With a nice guy, you know he'll call when he says he will. With a jerk, you never know. Nice guys are easier to trust. You may be afraid to give your trust to anyone, so you avoid them.

I've finally grown up enough to know I don't need the excitement a jerk can create. In those scenarios, excitement and pain go hand in hand. A soothing, loving, constant relationship is healthier and more satisfying in the long run.

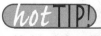

Unload the dishwasher without waiting to be nagged, if you want to keep all quiet on the home front.

I will agree that a challenge is exciting. We like the thrill of the chase, the roller-coaster ride of the challenge. We like to feel we have to work a bit to get him to come our way. It's always more fun to try to attract a man than to have him easily. Open your eyes, sisters—avoiding nice guys is not necessarily healthy for you. If you want a thrill, take your nice guy to an amusement park and go on the roller coaster!

Give a Nice Guy a Chance

Maybe you feel you don't deserve a nice guy. Subconsciously, some of us may not think we're worthy of someone decent. If someone is good to us, we may feel obligated to be good to him. Many of us are more comfortable giving in the sense of groveling to keep a jerk than giving because we're getting good things from a man. Are you open to a healthy relationship? Being with a jerk can take the pressure off because we don't have to take responsibility for our own happiness. If it doesn't work out, we can blame the jerk.

A man who lets us know he's interested can lead to wonderful feelings. How nice if he calls when he says he will. How sweet when he gives us compliments and means them. So what if he's not a jerk—he can still be very attractive. At the last in a series of support group sessions, Barbara came in all excited and told us, "I met Steven a few months ago. We've been going out once in a while. I wasn't attracted to him because he was the typical nice

Seven Habits of Highly Annoying Men

There are no shortages of complaints by women about men's behavior, but some crop up more than others. The biggies:

1. Minutes after a conversation with your mate, you've forgotten three-fourths of what she said.

2. You don't pick up after yourself.

3. You're impatient when your partner wants to check her hair, her makeup, her horoscope, and so on before the two of you leave the house to go someplace.

4. Sports and news on TV, all night, all the time.

5. You promise to do something, then procrastinate, making her nag you.

6. "Reading" the Victoria's Secret catalog with the fervor of a minister studying the Bible.

7. Offering a solution every time she complains rather than just being a good listener.

guy. But I made the effort to give him a chance. I've been trying to appreciate his good qualities instead of wishing he were different.

"We do have a lot of fun together. I know now that if he were different, I'd probably be unhappy a lot of the time. I'm actually happy with Steven and can't believe it. Me, who always manages to get involved with the wrong man, is finally seeing a good one.

"The most exciting thing is that I had sex with him this weekend. I honestly didn't expect much, but he turned out to be a sensual and very pleasing lover. I sold him short at first, but I'm glad I got to know him better. Nice guys can be *very* sexy.

"After going through my phase of making snap decisions about whether there was instant chemistry between me and a new guy, I've learned to appreciate the goody guys. When you take the time to get to know a man, he may look much more attractive down the road. When you start by developing a friendship first, the rest may come later."

SEX WARS

" I SAID 'EITHER', HE SAID 'EYE-THER'. SO, I SHOT HIM. "

HELP ONLINE

CYBER-SESSIONS

You realize that the impasse you and your mate have reached won't be resolved without professional help, but you hate the thought of spilling your guts in a therapist's office. Consider couples' counseling online.
www.couplecounseling.com

12-STEP PROGRAM

If you're not sure how to even begin resolving your problems, click on Cyberpsych's site, which features 12 effective problem solving skills.
www.win.net/cyberpsych/adjissue.html

GIGGLES

Don't let your women problems get you down. Go to Jests and Jokes on the Internet and scroll through jokes—clean and bawdy—about women. Subjects include a "Guide to Womanspeak," "How to Score Points with a Woman," and "The Rules."
www.jestsandjokes.com/women.html

MAN'S GUIDE INTERVIEW

Men, Women, Anger, and a Dog with No Name

An Interview with John Gottman, Ph.D., D.Ph.

John Gottman, Ph.D., D.Ph., observes married couples the way some men study stamp collections, stock portfolios, or baseball box scores. A professor of psychology at the University of Washington in Seattle, Dr. Gottman has studied hundreds of couples for years at a time in a campus laboratory dubbed the Love Lab. His tools: video cameras and pulse, sweat, and movement monitors aimed at getting inside couples' heads and hearts. His research has led him to predict with 91 percent accuracy whether a couple will remain together or split—sometimes after watching them interact for as little as 5 minutes.

He is the author of several books, most recently The Seven Principles for Making Marriage Work. *At marriage workshops that Dr. Gottman and his wife, a fellow psychologist, have run, he's heard the gamut of complaints that perplexed men have about women's unfathomable ways. We asked him for his take on the gender wars and the future of marriage.*

MAN'S GUIDE: You've said that men aren't from Mars and women aren't from Venus. How do men and women differ?

> **DR. GOTTMAN:** In marriages that are going well, there are almost no gender differences. In general, for example, women exhibit nine facial expressions of emotion a minute in marital interaction, and men exhibit eight. When you look at couples in happy, stable marriages, you find that the gender differences are really tiny in terms of physiological responses and so on. But when the marriage is ailing, you do get big gender differences. So one of the things that I found that led me to say that men and women are really from the same planet was an analysis we did on the variants of romance, passion, and good sex in a marriage. For women, 70 percent of the dissatisfaction was tied to the quality of the friendship. For men, it was just about the same thing— very close to 70 percent.
>
> Guys may have a little bit different idea about what the friendship is about, but not that different. The major complaint we get from men

when the marriage is really hurting is that they feel like their wives don't even like them and are not their allies. They feel kind of alone and isolated.

MAN'S GUIDE: How does a man be a good friend to his wife?

DR. GOTTMAN: The elements of the friendship are, number one, really feeling known by your partner, feeling like your partner is interested in knowing you and continuing to know you, feeling interested in your partner and knowing about your partner's psychological world.

> " We haven't evolved enough that we can tell the difference between a saber-toothed tiger and a critical wife. We're angry. And we're going to get even. "

Number two, really having a culture of appreciation in the marriage, rather than a culture of criticism. When you have this, people are really thanking one another, looking for positive things and expressing appreciation. There's affection and respect communicated in the marriage.

The third principle is turning toward versus turning away. By that, I mean everyday, mundane conversations in which a couple takes an interest in what each of them is saying, rather than just grunting or shrugging. It's not glamorous, but these interactions turn out to be the basis for good romance.

That's what I mean by the marital friendship—those three ingredients.

MAN'S GUIDE: Are the differences that do exist between men and women primarily biological or cultural?

DR. GOTTMAN: I think they're mostly biological and amplified by culture. Where you get the biggest differences between men and women is in what you might call the vigilant system, that is, the system in the brain that detects and responds to danger. There's pretty good evidence that we have evolved from ancestors whose men were specialized for cooperative hunting and protecting the tribe. Cooperative hunting usually requires being quiet, hunting over fairly large distances, communicating and maintaining vigilance, and being ready to respond with aggression—and anger.

The females in our species who survived were the ones who were really able to nurture the young and nurse them. They had to be calm. When you have women who are trying to nurse and there's a lot of stress in their lives, it usually disrupts the nursing.

If you do experiments in psychology laboratories in which you make men and women angry and then ask them to calm down, the women can calm down. Guys don't calm down when they get really angered. You ask women what they're thinking, and they say, "Oh, I have to go shopping this afternoon. I was thinking about what I will be buying." You ask guys what they're thinking, and they say, "That son of a bitch. Nobody treats me like that." They're rehearsing these stress-maintaining thoughts.

> **" Why is it the minute you dolls get a guy that you like, you take him in for alterations? "**
>
> *—Guys and Dolls*

Well, after a marital fight, you get the same gender difference. Guys either feel righteous indignation or they feel like innocent victims. It's either fight or flight. And the vigilant system gets activated. Men have a bigger heart-rate response and it takes them longer to recover. Basically what you find in all of these studies is that it's not really that men get more easily stressed out, but that the vigilant system is activated. Unfortunately, we haven't evolved enough that we can tell the difference between a saber-toothed tiger and a critical wife. We're angry. And we're going to get even.

MAN'S GUIDE: Is that fight-or-flight response why you say that when one spouse stonewalls during an argument, 85 percent of the time it's the man?

DR. GOTTMAN: Yes. What predicts stonewalling is an elevated heart rate. We interviewed people about what they were thinking during these moments. We showed them the videotapes of themselves and asked, "What were you thinking right there?" The guys said, "I was just thinking, 'I'm not getting into this. I'm going to cool out.'" And of course, their wives were thinking, "He's so disapproving right now."

She was seeing him as withdrawn and hostile. But he was saying,

"I'm neutral. I'm just going to cool out. I'm going to calm down. I don't have to take this personally." He was trying to soothe himself in those moments. Unfortunately, it doesn't work very well. It intensifies her attack.

MAN'S GUIDE: You say that these gender differences can contribute to, but don't cause, marital problems. Explain.

> **❝ Sometimes it's worse to win a fight than to lose. ❞**
>
> —Billie Holiday, "Lady Sings the Blues," 1956

DR. GOTTMAN: Well, I think they're very important. What I'm saying is, you don't see the gender differences unless the marriage is ailing. Until the vigilant system gets activated, there really aren't any gender differences to speak of. They exist, but they're trivial.

Of course, it's very logical, if you think about it for a moment. Gender differences can't cause divorce because a couple that gets divorced has a male and a female and so does a couple that stays married. It has to be the interaction of gender differences with something else.

What we find is that it's chronic conflict that activates this vigilant system in guys. What drives women crazy is when it progresses to the later stages of emotional withdrawal by men. Then men go nuts. They get physiologically aroused. Their immune systems suffer. That's how I think the gender differences work.

MAN'S GUIDE: Are men and women bringing a lot of the same needs into a marriage, insofar as everyone wants to be loved and respected—that sort of thing?

DR. GOTTMAN: Exactly. In our apartment lab, we look at really mundane interactions, like people reading the paper together, or eating dinner and stuff. People make bids for attention, interest, conversation, humor, affection, support. All these sort of very simple statements, like somebody will say, "Last night I had a disturbing dream." Or, "Do you think we should buy some more of that great steak that we had for the barbecue?" Here's one of our findings: In marriages where couples are getting along, there are 70 of these bids for attention in 10 minutes. Isn't that amazing?

MAN'S GUIDE: I think so.

DR. GOTTMAN: And in marriages where they're not getting along, there are seven, on the average. One-tenth as many bids are getting made for connection when the marriage is ailing. And then the number of the bids that get responded to declines over time, such as when the person says, "What did you dream? Tell me about it." As opposed to just sort of grunting or not responding at all. These very small moments turn out to be the basis for emotional connection, for attention.

The probability of rebidding when your spouse is unresponsive is almost zero in all marriages. In other words, nobody says, "Hey, I just said, 'Here's an interesting article.' Did you hear me?" Instead, they seem to sort of crumble a little bit and sort of slink away. And there don't seem to be any gender differences here. The men are making bids for attention, interest, and affection the same way as women are.

It matters how your partner responds to you. Really having knowledge of your partner's inner psychological world. Knowing what's stressing your partner out and stuff like that. Just about all the women are doing this. They're staying in touch with their men. They know about their jobs. But there's a huge variability in the extent to which guys do that. One pediatrician we saw didn't know the name of the family dog. They had had the dog for 3 years.

MAN'S GUIDE: Come on. Really?

DR. GOTTMAN: We said, "What's the dog's name?" He said, "Lisa, what's the dog's name?"

And we went on, "How long have you had this dog?"

"Lisa, how long have we had the dog?" She said 3 years. And he said, "We've had the dog 3 years."

We asked this guy where the back door was at his house. He said, "Lisa, where's the back door?" Hey, wait a minute. You've lived in this house for 5 years, and you don't know where the back door is? He said, "I just go in and out the front door. I go to work and come home."

But some guys are amazing. They really know stuff about their wives. They know their wives' best friends. They know what stresses them out, what they're worried about, what their aspirations are.

There's huge variability in guys. There are some guys who are much more emotionally intelligent about relationships. They've figured it out.

MAN'S GUIDE: You've written that anger is not necessarily a bad thing in an argument. Explain how to use anger constructively.

DR. GOTTMAN: First of all, it's taken us about 15 years to code specific emotions. And we all are trained to know how to read facial expressions. So we know what the brow looks like when people are sad. We know what the mouth looks like when people are angry. We look at facial cues, vocal cues, what people are saying, their timing, and so on. When I'm talking about anger, I'm talking about really pure anger, without contempt, without defensiveness. And that doesn't predict anything negative. It doesn't predict anything positive, either. It's not what you'd call a constructive thing.

In marriages that are going well, when you interview people about their partners' anger, particularly when you interview women, they're not taking it personally. In fact, they kind of score the anger. We have a rating dial where they have to tell us what they were feeling when they watched their videotapes. And in marriages that are going well, the women score their husbands' anger at neutral, not negative or positive. Whereas in marriages where people aren't happy, the wives score their husbands' anger as very negative.

In one case, the husband gets angry and his wife says, "Man, is he stressed out." In the other case, the wife says, "I hate the way he treats me. He's so mean." She takes it personally. Anger doesn't predict anything that's going to happen to the marriage, but the way it's perceived is very important.

Forty-seven percent of men responding to a *Mademoiselle* magazine survey said they bring their partners to orgasm every time. Only 30 percent of the women agreed.

. . . .

If this guy is typically contentious and defensive, then when he just gets angry—even when he's not contentious or defensive—his wife still sees that as more negative because he's a hostile SOB, you know. But if the husband, when he gets negative, tries to repair it, he'll say, "I'm sorry. I didn't mean to say it that way. Let me try again." And that can help his wife perceive it differently.

MAN'S GUIDE: **You also recommend that when an argument is getting pretty heated, a couple should take a break for 20 minutes and distract themselves with other thoughts. Why?**

DR. GOTTMAN: That turns out to be one of the most powerful things that you can do in your marriage. I have a hard time doing it myself. I remember one argument I had in which I made this point. My wife said, "I'm not talking to you when you're like this." She said, "You are physiologically aroused and you're being unreasonable."

I said, "I am not being unreasonable, and I want you to sit down and listen to me." She said, "I'm not talking to you until you calm down." And she walked away.

I started relaxing myself and calming down, and about 20 minutes later, she came back and said, "How are you feeling?" And I said, "I'm much better. See what did I tell you?" I tried to take credit for it. Then we started talking about the problem again when I had calmed down, and we had a really productive conversation. In 10 minutes, we solved the problem.

> **" Men are highly overrated and vastly inferior to chocolate. "**
>
> —"Brenda Barrett,"
> *General Hospital*

MAN'S GUIDE: **What's the single biggest thing that men don't understand about women, or vice versa?**

DR. GOTTMAN: I think probably the most important thing is that guys have more trouble calming down. When there's a lot of conflict, it's harder for men to soothe themselves than it is for women. I think that's one of the big things that women take away from our workshops.

We talk about presenting the problem in a way that is really gentle, that says, "This isn't a big deal and I really appreciate all the things you've been doing lately, but I have a bone to pick with you. I want to talk about it. Now, don't get upset. Is this a good time for us to talk about it?" Raise the issue like that, totally different than if you raised the issue by suggesting that your partner has a defect in his personality. I think women learn that faster in the workshops. That's an important thing to clear up.

I don't find this thing that John Gray says—that when men come home from work, they need to go into their caves. I find just the opposite. Men want to connect at the end of the day. They like to be greeted by a really nice kiss and have their wives be happy to see them. Have their wives' faces brighten when they walk through the door. Certainly, nobody likes to be greeted by anger and frustration. I think that's true for men as well as women.

MAN'S GUIDE: So many marriages fail. Are you optimistic or pessimistic about the future of marriage?

DR. GOTTMAN: I'm very optimistic. And the reason I'm optimistic is that we've seen about 900 couples in our workshops now in the last 3 years. Our figures are that 86 percent of our couples make a major breakthrough on a gridlock problem in 2 days.

My vision is to try to help people establish a marriage clinic in every major town in the United States. There's no center where we can say, "Okay, here's this place that sees couples. They've seen, in the last 3 years, 4,000 couples, and 80 percent of them are doing well." I mean, wouldn't it be great to have a center like that where you could say that? Well, that's what we're going to build.

I think the reason I'm optimistic is that science hasn't been given a chance in this whole equation. There hasn't been a building of scientific approaches with clinical approaches. That's what I think the hope is—to use the same criteria that the medical world uses for evaluating a treatment for cancer or heart disease. For the public to really demand from clinicians, "Okay, what's your track record? How are you measuring this?" And to have managed-care systems say, "Yes, marital therapy is really important. We're going to reimburse, but we're only going to reimburse those centers that have a good track record." That's why I'm optimistic.

QUICKIES

BUT HONEY, EVERYONE DOES IT

Trying to offer a palatable explanation for your philandering may be as feasible as feeling pleasure with a double-thick condom. Still, here's something she probably hasn't heard: Most creatures that mate for life are unfaithful. Maybe it's your biological imperative to follow suit.

She won't accept your word on this, so cite the studies that support it. Stephen T. Emlen, Ph.D., a professor of behavioral ecology at Cornell University in Ithaca, New York, concluded that only about 10 percent of mammals and birds that mate for life are faithful to their partners.

Some researchers believe that males are biologically driven to roam by the desire to spread their genes into as many future generations as possible. This leads some species—including lions and mountain gorillas—to kill and eat the offspring of rival males.

So there you go. Tell your honey that you've strayed simply because of your need to propagate your species far and wide. She may well tell you to go propagate yourself, but she was probably going to say that even before you educated her about the animal kingdom.

Incidentally, the impulses that spur humans to seek sex outside their partnerships are a lot more complicated than those of chimps or bluebirds, says Dr. Emlen. He suggests that you should not be hasty in drawing simplistic conclusions. That's the part you may want to neglect telling your partner.

MAN IN FOWL MOOD WANTS SEX

The next time your partner balks when you plead with her to wear that body stocking you bought her, point out that your fantasies are pretty tame compared to those of some men. Like the guy with the biggest passion for poultry this side of Colonel Sanders, whom New York City psychiatrist and sex therapist Avodah Offit, M.D., described to *New Woman* magazine.

"He complained that he couldn't get erections unless he watched a chicken being killed. Apparently, it stemmed from when he was a teenager and used to watch the young girls killing chickens for dinner. The excitement, the heaving of their breasts as they caught and killed the chickens, was associated in his mind with sexual arousal.

"So to satisfy himself, he orchestrated parties on farms where he invited his friends and ordered that a chicken be killed and roasted. The sight of it lasted him several weeks as a fantasy and he was able to have sex with his wife. But then he started asking her to kill the chickens for him; when she objected, they came to see me."

There could, however, be a simpler explanation for the man's poultry penchant: He was from Turkey.

VIRGINITY TESTS VANISH

Women and girls in Turkey will no longer be forced to undergo virginity tests, that country's government decreed. Orphans, prisoners, and sometimes foreign tourists staying in hotel rooms with male companions had been forced to undergo gynecological tests against their will. Turkish families had defended the tests as a way of deterring girls from damaging their marriage prospects.

DEAR DR. MANLY

Q: *Why can my wife always find things that I've misplaced* when I can't?
—T. M., PHOENIX

A: I would have answered earlier, but I misplaced your letter in the clutter here on my desk and had to have my secretary come in and find it for me. Seriously, this is a for-real phenomenon. Robin L. West, Ph.D., a psychology professor at the University of Florida in Gainesville led a study of more than 300 men and women about this very thing. He used a digital blueprint of a 12-room house on a computer screen and 20 icons, each representing a different household object. Those in the study were asked to place each of the objects somewhere on the blueprint. Forty minutes later, they were asked to remember the location of each object. Guess who did best?

It may not seem like much difference, but women scored 14.4 finds versus men's 13.5. That little difference is significant, says Dr. West, because it happens in study after study. Adds another dimension to the phrase "She's a really good-lookin' woman."

Q: *My wife and I have taken marriage clinic programs and night courses that teach couples communication skills. Seems the more we study, the better we get at putting each other down. Are all these communications techniques really helping anybody?*
—P. W., SANTA BARBARA, CALIFORNIA

A: Learning to communicate may just be another way of talking yourself into trouble. It flies against conventional wisdom, but a study at Purdue and Wake Forest Universities, in West Lafayette, Indiana, and Winston-Salem, North Carolina, respectively, seems to support your suspicion. Of the 60 couples studied (married an average of 7 years), those who were less skilled at communicating their feelings were actually happier than couples who were more skilled.

Just like you and your wife, those who were the better communicators simply insulted each other more effectively. A partner with negative intentions who is skilled in communication can wield a pretty wicked tongue. "It could mean that she knows just where to put the knife," says lead researcher Brant Burleson, Ph.D., a psychologist at Purdue.

We all know we're not supposed to let grievances fester in a marriage, but clearing the air can kill a marriage, too, if the process revives past conflicts, the researchers say. The happy couples, they found, had at least one mate who could sense the other's feelings and take preemptive action before shouting started and dishes flew. That is a sense that can be cultivated. Learn to pay special attention to the hints she drops and back away from the big bad buttons she's daring you to press. Just ask yourself, "Is it more important that I win this one or that I have sex sometime in the next month?" You'll do what's right.

Dr. Manly is a fictional character.
The actual advice was provided by a variety of
medical doctors and other qualified experts.

2

SUPERCHARGE
YOUR INNER
HUNK

 Most of us men try. We really do. We try to wear clothes that look good and are appropriate to the setting. To get our hair cut in a way that flatters our faces. To wear cologne that piques a woman's interest. To do whatever we believe will enhance our natural sexuality and maximize our magnetism. We want women to like what they see when they are looking our way. We want them to look our way. And keep looking. For the right reasons.

Too often, however, we choose attire that wasn't even hip in our fathers' day. We get haircuts that make Moe of the Three Stooges look stylish, by contrast. We splash on so much of a foul-smelling fragrance that we repel women more effectively than deet does mosquitos.

Having a sense of style is important. Not just to entice women, but for what it says about a man to everybody. It says you have self-confidence. Self-respect. That you are competent.

In this section, you'll learn how to better present yourself as a man of substance. A man to be reckoned with. A man that women would like to know better. This chapter is about how a man can radiate sex appeal.

TOP TEN

Fashion Mistakes

What sets off her "geek meter"? Here's what women around the Rodale offices cited.

① Pants that are too short or too tight

② Tube socks with shorts

③ White socks with dress shoes or dark slacks

④ T-shirts emblazoned with images of cartoon characters, oversized beer mugs, car races, women in bikinis, or rock bands

⑤ Ties festooned with the above. Ditto for boxers

⑥ Wrinkled fabric. Any wrinkled item of clothing. "A man wearing pressed clothes says to me, 'I've got it together,'" says one woman

⑦ Fishnet shirts

⑧ Socks with sandals

⑨ Pants worn with the waistband around the chest

⑩ Silk shirts. "Only a woman—or George Hamilton— should wear silk," says one of our female respondents. Hint: You're not George Hamilton

Bedroom Basics

You may do a wonderful job of wooing a woman only to go to your place and have the mood turn as sour as the month-old milk in the back of the fridge. The reason may be that seeing your bedroom—or you in underwear—is about as sexy to her as Walter Matthau in Grumpy Old Men. *Authors Perry Garfinkel and Brian Chichester know exactly what to do. They'll help you save the day and the night and possibly the relationship in this excerpt from* Maximum Style.

At most places, the dress code is clear. At a restaurant? No shirt, no shoes, no service. At work? No tie, no jacket, no promotion.

Sartorial things in life are generally spelled out on a sign or in a book somewhere.

Except in the bedroom.

It may seem simple at first blush: Get naked. And get in bed. But like most things in life, it's more complicated than that. For example, what if you're spending the night in someone else's quarters for the first time? What if you're looking to jump-start your love life? What about loungewear? Cold nights and colder feet? And then there are all the tricky issues revolving around how to act and what to say. Being a stylish lover—now *there's* a goal worth pursuing.

Room for Style

Style in the bedroom is important. Not only are you sleeping there every night but also it's where your most intimate moments occur. Statistics show that one in three of us between the ages of 18 and 59 have sex twice a week or more. Another third "do the deed" at least a few times a month. One thing that you can bet on: What you wear and how you conduct yourself in the bedroom will have a direct impact on how often you have sex—and how much fun it is when you do.

"Men don't think about subtle sexy things, like what they wear to bed. We're conditioned to be fighters, not lovers," says Sam Baker, president, chief executive officer, and chief designer at Male Power LTD, an exotic-underwear manufacturer in Bay Shore, New York.

That's sad, Baker adds, because "style matters

hot TIP!

Keep an electric razor in your glove compartment or briefcase for a quick touch-up when you need to look presentable late in the day.

so much in the bedroom. It's part of the mood. Underwear, lingerie, your bedroom eyes, everything you say or do in the bedroom perpetuates the feelings. It's your job to make the most of them, and clothing helps."

And we're not just talking sex. Your sleeping quarters also play host to a variety of activities: lounging, reading, deep discussion. When it comes to what you're wearing, the bedroom offers latitude to prove that your style sense doesn't end at the office.

"Men have always had it easier at this. We're beneficiaries of laxer dress standards and have more freedom," says Ross E. Goldstein, Ph.D., a psychologist and president of Generation Insights, a consulting company in San Francisco.

That's because there's a bit of a double standard between men and women when it comes to the dress code, including nighttime dress code. A man, for example, can wear boxers and a T-shirt to bed and be normal. A woman in boxers and a T-shirt, or in sweats and a sweatshirt, is frumpy.

Here's how to improve your image in the bedroom by wearing—and doing—the right stuff.

● **Be a man with a plan.**
What to wear in the bedroom depends largely on what you're planning to do. If you're spending the night at someone's house for the first time, or vice versa, you'll dress differently than if you're recovering from a back injury for 2 weeks. Think ahead and plan your nighttime wardrobe with as much forethought as your daytime outfit.

"Black socks and white baggy underpants aren't all that attractive at the end of a good date, but I suppose if you've gotten that far, you're home free," quips David Wolfe, creative director and chief trend forecaster at The Doneger Group, a buying house and fashion forecasting firm in New York City. The question you may want to ponder is, Will there be a repeat performance?

SEX ✠ TRENDS

FRAGRANCE SALES ARE SWEET

Sales of men's fragrances are booming, but it may not be because we've suddenly become more sensitive about our odors. One school of thought is that increasingly clever advertising and slick packaging is at least partly responsible for the renewed interest by Dave in aftershave, or by Carl for cologne.

Swiss Army, for example, makes a cologne set inside a brushed aluminum canister. Calvin Klein's CK (for Calvin Klein, we guess) is sold in a sleek, minimalist glass bottle. Then, too, there are all those free toiletry bags and other gifts tacked on when you buy a fragrance.

⦿ Don't dis robes.

Hugh Hefner you're not, and maybe you never want to be. But the old playboy is on to something when it comes to loungewear. Robes are comfortable. Any woman will tell you that the thin, cheap Kmart-type robe that you wore as a kid won't cut it. Nothing cuts it short of thick, luxurious, warm, and full-length. Good robes can cost $40 or more, but they'll last and are worth every penny. (And they'll look great on her, too.)

⦿ Climb in the ring.

Forget those saggy, white briefs you've been wearing. "Aesthetics is very personal, of course, but a lot of women, especially younger women, think that boxers are sexy because they look good on different types of men," says Jeanie Wilson of Sara Lee Knit Products in Winston-Salem, North Carolina, director of marketing for Hanes underwear.

Bikini briefs are still worn by many men, and preference seems to be regional as well as personal. For example, Wilson says, Europeans tend to prefer bikini briefs

perfect figures

If you've spent thousands of hours in the gym building your biceps and pecs, it may disappoint you to learn that it's facial features, not muscles, that women find most attractive in a man. In a survey of women conducted for Rodale, 27 percent of women said a man's eyes were his most attractive physical feature. Another 24 percent said his face, and 22 percent cited his smile.

Only 6 percent of the women said a man's chest was tops, while fewer than 3 percent mentioned arms.

and flashier colors in underwear. Our advice? Unless you have a body that can carry off Speedos on the beach, choose boxers. Preferably silk ones.

⦿ Get exotic—and erotic.

Male Power LTD's line of exotic underwear, and others like it, are surefire style enhancers.

"A lot of this stuff is frowned upon by guys, but it works. Wearing exotic underwear makes you feel sexy," says Baker, whose product line includes underwear in animal prints, sheer material, fishnet, lace, thongs, G-strings, and novelties.

"Today, we're more open about these things. Exotic underwear is gift wrap for your lover. You're bringing her yourself in style," Baker says.

⦿ Smooth out the wrinkles.

No matter what you're wearing, consider making it a cotton/polyester blend, suggests Wilson. Blends are popular choices for loungewear, underwear, and lingerie because they don't wrinkle easily, guaranteeing a fresh-pressed look, even after your outfit has been under your suit all day.

● **Wear a sleek physique.**
Fitness and good health are always in fashion, and nothing looks better on a

Things You Should Keep in Your Bathroom

The well-rounded man keeps a well-stocked bath. Put these items on your shopping list.

● **Moisturizer**
Use a nickel-size dab on your elbows and a quarter-size blob on the front and back of each leg. Rub it in gradually. "Use a body moisturizer with urea or lactic acid, two strong moisturizing agents," says Patrice M. Healey, M.D., a dermatologist in Beverly Hills, California. Use only oil-free products on your face.

● **Antiperspirant**
Apply four to six swipes after a shower. "Test-drive a new antiperspirant by wearing it through a tough workout," says Eric Kraus, director of communications at the Gillette Company. "If it works then, it'll work anytime."

● **Soap**
"If you can't get soap to lather, you probably need a water softener," says Dr. Healey.

● **Cologne**
Use three sprays or four finger dabs, max. Apply once a day, with a booster shot at night. "Don't put cologne on your face," says Jack Wiswall, senior vice president of Cosmair, the American subsidiary of L'Oreal. "It can irritate your skin, and the smell will overpower you."

● **Wet razor**
A new blade should yield two or three close shaves.

● **Dental floss**
Floss daily from the bottom of your tooth outward, so you don't imbed anything in your gums.

● **Shaving cream**
Use a blob about the size of a cherry tomato. Take a warm shower first, and then shave with hot water. "It opens your pores and softens the hairs," says Eric Malka, owner of the Art of Shaving in New York City. Wet your face, then cover your entire beard with at least ½ inch of lather. Shave with the grain; if you insist on a

guy than well-toned muscles and low body fat. "Women talk about men's physical appearances these days—their bodies, shoulders, and butts," Wolfe says. "Women are looking at you more as a sex object and not as much for security, because they don't need that as much. And, hey, if you're in better shape, even cheaper clothes look good on you."

● Shoot for silk and its ilk.
Silk is "special-occasion" material in the bedroom. Silk boxers, silk pajamas, even silk sheets are famous for their luster and luxuriousness. If silk is too expensive, consider satin. Or "sand-washed" silk, which, after debuting in 1991, is nothing more than microdenier polyester treated with chemicals and roughed up by sand for a smooth, silky finish.

second pass against the grain, reapply shaving cream first.

● Toothpaste
Squeeze out a dollop that runs the full head of a small, soft-bristled toothbrush. Brush twice a day. Skip fancy toothpastes (like tartar control) unless you have specific problems.

● Shampoo
A quarter-size dab will do you. "Use a clarifying shampoo once a week to get rid of buildups from other hair products," says Damian Miano of Miano/Viel Salon in Manhattan.

● Conditioner
Apply a squirt the size of a dime. Conditioner moisturizes your hair so that it doesn't become dry and brittle. It's best to use one that contains an ultraviolet-ray blocker.

● Decorate for love.
Your bedroom's decor tells a woman a lot about you. Ditch those old, pilled sheets that you've been using for too long. Buy nice satin ones for the summer and warm, soft flannel ones for the winter. Invest in new pillows—easily camouflaged sex accessories—and stick a stool in a corner. It's a great shelf for books and papers and can come in handy for certain sex positions. Pay attention to music and lighting, too. A radio or CD or tape player should be the only electronic device on in your room if love is in the air. If you have a TV, make sure that it's off. The 11 o'clock news doesn't quite set the right mood. Lighting should come from candles, dimmer lights, even black lights near the headboard. (Black lights give you and your lover the appearance of a healthy tan, without the adverse side effects of tanning.)

● **Keep it clean.**

A clean, well-organized bedroom can make a big positive statement to that first-time visitor by showing that you respect yourself. It also is far better than the alternative. Do you want women to see clothes piled on the floor, closet doors open, shoes and magazines everywhere, an unmade bed?

How Women Size You Up

Every dame you meet is checking you out. But who wants to hear from men what women like in a man? Men's Health *magazine knew better. They went to the source. They asked a good-looking woman who has given ogling men a good deal of thought. Here's what Stephanie Williams had to say.*

As a woman, I know that within seconds of laying eyes on me you'll have decided whether you'd like to have sex with me. Well, guess what, Gus: I've been doing the same thing to you. So has every other woman you've ever met. I also know how you're checking me out: breasts, butt, legs, and—if I make it that far—face. The way women check you out is infinitely more complex. You seem like a nice boy, so I'll let you in on exactly how my eyes roam over your body during the first few seconds we come in contact.

Before continuing, I should warn you that the things women check may seem a little odd to you. I once chose a boyfriend based largely upon the length of his sideburns. As it was, he looked a little young; if those burns had been any shorter, I would have thought he was a Boy Scout. If they'd been longer, he would have seemed seedy. My friend Allis recently shot down a guy in a bar because he wore

SEX TRENDS

SMILE, LASER MOUTH

You may wonder where the yellow went if you try one of the latest tooth whitening methods available. Dentists can now use a carbon dioxide laser to brighten that black hole inside your mouth. It's expensive—$900 to $2,000— but one 3-hour session should do a better job than over-the-counter or dentist-assisted at-home bleaching treatments.

his polo shirt with both buttons open, to flaunt his chest hair. She figured that his pal was more trustworthy (in other words, datable) because he had fastened one of the buttons on his polo and had also worn a T-shirt underneath. After Allis and I got drunk and told the guys about her analysis, T-shirt Man said he'd worn the undershirt because he sweats profusely. He was immediately transferred to the shot-down list.

You probably call this nit-picking; I call it being choosy. Men are always on the make; women are more likely to be using a process of elimination. "Women are always a little more conscious of the question, 'Does this guy have potential as a mate?'" says Anita Barbee, Ph.D., a social psychologist at the University of Louisville. "We look at more dimensions than men do, and we're more critical because if we get pregnant, we have to deal with the consequences." Women have to play Sherlock Holmes to figure out whether you're datable, boyfriend material, or merely—to borrow your lingo—doable. All this sleuthing happens in seconds.

perfect figures

Nearly 60 percent of women have some changes in mind that would make their partners sexier.

This type of scrutiny can actually work to your advantage. "Research shows that if a man doesn't find a woman attractive, she's generally out of the ball game," points out Jennifer Maxwell Parkinson, an image consultant and president of Look Consulting in New York City. "Women don't do that. They're more interested in who the person is." Our decisions, therefore, are much more thoughtful, realistic, and capable of being influenced than the ones that you reach with your simplistic little formula (nice tomatoes = yes; no tomatoes = no way).

So let's say you're heading for a table at an outdoor café. See that hot babe sitting across the aisle? That's me. By the time you've reached your table, I've already checked out . . .

❶ How "put together" you are

In this initial once-over, I'm looking for hints. I'm not going to go for an untucked, unmatched guy who hasn't had a good haircut since Lord knows when, for the same reason I wouldn't buy a fixer-upper if I were house hunting: It's too much work. If I see major structural damage—a brown belt with black slacks, for instance—it means that no woman has ever loved you enough to make you presentable.

The other extreme is no good, either. If your suit, suspenders, shave, and shoe shine are perfect, I'll look down at my simple frock and assume that I could never please you. I need to see some vulnerability, some sign that you'll need me. I'll also probably assume that, as a control freak, you'd be awful in bed.

If I don't like your style, the scan stops here. If I do, I'll sneak a peek at:

Where You Are and What We Notice

We "nice girls" have to gather our info on the sly; we can't just all-out ogle the way you can, or we'll inadvertently send a signal that we want you to make The Approach. The Approach is always on our minds—we're constantly evaluating whether we want you to know we dig you (smile, eye contact) or whether we absolutely don't want you to head in our direction.

How hard we stare and what we stare at depends on the circumstances.

● At the office

We have all the time in the world to look you over, so we'll do it very slowly, maybe over the course of a week. It can be hard to learn anything useful at the office, since most clothing clues aren't there: Guys pretty much have to wear the same thing. We'll look for men to show a little flair—something, anything, different from other guys. Like a tie.

● On the beach

For once, physique comes first. How big are your muscles—too big? Nonexistent? How firm and shapely are those buttocks? How good are you on the volleyball court? We won't search too hard here for the perfect guy; a fling is fine. Especially since we don't have enough clues (clothes, for instance) to make any real deductions.

● At Chippendales

This is the one place where it's socially okay for us to ogle you the way you ogle us. Men are always pointing out how women go overboard, hooting and hollering when we visit a strip bar. If you had to practice the restraint that we do on a day-to-day basis, you'd holler, too. Or implode.

● In a bar

Often, women are here to meet a man, so they'll be pretty open about letting you see them looking. If she looks at you, then away, then back at you, you're in business. But be careful; some women will be defensive since there are so many guys here who are just looking for a one-night stand. A woman may be in all-out judgment mode, looking for any reason to shoot you down.

❷ That thing you're carrying

You call it a prop. I call it a way for you to introduce yourself without saying a word. A tennis racket says, "I'm in good shape, boyishly competitive, and pretty well off." A squash racket says, "I went to an Ivy League school." A book says, "Wow! I read! I'm probably even sensitive!" (If it's something I've read and liked, it screams, "I may be your soul mate!")

perfect figures

Three out of 10 men enjoy shopping for clothes.

Reading the newspaper? Bet you're a good conversationalist. Carrying a backpack? I'll chastise myself for robbing the cradle, no matter how old you look. A worn, soft leather bag or briefcase is a total turn-on—the closest a modern guy ever comes to carrying a saddle. It shows that you're a hard worker. But a fake-leather bag with strips peeling off to reveal the white synthetic underneath means that you're stuffy and cheap. A cell phone says, "Either I'm extremely important or I just think I am"—probably the latter. If you have a dog with you, you're probably sort of lonely—and you may make a great dad.

I'm not always right, but I have to start somewhere. "You look at the package to gain an understanding of the product," says Michael Cunningham, Ph.D., a psychology professor at the University of Louisville (and Anita Barbee's husband). "If you're disappointed with the product, you may learn to be more careful about the packaging."

Now that you're close enough for me to take a good look at you, I'll peruse . . .

❸ A bit o' your brain

That's how Dr. Cunningham refers to the eyes. "Retinas are directly

◉ On the train, bus, or subway

"Women have to be more surreptitious here because they can't escape if they erroneously convey the message that a guy should approach," says Michael Cunningham, Ph.D., a psychology professor at the University of Louisville. In other words, sometimes women are looking at you out of boredom, so don't get too excited.

◉ In a café or bookstore

Women here are just as likely to be window-shopping as to be eating or reading. They'll look at what you're eating (or reading) to try to figure out why you're there. Approach with caution.

locked into the brain," he says. "Eyes are highly mobile and convey a lot of information." If you asked me, I'd probably say that I'm looking for honesty or sincerity in your eyes, which sounds like hogwash. But Dr. Cunningham says that your eyes can tell me how smart you are (do they look active or glazed?), how healthy you are (are they clear or yellow or bloodshot?), and even how turned on you are (your pupils dilate when you're aroused). A lot of that is subconscious. What I'll really decide is whether I like your eyes.

Something else I'll size up about your eyes is size. "The larger a man's eyes are, the better-looking he is; it brings out a nurturing feeling in women," says Dr. Barbee (who, with Dr. Cunningham, studied facial features and attraction). Big eyes, she says, are a "neonate" feature: They're associated with cute babies, and you know how chicks dig those. Color doesn't matter very much; but if your eyes are deep blue, I wouldn't kick you out of bed. Ditto long eyelashes.

If you're wearing glasses, I'll be far happier with you if they actually fit your face. Avoid excessively large frames or reddish-brown lenses like the ones that James Garner used to wear in the *Rockford Files*.

10 Things That May Knock You Out of the Running

1. Being shorter than I am

2. Too much pride in your body or your clothes. You can look good without straining

3. An earring in your right ear

4. A very loud shirt or tie

5. A comb-over. It's just dishonest to pretend you have more hair than you do

6. Excessive dandruff

7. A unibrow. Be a man; buy some tweezers

8. Sweat rings under your pits

9. A Beavis and Butt-head T-shirt

10. Body odor or too much cologne

Once I'm done with your eyes, I'll eyeball . . .

4 The rest of your mug

According to Dr.'s Barbee and Cunningham's research, women look for men who have lost the baby fat in their faces and who have high cheekbones and large chins. These features supposedly show maturity, to balance those babyish eyes. We're also suckers for expressive mouths, and we may subconsciously notice what color your lips are. Aroused lips turn red.

A recently published study found that most women prefer men with feminine features, such as a slender nose, "Cupid's lips," a cute chin, and a light brow. Dr.'s Barbee and

Cunningham have found that the women most likely to go for this type of quasi-guy are ultra-femme, since both men and women seem to seek someone who'll match them. (Masculine women seem to fall for men more masculine than they are.)

If you look like a girl, I'll want to look at . . .

Four Things That Most Women Don't Check Out

❶ The fabric of your shirt

❷ Your legs

❸ Your penis

❹ Hmm. You know, we actually check out everything else

❺ **Your chest**

If we weren't sitting down, I'd look at your butt, but this time I have to settle for judging your build up top. Are you a Jerry Seinfeld or an Arnold Schwarzenegger? I'll take no more than a quick peek, though; I won't stare the way you do. A recent study done at the University of Mannheim in Germany showed that men look at women's and men's chests more often than women look at either sex's chests. You weirdos.

Next I'll scrutinize . . .

❻ **Your hair (the stuff on your head)**

One question comes before all others: Could I run my fingers through it? I'm looking for a yes. If you have the standard guy haircut, here's a secret: Ditch the part. Simply run your hand across the top of your head to achieve that artfully mussed look. It will give me fantasies of mussing your hair even more by grabbing it in ecstasy as we tumble around in bed.

"To some women, overly long hair may be a little too much—too creative or artistic to live with," says Parkinson. If you go this route, make damn sure you have the hair for it. Do people compliment your long hair constantly? Do women ask to touch it? If not, think about a haircut.

If you're bald, there's a bright side. "These guys are seen as less romantically sexy and less dominant, but more wise and gentle," says Dr. Cunningham. "Baldness signifies that men are past the competitive stages of their lives and are ready to settle down." This may be why every woman you date pressures you for a rock.

If you're bald but still sowing your oats, buy a red Camaro or something, to let us know where your priorities are.

If you have dark hair, you'll appeal to more women than your blond pals do—because you will seem mature. You prefer blondes for the opposite reason.

Are You My Type?

Women tend to prefer either liberal or conservative men; in other words, the same woman may like Bad Boys and Musicians, but probably not Bad Boys and Executives. But it's always best to learn to live with your type; a Granola Guy in Executive clothing just doesn't work. This handy chart is permanently stamped on the brain of every woman you will ever meet. It's how she tells whether you're "for real."

THE ARTIST OR MUSICIAN

How we know you're this type:
You're probably smoking, and wearing something weird or disheveled

What kind of woman goes for you:
A hopeless romantic who feels things intensely. You obviously have a commitment problem; she wants to be the woman who makes you want to settle down

THE INTELLECTUAL OR POSEUR

How we know you're this type:
The book you're reading (it also determines which camp you fall into)

What kind of woman goes for you:
Brainy women with high self-esteem who want to spend their evenings talking and who don't mind that you're poor

THE GRANOLA GUY

How we know you're this type:
Tie-dyed T-shirt, Save the Whales knapsack, Birkenstocks

What kind of woman goes for you:
Women who look like female versions of you. They admire your "integrity." Other guys don't understand them

THE BAD BOY

How we know you're this type:
Leather jacket, long hair, concert T-shirt, tattoo

What kind of woman goes for you:
Meek little "good girls" who are too afraid to cut loose themselves, so they rebel by dating you

THE NICE GUY

How we know you're this type:
Bland clothes, medium build, boy-next-door looks

What kind of woman goes for you
Most women, as long as you avoid seeming too nice. Cultivate an air of mystery—a secret past or something

THE EXECUTIVE

How we know you're this type:
Razor-sharp haircut, top-of-the-line clothes, the *Wall Street Journal*

7 Your hair (the stuff on your face)

You know how I feel about this one: I like medium-length sideburns. I dislike goatees (too collegiate), beards (too ZZ Top), and mustaches (too Magnum, P.I.). Opinions differ, but your safest bet is to go without.

I should note, however, that many women like to see a little scruff on the weekend—it shows us you have testosterone. My friend Marilyn didn't give the man she eventually married a second look the first time they met; the second time, he had a five-o'clock shadow.

Next, my eyes will jump down to . . .

8 Your shoes and socks

Warning: crucial area. "A guy can wear the nicest clothes with the cheapest shoes and think women won't notice. Well, we do," says my friend Rosie, a tall, gorgeous Italian-American babe. "We look at the heel to see if it's worn, and at the leather to see how good it is. Also, if he wears white socks with dark shoes, it's over."

Old running shoes are also a no-go, unless you're running. There are plenty of aesthetically pleasing sneakers out there, so buy some.

Women will also check out how big your feet are. Let me put it this way: Most women won't look directly at a guy's "package" until, like, date three, but we are curious. So we're forced to follow that old myth about your feet and . . .

9 Your fingers

After I'm done gauging the girth of your digits, I'll zero in on one in particular: the ring finger.

What kind of woman goes for you:

A woman who is very organized herself, or one who needs organization in her life. Someone who wants a provider

THE BLUE-COLLAR WORKER, MAN IN UNIFORM, OR JOCK

How we know you're this type:

Muscles, jeans, workout clothes, uniform, camouflage

What kind of woman goes for you:

All these guys appeal to conservative gals (especially Catholics) who want an old-fashioned man who will settle down but still fill their nights with ecstasy

THE PREPPY

How we know you're this type:

A wardrobe from the Gap or J. Crew

What kind of woman goes for you:

Women who look like Hope on *thirtysomething*

"Women are going after a relationship; men are looking for a moment," says Parkinson.

Next, I'll scout for . . .

🔟 Watches, gold chains, class rings, and pinkie rings

I hate to admit it, but I'll look at the watch to try to calculate how much money you make. "Statusy things attract women," says Gilda Carle, Ph.D., a psychotherapist and the author of *Don't Bet on the Prince! How to Have the Man You Want by Betting on Yourself.* "They suggest that the man can take control of his life and his business situation, and that he can take care of her, too." If you wear a Rolex, I'll think you're a sugar daddy and find you intimidating (though many women would be all over that). A sports watch is almost always good, unless you're wearing it with a suit. A Swatch means you may still watch Saturday-morning cartoons (not necessarily a bad thing). Off-label watches with cheap-looking bands say you're cheap (definitely a bad thing).

Most women find other jewelry gaudy. But if you're looking for a hippie chick, feel free to pile on the crystals.

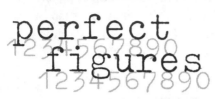

perfect figures

More than 9 out of 10 women say a man who is losing his hair should not worry about it, according to a survey conducted for Rodale.

About 42 percent of men between the ages of 18 and 49 have male pattern baldness, a recent study found. That's more than the 33 percent that other surveys have found.

· · · · · · · · ·

There's one more thing that can make or break our love:

🔟 Your _____

It's not your package, but I can't say exactly what it is—because it's that one thing that makes you stand out. For Clint Eastwood, it's those badass wrinkles. Some guys are bland-looking but jazz themselves up with, I don't know, blue hair. That will either speak to me or not, but if I like it, I'll really like it. So hit me with your best shot—the best you can pull off.

At this point, if I'm still digging you, I'll make eye contact and maybe even throw you a smile to let you know you're doing just fine. But then I have to run. I have a date with Sideburn Boy. That's the other thing to remember: Sometimes, like you, women are just looking.

Does Propecia Work?
Can You Leave a Little More on Top?

Men whose hair is falling out like autumn leaves tumbling to the ground may be wondering if Propecia or Rogaine is worth a try to halt that barren look. Ron Geraci checked into what's true and what's bald-faced hype in this piece for Men's Health *magazine.*

Enough time has passed since Propecia, the first and only pill created to treat male pattern baldness, was approved for sale in the United States. High time, we thought, to find out just how much hair the drug is actually capable of germinating.

The short answer, we discovered, is . . . some. If you've already lost a significant amount of hair, Propecia won't cause any pressing need to go out and buy a blow-dryer. Even in ideal circumstances, it can't transform a Bruce Willis dome into a Michael Douglas mane. If, however, you're only beginning to go bald, the drug is very likely to halt, or significantly slow, your hair loss, say dermatologists who have been prescribing Propecia. "About 90 percent of my patients on Propecia have stopped losing their hair," says Ken Washenik, M.D., Ph.D., director of dermatopharmacology at the New York University Medical Center in New York City. The drug's maker, Merck, found similar results in tests.

In case you haven't been following the Propecia story (in which case you probably have a full head of hair, you lucky dog), the pill is a 1-milligram version of finasteride. Merck has sold the drug since 1992 as Proscar, to treat enlarged prostrates. Finasteride decreases the body's amount of dihydrotestosterone (DHT), a male hormone that apparently encourages prostate and tissue growth and baldness. Without a steady supply of DHT, your hair follicles stop dying, and a few may even resume sprouting hair.

So far, indications are that about two-thirds of the men who take Propecia grow some hair. "My results have been almost too slight to notice," says Bob, 46, an Anthony Edwards look-alike, who has been taking Proscar since mid-1997. "My wife noticed that my bald spot was filling in slightly, mostly in the form of peach fuzz. But I assume the drug is preventing further loss, and I want to hold on to what I have until the real cure comes along."

That seems to be the right way to approach taking Propecia. "If your goal is to regrow your hair, you'll probably be disappointed," says George Cotsarelis, M.D., director of the hair and scalp clinic at the University of Pennsylvania in Philadelphia. Like Rogaine (the nonprescription minoxidil spray), Propecia works best on younger, newly balding men who still have a lot of hair to save. But even many of them aren't completely satisfied.

"Honestly, I expected better results," says Jeff, a 22-year-old from Baltimore who has been using Propecia for 8 months. "But knowing that I'm doing something instead of just complaining about it makes it worthwhile."

At this point, there's no way to predict what Propecia will do for you, but you'll know fairly soon after you start taking it. "If you're going to see any regrowth of hair at all, it will happen within a year," says Dr. Washenik. "Men who stop using Propecia before that point may be giving up prematurely." If Propecia doesn't regrow hair after a year, he adds, "you have to ask yourself if keeping your hair is worth $50 a month."

Another shortcoming shared by both Propecia and Rogaine is that while they may *slightly* thicken your front tuft, they work best on bald spots at the back of the head. If you're losing hair at the temples, the odds of either drug producing noticeable results are slight. Why? Your frontal hairline responds to male hormones differently, explains Dr. Washenik. These hairs often fall out rather quickly; the hair on your crown and the center of your scalp usually takes years to thin. "Every man still has a certain number of salvageable hairs in these areas," says Dr. Washenik. "But the hair at the temples and forehead is usually not salvageable. We don't know why."

To keep their edge in the hair-loss marketplace, the makers of Rogaine introduced an "extra strength" version of the spray that contains more than twice the concentration of minoxidil of the original and costs about the same—$30 or so for a month's supply. The company's studies on 825 men have shown that the stronger solution produces 45 percent more hair growth and works a bit faster than the 2 percent solution.

"The 5 percent minoxidil solution is definitely more effective than the 2 percent, and I've seen it foster more frontal hair growth," says John Romano, M.D., dermatologist at the Cornell Medical Center in New York City.

It took Karl Malone 6 months to grow the new hair he sports in the Rogaine ads, but only about 5 percent of men can hope for even his success, says Dr. Cotsarelis.

The most effective—if not the cheapest—

hot TIP!

When using mousse on your hair, apply a glob the size of a Ping Pong ball. Comb your hair gently while it dries, or your hair may clump together.

strategy may be to use Rogaine and Propecia simultaneously. Because one reduces baldness hormones and the other stimulates hair follicles, these drugs seem to complement each other well.

"The combination appears to work better than using either Propecia or Rogaine alone," agrees Ronald Savin, M.D., clinical professor of dermatology at Yale University. "Instead of seeing moderate regrowth in one-third of my Propecia users, I believe that adding Rogaine is pushing the success rate to two-thirds. It's my own subjective opinion, but it's a strong one."

There's no clinical proof, though, since no dual studies of the two drugs have taken place. Like stubborn competitors unwilling to share the market, both companies say no such research is planned.

If you start using Rogaine, you may lose *more* hair during the first month, says Dr. Washenik. Minoxidil purges hairs that are naturally preparing to fall out, exposing more scalp and no doubt scaring the hell out of lots of users. The accelerated shedding is temporary and usually stops in a few weeks, he explains. "Take it as a sign that minoxidil is working."

perfect figures

Average number of days per month that men wear a fragrance: 21

Some men may be staying away from Propecia because they've read about two side effects that arose in Merck's studies: Finasteride caused erection problems in 1.3 percent of subjects, and it caused birth defects when given to pregnant animals. Male fetuses need DHT to develop genitals, so some doctors wanted men to stop using Propecia for 3 months before trying to conceive a child, and the Propecia label warns that pregnant women shouldn't even touch the pills.

Take a closer look, however, and there may not be much to worry about. The erection problems also occurred in 0.7 percent of the placebo group, "so you're talking about a minuscule difference," says Marty Sawaya, M.D., Ph.D., principal investigator at Aratec, a Florida foundation that conducts hair research. "In my practice, I've never had a patient on Propecia complain about this."

Also, several dermatologists acknowledge that the birth defect cautions are probably worded a bit strongly. According to Dr. Sawaya, your wife would have to be exposed to a large number of crushed tablets every day to absorb enough finasteride through her skin to harm your unborn child. And you'd have to ejaculate "several buckets' worth" of semen—regularly—to endanger his development. If you can do that, don't complain about losing your hair.

One little-known side effect does concern some doctors. There's no doubt that Propecia can slightly decrease your prostate-specific antigen (PSA) results during a prostate cancer test. Since skewed results may mask a possible problem, men should always remind their testing doctor that they're taking it.

Other than these rare problems, taking a daily milligram of Propecia seems relatively harmless. "The 10-year data on finasteride show it's very safe," says Dr. Cotsarelis. The prospect of a man taking Propecia "forever" is unsettling to him, but that's not likely. "My hope is, there will be a better treatment soon."

And indeed, at least 70 new baldness drugs are being researched right now, says Dr. Sawaya, and half of the big medical firms are working on hair-growing potions. (After all, the potential market is huge; there are at least 25 million balding men in the United States alone.) If the clinical trials are successful, several new drugs may surface in the next few years. They'll fit into two categories: follicle stimulators like minoxidil, and hormone inhibitors like finasteride.

Currently, the most promising candidate is a DHT-blocking pill being researched at Glaxo-Wellcome.

SEX WARS

"MY FIRST WIFE DIDN'T THINK I WAS SEXY."

HELP ONLINE

TYING THE KNOT

Do your neckties look about as stylish as a hangman's noose around your neck? Then check out *MBA Style* magazine's Web site for necktie tying tips.
members.aol.com/mbastyle/web/necktie.html

PERSONALITY TEST

Been a little gruff or grumpy lately? Sometimes we all need to see ourselves as others do—take a reality check—and make some needed adjustments. Just so we remain our charming, attractive, likeable selves. Here's a quick personality test that covers the main points and lets you grade yourself.
ag.arizona.edu/aed/aed301/scale.htm

FINAL APPROACH

Any suave-man wannabe needs this advice on how to read a woman's body language and best approach her without causing her to flee like a startled deer. If you succeed, perhaps you'll move on to reading her body in braille.
www.dowco.net/purelove/body.htm

MAN'S GUIDE INTERVIEW

Clothes Help Make
the Man Make the Woman

An Interview with Bruce Boyer

Caught you. I saw you glancing at the woman over there with the chocolate-brown eyes and café au lait skin, her suede skirt hugging her hips just right.

Or maybe it was the petite blonde with the full, pouty lips who's wearing those painted-on jeans.

And I know what you were thinking, too: Do they have nice personalities? Have they ever read Dickens or Hemingway? What were their grades in college?

No?

I guess you were thinking about how you might get a little closer to one of them, crack a joke, make her smile, and move on to the exchange of phone numbers. And from there to a date and a warm body to dance with or . . . more.

No shame in that. It's the first time you've ever laid eyes on either of these women. What else do you have to go on initially but their outward appearances? It's no different for women. Sure, they have different standards and they leer less often, but they'll judge you first on your packaging. And if your image is not up to par, you face an up-hill battle just to make small talk.

So, in the interest of enhancing your inner hunk—or at least minimizing your shortcomings—we have consulted with Bruce Boyer, the author of three books on men's fashion and a freelance writer who has discussed the do's and do nots of male style in such publications as Esquire, Town and Country, Forbes, Mr, Mirabella, L'uomo Vogue, Harper's Bazaar, *and the* New York Times.

MAN'S GUIDE: Women often like to make this psychobabble claim that it is what's inside a man that really counts. Now, that may be true in the long run, but we know they see the outside package first. So what is the biggest fashion "do" if you want to bring out the hunk inside you or at least make her think there is a hunk inside you?

BOYER: I guess my first piece of advice would be that despite the popularity of that casual-Friday type of grunge look, it does pay to be neat and clean. Grooming is very important.

And my second piece of advice would be to dress according to the person that you are. That is probably the easiest way to make an impression and the quickest way to let women know who you are.

MAN'S GUIDE: What if the person you are is someone who wears button-down plaid shirts with some pinkish slacks? What if the person you are is a person who is used to dressing in an uncoordinated manner?

> **"** Never buy anything on sale just because it is on sale. . . . You just spit your money out the window. **"**

BOYER: My feeling is: Fine. One man's uncoordinated and sloppy is another man's hip and stylish. I don't like to prescribe a "look." A lot of the time, a guy's style is inherent in the little inconsistencies.

For example, I have maybe 20 pairs of shoes. Probably 15 of them are brown suede. And I wear brown suede shoes with almost everything, including blue-striped suits. And a lot of times, people—particularly the designers—say, "You can't wear brown shoes with a blue suit." I say, "Hey, that's me."

There are, in fact, rules about dress, but a lot of times they are not what people think they are.

MAN'S GUIDE: So what *are* the rules about dress?

BOYER: Maybe a better way to handle this is to talk about the myths that are not true. There are all sorts of made-up rules, like a heavyset man shouldn't wear a double-breasted suit, or a thin guy shouldn't wear stripes. Frankly, those kind of rules are a load of crap. They are just somebody's idea of what is true.

Another thing that is not really true is this color business. There are all of these people going around, predominantly women, saying, "You should wear beige and orange because you are an autumn person." That is ridiculous. That is about the most pervasively stupid gimmick I have seen in years.

Most of the rules are very simple. With collars, for example, the rule is that the bigger the man is, the bigger his collars should be. I mean that not only in terms of being big enough to fit his neck but also that the height of the collar and the length of the collar point should be greater.

MAN'S GUIDE: I know you just said there are few, if any, hard-and-fast rules, but what about this monochrome thing? This idea that it is fashionable for the color of your shirt and your tie and your jacket to all be pretty close. Is this a good strategy, a neutral strategy, or a trick that most men should think twice about?

BOYER: The monochromatic look is something that is more a matter of fashion than of style. In other words, it is current. It is seen as the thing to do at the moment. Yesterday it wasn't seen as the thing to do, and tomorrow it won't be seen as the thing to do. Tomorrow's fashion may be to wear lavender jumpsuits.

> " Clothes make the man. Naked people have little or no influence in society. "
>
> —Mark Twain

I don't think that this particular fashion idea does any harm, because, to my mind, it is a very easy way to dress. And I am all for helping guys get dressed more easily.

Dressing should not be an occupation, unless you are a designer. Most guys want to get up, get dressed easily, get off to their jobs, and know that they are appropriately attired. I think that the monochromatic approach is probably the safest way to do that.

I should add, however, that it is the most boring way to dress. "Safest" and "boring" almost always go together. I would like to see a man get beyond the monochromatic approach and start putting some individuality and a little bit of a spark and a little bit of real personality into his clothing.

MAN'S GUIDE: Is there anything that is really a fashion "don't," aside from wearing bright orange department-of-corrections coveralls?

BOYER: Prison attire might be very fashionable in the right crowd. But seriously, one of the biggest items on the "do not" list is that you do not buy an accessory that you can only wear with one outfit. If a tie only goes with one outfit, that is an expensive tie, no matter how little you paid for it. Hypercoordinated outfits are an incredible waste of money.

Second, never buy anything on sale just because it is on sale. Ask yourself, "Would I still want to buy this item if it were the regular price?" Because if you see the item and you say, "It is such a good buy. I am going to take it," then you will typically get home and you will never wear that item. It isn't the right color. It doesn't quite fit. But it was a hell of a good buy. Yeah, it was such a good buy that you just spit your money out the window.

Third, the most important thing is not to buy clothes that do not fit well. If it doesn't fit well, you could have the most expensive cloth and the nicest colors and the nicest pattern and you will still look bad. Conversely, even a suit that is a little wild, if it fits well, at least will make you look well-tailored.

MAN'S GUIDE: Are there any timeless styles or fabrics, or are men as much slaves to the fashion industry now as women have long been?

BOYER: We didn't used to be as much victims of the industry as women are. But that has been changing over the past 20 years, and the closer you get to the present, the more that victimization has increased. Still, a lot of men have retained enough sanity to understand that there still are essentials and basics and classics that belong in every wardrobe.

You need a gray worsted suit, a blue Oxford button-down shirt, and a striped or polka-dot tie. Let's see, what else?

A tweed sport jacket. A single-breasted navy blue blazer—preferably in lightweight flannel. Gray flannel trousers. Simple slip-on penny loafers. In the summer, khakis and maybe a seersucker sport jacket.

I would say that the higher-priced items in the wardrobe, such as suits, sport coats, overcoats, good shoes, and things of that nature, should be fairly classic and conservative and traditional.

Use the less expensive accessories to brighten up your wardrobe and make it individualized, because those are items you can change more easily. For example, I might recommend that if a guy really wanted to step out and be a little different, he should buy a pink button-down shirt. Give it a try. It might work. I would not, however, recommend buying a pink jacket.

I might recommend buying a colorful pair of argyle socks to try. But I wouldn't recommend buying a pair of sky-blue lizard-skin shoes.

I might recommend buying a yellow striped tie to try. But certainly not a yellow striped suit.

MAN'S GUIDE: Obviously somebody buys this stuff, because I've seen wild items like those in store windows.

> **BOYER:** Yes, but there is a point where economics should meet reality when it comes to style and clothing.

MAN'S GUIDE: You mentioned that you have quite a few pairs of brown suede shoes. I myself just bought a pair from Coach. And my wife, who insists that shoes make the man, was all over me when she saw me in these $190 shoes. Is it just my wife, or do a lot of women look at the bottom of your legs before they even consider moving up from there?

> **BOYER:** I think that is probably true. It is funny, though, because this is the kind of thing our grandfathers used to say. They would tell you that when you go out for a job or you want to make an impression, the main thing is that you have on good shoes or clean shoes or well-polished shoes or something along those lines.
>
> And we said, "Oh, come on. What about your hair; what about your character; what about your sparkling dialogue?"
>
> And they said, "No, it's your shoes."
>
> We thought they were completely full of it, but it turns out that a lot of times they were right, and we kind of grudgingly have to admit that.
>
> My father said to me once when I was young and wearing jeans that I could get away with wearing basically anything because I was young and active and built decently. Then he said to me, "You know, you are going to find that the older you get, the more you need a good tailor."
>
> Dad was right.

MAN'S GUIDE: Let's switch gears here, from everyday wear to workout wear. Now that Bally's Total Fitness, World Gym, Gold's Gym, and so many other health club operations have all these locations and these huge windows facing the streets, the health club has become a place to be seen.

> **BOYER:** . . . And to meet people.

MAN'S GUIDE: So if you are going to the gym to be seen, what can you do to enhance your appearance, aside from having firm pecs and washboard abs and a tight butt?

BOYER: There are two main schools of thought here, and I would rather establish a third point of view.

One of the two major categories are the guys who hang around the health club a lot and think of themselves as "real athletes," whether they are or not. They wear the sweatshirts with the arms raggedly pulled off, and they put on either cutoffs or these grungy-looking shorts that they bought at the Army-Navy surplus store. And they wear these big, thick leather belts that apparently don't do anything. Sometimes, they even wear construction boots. Because they are *real* weight lifters. Of course, along with all that, apparently you have to smell like two hot horses rubbed together.

The other major camp consists of those people who obviously are not interested in any real exercise at all, because they are wearing Calvin Klein cashmere sweat suits. I have asked the designers about this, and they tell me, "Bruce, these things are not made to sweat in." So you pay $700 for the trousers and $500 for the top, and you don't dare sweat in them. But you look good. You look good.

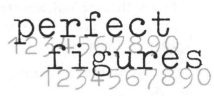

perfect figures

Nearly 25 percent of women in a survey conducted for Rodale said that the sexiest clothing a man can wear is a finely tailored suit. In second place, with 18 percent of the vote: jeans and a sweatshirt.

If you want to really work out, it is okay to wear the former style, and if you really want to meet people, it is okay to wear the latter style.

But I would want to spend more time working out and less time meeting people. Because if I have to meet people in a gym, I am not sure what that says about my life. I would just get moderately priced clothing that is effective for what I want to do. There are some wonderful new fibers and fabrics out there that wick away sweat and can be easily washed and are very soft and comfortable to wear, and that is what I would go after.

I would go after clothing that was supremely comfortable for the job to be done. You can find workout clothing that also has some interesting designs and colors. But I just cannot see being a slave to fashion in a situation like this, unless the gym is your idea of a great place to go to meet people.

If the gym is your idea of a good place to meet people, then you can just sit around drinking your diet Snapple in your cashmere outfit, mopping your brow on a Ralph Lauren designer towel and saying, "Oh, I feel so wonderful after that workout." And hope that somebody comes over and sits down and starts talking to you.

MAN'S GUIDE: We have talked a lot about clothes, but not much about hair. What about the top of the head? The styles obviously vary from long hair to the bald look and everything in between. But what if you don't have much choice in the matter and you are, shall we say, follicly challenged. What are your thought on rugs versus plugs versus just the natural look?

BOYER: Let me preface this by saying that I myself am bald.

MAN'S GUIDE: For my part, I am quite receding, so I'm with you.

BOYER: I am not speaking just from my misfortunes regarding lack of hair, but my feeling has always been that guys who wear rugs—any kind of rugs, whether good, bad, or otherwise—look like guys who are wearing good, bad, or otherwise rugs.

You don't fool people. No one says, "There goes a guy with great hair." They say, "There goes a guy with a great rug."

" Style is to gamble with your image, how others see you. **"**

—Alfred Paster,
The Roots of Soul, 1982

MAN'S GUIDE: So it's the Burt Reynolds syndrome. He finally ponied up for a good toupee that looks right on him, but you still know it is not his hair.

BOYER: Exactly. A guy who is thinking about getting a rug should understand that. He is not going to look like a guy who has good hair.

My feeling is, getting back to this idea of dressing for who you are, why don't you just get a good haircut that takes the best advantage of whatever you have? I mean, if you only have a little hair around the fringes, get it cut well and flaunt it, baby. There is nothing wrong with that.

When I finally went pretty-much bald, I said, "I am just going to shave it off." At first, I thought it was funny-looking. I don't know how I got used to it, but it's funny, it doesn't matter anymore.

I've talked to women about my hair, and I ask, "What do you think of this?" And they say, "Oh, I didn't even notice it, Bruce," or "I think you look great." Or whatever. But it doesn't make that much difference.

In my mind, the hair thing with men is exactly the same as the breast thing with women. Women think, "Oh, I have to have great, big breasts; and I have to get implants and push-up bras and all of that."

If they only understood that real guys don't care about any of that.

MAN'S GUIDE: Most men are just happy to see the breasts up close at some point.

BOYER: Exactly. And the real ones don't taste like silicone.

MAN'S GUIDE: How do we get all of these messed-up views of fashion and appearance? Is it well-meaning experts giving us bad advice, or some more insidious reason, like ensuring that we always go broke trying to look right?

BOYER: That is a good question. Someone should trace back one or two of the major myths and find out which schmucks first tried to push them on the unsuspecting public.

Maybe it is the sociology of propaganda or the sociology of retailing. I don't know. Maybe there are just too many fashion writers looking for something to write about.

Who knows where craziness is born?

QUICKIES

FIRST IMPRESSIONS

Nine women told *New Woman* magazine what attracted them to a stranger. Their comments may leave you more confused than ever as to what women like.

JEAN DREAMY

"The way his jeans fit perfectly. I knew he was someone who cared about details, who was aware of himself, even in casual situations."

—SUSAN, 30, MINNEAPOLIS

ACTION HERO

"The lights hadn't gone down in the movie theater yet, but I spied him 20 rows away as he leaned forward and asked these loud people if they'd refrain from talking when the movie started. I knew he was a take-charge man of action, and that was sexy."

—RHONDA, 32,
HOBOKEN, NEW JERSEY

LEMON-FLAVORED

"I was at a barbecue when a guy tripped down the stairs and spilled lemonade on himself. He stripped off his shirt, wrung it out, put it back on, and went to make more lemonade. Granted, it was like a Mentos commercial, but it made me think he knew how to handle a crisis calmly."

—SARAH, 27, AMES, IOWA

COFFEE MATE

"I was online at Starbucks; he was working the cash register. It was morning in New York City, and people were arguing about who was next in line. He shouted out, "People, it's just coffee!" and made everyone laugh. I definitely wanted to be with this life-of-the-party guy."

—JILL, 28, SAN FRANCISCO

HOLEY MOLEY

"He had a big hole in his sweater. I don't know why I liked it; maybe because it meant he could deal with imperfection."

—JULIE, 38, SAN FRANCISCO

LOCKED IN

"His hair. He had a thick head of hair, and I just wanted to run my hands through it for hours."

—DEBORAH, 37, NEW YORK CITY

HANDY MAN

"He had enormous hands. We sat in meetings together and I would just fixate on them."

—JOCELYN, 35, ATLANTA

MINTY FRESH

"He showed up at a party with dried toothpaste all over his lips. To me, this meant that although he was gorgeous, he wasn't so vain that he was checking the mirror all the time."

—Becca, 30,
Colorado Springs,
Colorado

DOWN AND DIRTY

"This guy wasn't my usual type, but he was walking out of the park covered in grass stains with actual clumps of mud still on him. Imagine what he'd be like in bed!"

—Cynthia, 29, Phoenix

THINK OF HER SIDE OF THE MEDICINE CABINET AS YOUR UTILITY KIT

She's going to keep cluttering the bathroom with expensive, perfumed junk, so you may as well use some of it for your own evil purposes. "Men can use any product that women can," says Wilma F. Bergfeld, M.D., a dermatologist at the Cleveland Clinic. You know how to use her $15 shampoo, but some of her other beauty aids have surprisingly handy uses. Here's a guide.

● Baby powder
A few sprinkles will stop sweat and chafing around your groin or on your feet, and freshen unwashed sheets before an unexpected sleepover. Also, combing some Johnson's powder into your hair will degrease it when you can't shower, says Billy B., a makeup artist in New York City.

● Soap-free cleansers
Products like Cetaphil Gentle Skin Cleanser by Galserman ($9 for 16 ounces) remove surface oils and dirt without water; they're perfect for camping trips.

● Moisturizing lotion
Use it just the way she does. Lancome's Vitabolic and similar lotions can help rehydrate dry skin.

● Hair conditioner
You can use it as shaving cream.

● Toner
If she uses a spray like Aveda Toning Mist to remove facial oils, you have a dandy aftershave.

● Pomade
She uses a thick, waxy goop like Sebastian's Molding Mud to style her hair. You can use a thin film to buff your shoes. Really.

● **Eyebrow pencil**

Clean up a crooked goatee or fix shoe scuffs.

● **Mascara**

It can darken gray mustache or eyebrow hairs.

● **Nail-polish remover**

Some brands contain acetone, a solvent that will remove some types of ink stains from clothing. Be careful; it can also remove some dyes and put holes in delicate fabrics such as rayon and satin.

● **Petroleum jelly**

A dab makes an emergency hair gel. Rub a small amount between your hands to liquefy it before putting it on your head.

NO WONDER WE CAN'T FIND BIGFOOT

Years ago, a hairy chest meant machismo—the follicular equivalent of a 1975 Camaro. Soon, it may be a sign of intelligence. For 23 years, Aikarakudy Alias, M.D., a clinical psychiatrist in Chester, Illinois, has examined male medical students, Mensa members, and manual laborers and rated their body hair on a scale of 1 to 9 (1 = Leonardo DiCaprio, 9 = Ed Asner). In his study on 117 Mensa men, half had thick body hair (rating between 5 and 9), while only about 28 percent of the male population has such fur. Alias believes that dihydrotestosterone (DHT), a by-product of testosterone that fosters body-hair growth, may also enhance brain-cell development. "Then again," says Dr. Alias, "I become skeptical every time I see a hairy fool."

I CAN SEE CLEARLY NOW

Hate the way you look in glasses? Can't bear to poke around your eyes with contact lenses? Looking for an alternative to laser eye surgery? Now there are Intacs—two tiny, crescent-shaped pieces of plastic inserted by a surgeon in the outer edges of the cornea. They reshape the central cornea so that light rays hit the retina correctly says a clinical-trial investigator. In trials on 410 subjects with mild to moderate nearsightedness, 78 percent achieved 20/20 vision, and 98 percent improved to at least 20/40. Intacs should be available soon.

SCENTED SUITS WOO WOMEN

A Korean company is selling men's suits containing lavender microcapsules that pop as the wearer moves around, to the delight of women steamed over the stench of cigarettes and booze on their partners. The next suit scent arriving on the scene: peppermint.

GET SMART

Want to impress your new honey with how erudite you are? Want to know the meaning of erudite? Try listening to the *Instant Genius* audiotape series. It gives you a primer on topics that include philosophy, wine, etiquette, and the stock market. Each tape runs about an hour and costs $12. They're available in bookstores.

DEAR DR. MANLY

Q: *You probably don't hear too often from guys complaining that they are growing too much hair. But for the last couple of years, I've been sprouting wiry hair on the shaft of my penis. It's long enough I could comb it. Not a pretty picture. And now my lover is complaining that it hurts her— that it's scratchy during sex. How can I cut it off? The hair, Doc, just the hair.*
—L. D., Baton Rouge, Louisiana

A: I've heard it before. In fact, it's just about the most common question that guys ask. It comes in right behind, "Pamela Anderson or Cindy Crawford?"

Men tell me they're using razors, tweezers, even depilatories on their penises. I'm sure you can think of obvious reasons why you may regret using a razor. Tweezing the hairs or using caustic depilatory creams is pretty likely to irritate the sensitive skin on your shaft. I can't really get too enthusiastic about those techniques.

In fact, skip the depilatory altogether. I looked at a few bottles in the stores. None of them say, bluntly, "Guys, don't put this stuff on your penis." But if this isn't a stop sign, I don't know what is. Quoting from the back of a Nair bottle: "*Do not* use near eyes, nose, ears, nipples, perineal or vaginal/genital areas."

Ever heard of conditioner? I mean it. Use a gentle shampoo on your penis, like Johnson's Baby Shampoo, and follow it with good hair conditioner. That will soften the hairs so they won't scratch and won't irritate your partner. And as an extra bonus, the labels say it will untangle the hair and make it bouncy and shiny, too. I can't take credit for this tip. I consulted with Victor Newcomer, M.D., a clinical professor of dermatology at the University of California, Los Angeles, UCLA School of Medicine.

If the hair *must* go, you can try an electric razor. The spinning heads should be gentler to your privates than a blade would be. If you want a permanent solution (permanent as in lasting, not as in permanent wave), then think electrolysis. Let a certified electrologist zap those hairs, one by one, with an electrified needle that slides right down into each hair follicle. I know this may sound painful, so ask your doctor to prescribe an anesthetic cream for you to rub onto your penis before the treatment. Electrolysis burns and damages the bulb beneath the skin from which the hair grows. It may take a few treatments, but sooner or later, the root gets so damaged that it quits growing hair.

To find a skilled electrologist who specializes in genital hair removal, contact the International Guild of Professional Electrologists at 803 North Main Street, Suite A, High Point, NC 27262, and tell them what you're looking for. They'll search their database for you.

Q: *I want to break the nightly routine of just crawling into bed with my wife and turning out the lights. Anything I can do to seem sexier to her?*
—J. J., Chula Vista, California

A: Light a candle before you turn out the lights. Better yet, install a soft reading lamp on your side of the bed. Light a candle, turn out the lights, and turn on the reading lamp. And read to her in a gentle, pleasant voice.

I suggest you read to her from *My Secret Garden*. In this 1970s-era book, author Nancy Friday quotes dozens of women describing their explicit sexual fantasies. The book is full of erotic short passages. They are great to read and talk about together. And when you read these out loud, you'll be talking your wife's language. This is female erotica. You read it to her, and you look better and better. Do this a couple of nights a week, and pretty soon, she'll be begging you to read her bedtime stories. You'll find that *you* won't have to beg at all anymore.

Dr. Manly is a fictional character.
The actual advice was provided by a variety of
medical doctors and other qualified experts.

3

PROMOTE
PERPETUAL
PASSION

 If you're married, chances are that you promised to remain with your wife through sickness and health, till death do you part, that sort of thing. If you're single but in love, you may hope she's the woman with whom you'll spend the rest of your life.

Either way, it's a serpentine road ahead. It's easy to forget that you have to burn real fuel—expend real effort and time—to keep passion and romance hitting on all six in a relationship. Especially when you are faced with daunting detours and road hazards like job pressures, debts, children, household chores, and even boredom due to being with the same person day after day.

The take-home message here is this: It is possible to keep rolling down Romance Road until you disappear into the sunset and the final credits roll. A challenge? Yes. Worth it? Oh, yes. Yes. And double yes. In this section, you'll find lots of good advice on how to jump-start a faltering love life and directions for how to find and cruise through an endless tunnel of love. We suggest you take this trip. For your sake. And the sake of the woman you cherish.

TOP TEN

Passion Igniters

If the sexual heat you once felt with your partner has escaped through the cracks—and now things are downright chilly—here are some ways to re-fire the furnace.

① Location, location, location. Just as with real estate, location can be everything in sex. If you always do it in the bedroom, liven things up by trying some alternatives. Think car, kitchen, desk, coat closet, back porch. You get the idea

② Work out together. Aerobic exercise such as jogging, bicycling, and swimming produces "feel-good" endorphins that can increase your desire—and hers

③ Enjoy a quickie. If the two of you seem to seldom have time for sex, have an occasional quickie. Don't fret if she doesn't have an orgasm. Many women don't mind having sex every now and then without climax. And remember, we're talking about an *occasional* quickie

④ Play with toys. Vibrators and other sex accessories can enhance lovemaking for lots of couples. The Xandria Collection, at P.O. Box 319005, San Francisco, CA 94131; and Good Vibrations, at 938 Howard Street, Suite 101, San Francisco, CA 94103, are reputable mail-order sex retailers

5 Be verbal. Tell her what arouses you most. Have phone sex if one of you is out of town. Talk dirty during sex. Moan and sigh if she's doing something you especially like during sex, so she'll know you appreciate it and will enjoy doing it next time

6 Learn her cycle. Her libido follows her monthly hormonal cycle, so pay attention. Best times to catch your honey craving some carnal knowledge: in midcycle and right before and during the first few days of her period

7 Create the mood. Spontaneity is fine, but a little planning can help trigger passion, too. Take a bubble bath together. Spring for some new sheets. Light some softly scented candles

8 Massage each other. Rub each other's backs using long, constant strokes. Circulate your fingertips on the scalp, slide down the nape of the neck, and gently pinch the eyebrows. Knead around the knees and elbows, and pull on the fingers

9 Compartmentalize. Practice mentally setting aside irritants that can kill your mood for sex. Problems at work, bills that need to be paid—put them on hold and think of sex as a reward for having to deal with them at all

10 Use condom sense. Before you get naked, remove the condom from the foil wrapper and lay it—still rolled—on top. If it's cold when it's time to use it, breathe lightly on it until it's room temperature. When you're fully erect, place a dab or two of water-based lubricant in the centermost inside part of the rolled-up condom. This will encourage the latex near the head to slide around in a pleasurable way

MUST READS

Drive a Woman Wild with Words

With apologies to Gary Cooper and Clint Eastwood, most women don't lust for the strong, silent type, the guy who grudgingly grunts or responds to her probing questions with yes and no answers. Nor do they covet a man who during lovemaking makes Marcel Marceau seem chatty. No, as writers Larry Keller and Christian Millman point out in their book, Guy Knowledge, *women like a little ribald repartee in the bedroom. Here's how to do it right.*

Try this the next time you're having dinner with the parents of your partner: Stand up, clear your throat, and announce, "I am a wild, hairy love beast, and I want to ravage your daughter until she mews like a helpless kitten."

Didn't go over too well? Well, there are two reasons why. First, it's downright hokey. Second, it's about as appropriate as a Willie Nelson song in a French restaurant. But if you learn when sexy talk is appropriate and make good use of it, you will have in your possession a key to a magical realm.

"When a man voices the depths of his desire for a woman, it unleashes something in her," says Bonnie Gabriel, author of *The Fine Art of Erotic Talk: How to Entice, Excite, and Enchant Your Lover with Words.* Gabriel, who is based in San Francisco, also teaches a nationwide seminar called The Magic of Making Love with Words.

Think your sweet pea just wouldn't be interested in something like dirty talk? Think again. According to *The Janus Report on Sexual Behavior,* men and women were virtually identical in claiming dirty talk to be very normal or all right (58 percent of men and 57 percent of women). The problem is often just putting the right words in your mouth.

"A lot of men get performance anxiety on the verbal level," says Gabriel. "Because of that, they get tongue-tied. They make wonderful lovers on the physical level, but they don't use their voices."

Sure, about half of all women think dirty talk is just fine. But how do you know if the woman you're with is one of the other half? A few ill-chosen words in the heat of the night could quickly turn your close encounter into the big chill. Dirty talk is very much a double-edged sword, says Gabriel. The same words we use to express lust and excitement are often also used to degrade and abuse people.

Good news, says Wendy Maltz, a certified sex therapist and counselor in Eugene, Oregon, and author of *Passionate Hearts: The Poetry of Sexual Love*. Women who like vociferous sex tend to also be vocal in requesting it. So, when you hear "talk sexy to me" or "I want to hear your voice" whispered in your ear, you need to be prepared. You need to spend some time now figuring out exactly *what* she wants to hear.

Aural Sex

In order to be a vocal virtuoso, it's important to have a good handle on what sexy talk is all about. "For me, erotic talk is any kind of expression that arouses passion," says Gabriel. So now you know the goal: to arouse passion. Here's how to reach it.

● **Start slowly.**
You don't want to jump right in with the kind of words you find scratched above a urinal at a biker bar. "Most women have said that as much as they enjoy lusty talk, they would rather it wait until they are feeling very aroused before you get into the graphic stuff," says Gabriel.

● **Ask her what she likes.**
Use what Gabriel terms erotic questioning. During your lovemaking, try different things such as varying your caresses or changing the placement of your kisses. Then ask her which feels better.

● **Let her know how she's doing.**
Your partner wants to know if she's pleasing you. Speak up, suggests Gabriel. Not only is it sexually stimulating to her but she'll also appreciate being appreciated. Tell her things like, "Yes, right there" or "Your touch is so incredible" or "I love it when you do that."

● **Create a safety zone.**
Tell your partner that you want to try an experiment. Spend some time just kissing and caressing, and then begin tossing out some phrases, words, and fantasies. Ask her if it increases the mood or dampens it. Make mental notes of the things she likes, and use them in the future. "This technique builds trust to the point where you can both really open up," explains Gabriel.

perfect figures

In one survey, 82 percent of the participants said that a satisfying sex life is important or very important, compared to 79 percent who said the same about job satisfaction. Fifty-seven percent of the women surveyed said women are blamed more often for sex problems. Only 37 percent of the men said that.

● Keep an open mind.

Say the two of you are happily ensconced in each other's voices. Out of the blue, she asks you to bray like a donkey. "Some people may have fantasies that turn the other person off," Gabriel says. The key here is to *never* mock or laugh at any of her fantasies. It will kill the trust you're working to develop. Instead, find a way to redirect her fantasy to something a little more palatable. Try saying something like, "Oh, what I'm really imagining is. . . . " Or, if you manage it without wilting,

Reach Out and Touch Her

Sometimes fate, business trips, or an angry, stick-toting father can conspire to keep you away from the woman you love. That's when technology can be your friend.

"Phone sex is a wonderful way to keep the spark alive when you can't be together," says Bonnie Gabriel, author of *The Fine Art of Erotic Talk: How to Entice, Excite, and Enchant Your Lover with Words*.

Here are some tips that Gabriel suggests you keep in mind when love is on the line.

● Play off the fact that you're not there.

Describe to her what you would do if you *were* there.

● Book a trip to Fantasy Island.

Dig around in the sexual closet for a while and pull out some of your favorite shared fantasies. Tell her how you imagine the two of you together in the fantasy.

● Delve into the past.

Talk throatily to her about things you've done together. Tell her how good it felt when she did that . . . or that . . . or especially *that*.

There's another avenue of long-distance communication that can work almost as well—computers. Chat rooms and instant messaging can provide you with a way to sweet-talk your lover without all the toll charges. Of course, says Gabriel, the sound of your voice is missing, so you'll have to adapt.

You'll need to be more descriptive to make up for the lack of sounds, Gabriel says. A good way to do that is to describe what your voice would otherwise convey. Tell her how you're moaning, how excited you are. With a little practice, you'll be as good as you are on the phone.

Practice is also the only way to get around that other difficulty of online sex—typing with one hand. "That can be a problem," admits Gabriel.

go ahead and be Eeyore. "You can just take turns being there for each other if you can't find a common fantasy to build on," says Gabriel.

● **Take her flying.**

Many women love the imagery that comes with sexy talk, says Maltz. You can use your voice to take her on that magical trip. You might try telling her about the two of you together in the rolling waves, the scent of the tropics in the air. Describe the scene to her in intimate detail.

Reaping the Benefits

It's understandable if you're a bit shy about this erotic-talk thing. You're not alone. In the book *Just Married* by Barry Sinrod and Marlo Grey, the authors point out that 74 percent of women in the first 2 years of marriage say they're the chattier of the couple during sex.

But if you switch that around and become a master of bedroom banter, the rewards can be great. "Both partners benefit tremendously," says Gabriel. "It helps people open up a new side of their sexuality."

In other words, it's about turning your good girl bad. In the best way.

SEX TRENDS

IS THAT YOUR DAUGHTER, OR ARE YOU RICH, FAMOUS, AND LUCKY?

If you're like many of us, good-looking young women are noticing you less and less as you grow older. In Hollywood, this doesn't happen. If anything, the trend is for the age gap between leading men and their love interests to be widening.

Some recent examples:

Movie	Actor	Actress	Age Difference
Bulworth	Warren Beatty	Halle Berry	32 years
A Perfect Murder	Michael Douglas	Gwyneth Paltrow	28 years
As Good as It Gets	Jack Nicholson	Helen Hunt	26 years
Six Days, Seven Nights	Harrison Ford	Anne Heche	26 years

Drive a Woman Wild
When You're Not in Bed

Women like sex, but they also like to be romanced. From the book Guy Knowledge *by Larry Keller and Christian Millman, here are some ways for men to do the latter in order to get the former.*

Romance has gotten a bum rap. If you think it's all about cloying novels with Fabio on the cover, boring English movies where nothing ever blows up, or fat little cherubs bouncing around, think again. It's really all about sex.

For starters, let's look at the root of the word. Romance is from the Latin *romanice*, meaning "in the Roman manner." All faults of ancient Rome aside, those boys had some major sex. And let's look at Cupid, the Roman god of erotic love. Today he's a pouty little pink bauble in dire need of a shot of testosterone. But he wasn't always such a wimp.

"Cupid was Venus's son," says Gregory J. P. Godek, author of the bestselling *1,001 Ways to Be Romantic* and *Love: The Course They Forgot to Teach You in School.* "He had a bow he used to make people fall in love. And let me tell you, his bow was *big.*"

Nudge, nudge, wink, wink.

So if the mere mention of the word *romance* creates an overwhelming urge to power up your buzz saw, it's time to change your attitude. And not just for her sake.

"For crying out loud, it's about being selfish," says Godek. "You want to have more sex? Have more fun? Enjoy your days more? I'll tell you how to do it—be romantic." It's not just a matter of more sex, he adds. It's better sex. You see, how you treat a woman outside of the bedroom most definitely affects her inspiration in the bedroom.

The Passing of Passion

If you want a relationship full of what the French call *joie de vivre*, you need to know about passion's Public Enemy Number One. "Routine can take the life right out of a relationship," says Carolyn Bushong, a licensed professional counselor in Denver and author of *The Seven Dumbest Relationship Mistakes Smart People Make.*

Consider this: You wake up, shave, shower, and rush off to work. Nine or so hours later you return, scarf down a hurried dinner in front of the television, watch a few more shows, and head off to bed. You repeat this until you retire. Then, you have an extra 8 hours to watch television.

And you want her to be thrilled by that? Not a chance. You're probably bored stiff, too, if you can wrest your eyes away from *Baywatch* long enough to admit it.

The cure? You guessed it—romance. Here's a crash course in the essence of tickling your sweetheart's fancy.

Let Her Miss You

Your goal is a passionate, exciting relationship. You would think that the more time you spend with her, the better.

Wrong.

Absence, said the seventeenth-century French writer Francois de La Rochefoucald, lessens the minor passions and increases the great ones, as the wind douses a candle and kindles a fire. Those aren't just the poetic words of a long-deceased duke—they apply very much today.

"You want to give her time to miss you," explains Carolyn Bushong, a licensed professional counselor in Denver and author of *Seven Dumbest Relationship Mistakes Smart People Make*. Absence breaks the routines that cripple so many couples' senses of romance. And it's just part of human nature to miss what you don't have.

But there's a caveat.

Gregory J. P. Godek, author of the best-selling *1001 Ways to Be Romantic* and *Love: The Course They Forgot to Teach You in School*, tells the story of a young, self-made millionaire. In his mid-thirties, after largely ignoring his wife while he made his fortune, he decided to switch things around. He took off from work and decided to devote every waking moment to his wife.

"You know what he found out?" asks Godek. "You know what she wanted from him? About 27 minutes a day." Now that's 27 minutes of his undivided attention, Godek notes, not just watching the news together. The point of this story? She likes you around, just not all the time.

So take that separate vacation, plan that weekend apart, go out in the evening by yourself. Just make sure that when you are together, your attention is squarely where it belongs—on her.

◉ Be spontaneous.

"Many women, when they say they want romance, mean spontaneity," says Godek. It's the unexpected that shocks and delights. The surprise trip, the fleeting kiss in the middle of yard work, the note on the bathroom mirror when she wakes up. Spontaneity, he adds, proves to her that you've been thinking of her when she least expects it.

◉ Turn off the tube.

Spend a week with the television off, suggests Godek. Not only will it spur you to action in other areas of your life, it'll free up time to spend passionately with your loved one.

perfect figures

Single guys have sex an average of 21 minutes per session. For married men, the average is about 14 minutes.

◉ Give the gift of unpredictability.

If you bring her roses every Friday evening, that's not romance, that's clockwork. If you're stuck for an unpredictable gift idea, ask her girlfriends, sister, or mother, Bushong advises.

◉ Take her car to work one day.

Bring it back washed and with a box of chocolates on the seat, Godek suggests. Don't mention it to her. Let her find out when she goes to work the next day. Unless, of course, it's the middle of a sweltering summer. Then you may want to put the chocolates in the fridge.

◉ Pretend you've just met.

Plan a night at a club where you don't normally go, says Bushong. "Choose a wilder one, one very different from your normal habitat," she says. "Let her go ahead, wearing something a little slutty." You hang behind for a bit, letting the wolves hover around her, and then come to her rescue. This works anywhere, adds Bushong, even in places like the supermarket. You could accidentally bump into her in the produce section. As tempted as we are to make a melon remark, we won't. Bushong suggests the more subtle: "Could you tell me how to cook my cauliflower?"

◉ Play Sherlock.

One of women's biggest complaints, according to Bushong, is that men are stone-deaf when it comes to picking up clues. "When she says, 'Gosh, I love purple roses,' make a note. Literally, make a note." Surprise her with them later.

◉ Be creative.

We gave you a few pointers to get you started, but from here on it's up to you. "Everybody is amazingly creative. Everybody. You have wells of creativity in you," asserts Godek. Dip down into those wells and pull up a bucketful for her.

You see, when it's all boiled down, she only knows you love her by the things you do. "It ain't the feeling, it's the action," says Godek. "You have to take the action."

And, buddy, a little bit of action is worth a whole lot in the big picture. "Do you remember how good you felt at the beginning of your relationship?" asks Godek. "That's what it can still be like."

Four Marriage Savers

If you find your marriage sinking into an abyss of indifference, there are practical steps you can take to reverse this. Writer Julia VanTine described four such steps to readers of Men's Health *magazine.*

If you think marriage is tough, try divorce. It has all the problems of your current entanglement, plus lawyers, settlement costs, a lingering sense of failure, and confused kids. To help you avoid that fate, we've identified four warning signs of a marriage in trouble, and strategies to help get it back on track. If your marriage is strong, try these tips anyway: Kathie Lee and Frank used to be a fun couple, too.

❶ Turn off the television.

"If the TV is always on, that indicates that neither partner has an interest in what the other has to say," says Frank Pittman III, M.D., a psychiatrist in private practice in Atlanta and author of *Private Lies*, a book about relationships.

One solution: Pry yourselves out of the matching La-Z-Boys at least once a week and go looking for adventure, suggests Michael Perry, Ph.D., a marriage and sex therapist in private practice in Encino, California. Trade off: One week you take her to the amusement park or

Almost half of all women experience heightened breast sensitivity before their periods that interferes with sex. Use a lighter touch when this is the case. For most women, this sensitivity occurs 1 to 4 days before their periods begin.

check out the seedy juke joint on the edge of town. The next week you do something she wants to do—take a Szechwan cooking class, go to the opera. You may have to grit your teeth, but those arias may save your marriage in the long run.

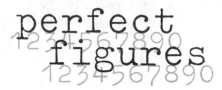

perfect figures

A mere 15 percent of American adults are responsible for half of all sexual activity. Eighty-five percent of all sex is being had by just 42 percent of us. Overall, Americans are having sex an average of 58 times per year, or a little more than once a week.

❷ Up your civility quotient.
"The heart of marriage is good manners," says Dr. Pittman. "A marriage is in trouble when partners stop treating each other with respect."

If you've both been less-than-chivalrous lately, dust off the manners you displayed when you were courting, advises Dr. Perry. It's a small thing to offer your wife a little more wine with dinner or to open her car door first before you open your own, but these things set a tone for the marriage. Too often, we reserve our best manners for work contacts and present our worst sides to the ones who matter most.

If your fights tend to disintegrate into insults, choose a "safe word" with your partner, recommends Dr. Perry. Uttering the word in the midst of a fight means that you immediately cease and desist. (Don't choose "stop." The word should be completely out of context, such as "peaches" or "sassafras.") "When either of you says the word, that means it's the end of that round," says Dr. Perry. "Physically separate yourselves and don't talk for a half-hour." That should clear the way for a truce.

❸ Stop giving yourself a hand.
Consistently preferring masturbation over sex can be a distancing maneuver, says Dr. Pittman.

If either of you seems to be avoiding sex, you have to strengthen your emotional bond first, then ease your way back into intimacy, says Dr. Perry. One way to get closer: Repeat after her. When you're discussing tough subjects with your mate, mirror what she says back to her. She'll know you're listening and she'll feel better understood. She'll also be more likely to extend the same courtesy to you.

That kind of understanding binds couples together. To break down physical distance, start giving each other full-body massages with the works—candlelight, oil, soft music. Getting the kinks out of one another's tensed-up muscles makes each of you feel cared for. Also, kneading each other's naked bodies—and hearing those guttural sighs of satisfaction—will soon trigger your lust, says Dr. Perry.

④ Bring her up to date on your bottle-cap collection.
The most common sign of a troubled marriage—and the deadliest—is apathy, says Dr. Perry. It's a bad sign if you don't care what she did at work today or if she's not interested in the progress of your hobby.

To cut through that fog of indifference, learn to ask specific questions about each other's interests and day-to-day lives, advises Dr. Perry. Don't ask, "How was your day?" Dr. Perry says, "That's just too general. You're going to get, 'Fine.' Ask your partner for specific details, and you're bound to learn something of interest."

Make Love Anywhere

One way to inject new life into a comatose sexual relationship is to make love in new and unusual places. Make your bedroom off-limits for anything but sleeping for a while and consider some of the following possibilities, suggest the editors of Sex and Health.

Before you start experimenting with easy-access outfits and set about convincing your partner that sex in an express elevator will bring your relationship and her climax to new heights, there are a few things you should know. Having sex outside the bedroom can be fraught with peril. For starters, there are a lot of hard surfaces in the world that can make thrusting, well, a little uncomfortable. And you can forget about long, romantic petting sessions: You'll probably have enough time only for the bare basics, with little opportunity for foreplay or fancy positions. Then, too, there's the risk of embarrassment and, if the authorities catch on, maybe a fine or a court date.

But learn to avoid the more obvious pitfalls and you and your newly adventurous partner can be well on your way to having great sex anywhere you can find a closet to pop into or a shrub to duck behind. Fans of this type of adventure wouldn't trade one fleeting quickie atop a national monument for a whole weekend of life-affirming lovemaking between the sheets. Here's all the logistical information you need for sex . . .

In Your Living Room

● Difficulties

Making love on your sofa won't be very different from making love on your bed, so it won't add much of a thrill.

● Solution

Use an armchair. You sit down first, then your partner straddles your thighs, hooking her legs over the arms of the chair and thrusting gently back and forth (it's even better if the chair rocks).

Start with your legs slightly apart and then, when the pace quickens, close your legs, pressuring your own genitals and boosting your ejaculation. If the chair arms are high, you might add a pillow or two underneath you to make it easier on her legs.

For the added excitement of being an exhibitionist, "accidentally" leave your curtains open.

In the Shower

● Difficulties

If you're taller, you'll have to bend your knees or lift her, which could hurt your back. You also risk penile damage if she slips free and comes down hard on your erection. And don't forget all that slippery porcelain.

● Solution

"Try rear-entry sex, with her braced with her hands on the shower wall," says Michael Seiler, Ph.D., a certified sex therapist and codirector of the Phoenix Institute in Chicago. This not only eliminates the height problem but it can also help you to better target your partner's G-spot. Invest in a good nonslip bath mat to avoid taking a spill, and stand out of the stream if you're wearing a condom, since water could cause it to slip off.

In Your Rec Room

● Difficulties

It's littered with toys, expired food snacks, and the occasional stray child.

● Solution

Wait until the kids are in bed, then clear away all the junk and find your way to the beanbag chair. Beanbag chairs offer the perfect opportunity to try one of those really advanced positions you've read about but have never been able to interest your partner in, such as the "wheelbarrow": Your partner lies with her chest supported by the beanbag, her elbows and hands flat on the floor in front of her. You stand between her legs, carefully grasp her by the thighs to lift her from behind, and insert yourself. Use her weight to rock forward and backward.

In Your Bathtub

● Difficulties

Water quickly washes away natural lubrication, making thrusting difficult and maybe even painful for your partner. Cramped quarters and exposed plumbing can make vigorous intercourse a danger to flailing body parts.

● Solution

Have foreplay in the tub, but sex on the floor nearby. Remember to leave a large towel handy to cover those cold, hard tiles.

In a Sauna

● Difficulties

It has to be a pretty big sauna so you can be sure you won't accidentally bump into those smoldering rocks in the corner. Plus, she's going to be awfully hard to hang on to with all that sweat dripping off her body. Did we mention it's hot?

About five men in eight said they would rather give up sex for 6 months than go without TV.

● Solution

Don't even think about exerting yourself in a sauna or steam room unless you're in peak physical condition and your doctor has given you a clean bill of health. "There's a risk of heat exhaustion if you stay in there too long, as well as dehydration, so be careful," says David Spodick, M.D., cardiologist and professor of medicine at St. Vincent Hospital in Worcester, Massachusetts.

Stick to positions that require no acrobatics and little exertion—we recommend side-by-side spooning. If it's not a private sauna, keep a towel over your waists so if somebody comes in you can play innocent.

In the Backyard

● Difficulties

This is probably the safest place to go if you want to make love in the great outdoors. But unless you have a high privacy fence or live on a sprawling Montana ranch, your bare backside could prove an irresistible attraction for nosy neighborhood kids, signature-seeking UPS drivers, and your local helicopter traffic reporter.

⊙ Solution

Wait until the sun goes down. After dark, you can safely sneak out and do your deed under the stars. Even if your neighbor's porch lights illuminate your actions, it's unlikely anybody inside will be able to see out. Bring a picnic blanket or old towel to protect yourselves from rocks and grass stains.

In the Car

⊙ Difficulties

As long as it's not moving, your car is the perfect place for everything from mutual hand jobs to oral sex. But when it comes to actual penetration, conditions are cramped, even in those giant utility vehicles everybody has now. Shifters, uneven seats, and fancy consoles make cars a ripe scene for freak accidents.

⊙ Solution

Push the passenger seat as far back as it will go, fully recline the backrest, and have her lie flat on it, says Dr. Seiler. Then gently straddle her, bracing the seat for support, and be prepared to moon anyone who happens by. She can take the top if she's much smaller than you, but be careful. Most seats don't have much room on the sides and if she takes a tumble, you could get hurt.

You might give this one a trial run in your garage before attempting it at a roadside rest stop.

At the Office

⊙ Difficulties

There's something deeply erotic about having sex in a place where the closest you usually get to each other is a global e-mail. But you could be risking your job. Plus, that fake oak desk or boardroom table could leave you both bruised.

⊙ Solution

If your "office" is a cubicle or a factory floor, it's probably best to let this one remain a fantasy. "Hop on your home office desk or your kitchen table and pretend you're at work," suggests Dr. Seiler.

If you have your own office and you're determined not to accept a facsimile, go in at night. Scout out the place for cleaning staff and take a good look around for video cameras. Once the coast is clear, lock the door and have your partner sit or lie on the edge of your desk or table (her back to the door, just in case). Then stand facing her and quickly execute intercourse.

At a Party

● **Difficulties**

At any minute, someone could burst in to retrieve that coat she has clenched between her teeth.

● **Solution**

Dress for speed. She should always wear a skirt and no underwear, says Tara Roth Madden, author of *Romance on the Run: Five Minutes of Quality Sex for Busy Couples*. Sneak into the basement, a bathroom, or a spare room with a lock, and go for quick, standing rear-entry sex. Don't take any longer than 5 minutes, or your fellow revelers might begin to miss you.

In the Ocean

● **Difficulties**

"Sand could irritate her vaginal mucous membrane," says E. Douglas Whitehead, M.D., a urologist and director of the Association for Male Sexual Dysfunction in New York City. And wading in cold water can make it difficult to get an erection.

perfect figures

Annual sales of Valentine's Day cards are approaching one billion. Women buy 85 percent of the cards.

● **Solution**

As long as condoms aren't a concern for you (water can cause them to slip off more easily), have foreplay on a secluded stretch of beach and, once you get an erection, apply a silicone or glycerin-based lubricant (like Eros) to your penis before heading out to sea. "Cold water won't affect your penis when it's already erect," says Dr. Whitehead. You stand in chest-deep water, she wraps her legs around your waist. Bonus: The water will make her lighter. If she wears a two-piece suit and keeps her top on, it'll just look like you're hugging. Vigorously.

In an Elevator

● **Difficulties**

Alarms will sound if you stop the car. Security cameras can capture the whole thing for posterity.

⊙ Solution

Use a freight elevator, advises Mike Hoover of American Elevator and Machine Corporation. Many lack security cameras—but inspect the ceiling to be sure. Shift the control switch into neutral (the center position) to stop between floors. This won't trip the alarm bells on most service models.

> " Coming soon: Airlines that will accommodate amorous passengers the same way trains and cruise ships do, with private sleeping quarters complete with hot tubs. . . "

Atop a Tall Structure

⊙ Difficulties

The Empire State Building, the Washington Monument, the Seattle Space Needle—they're all well-traveled tourist sites, and as such are patrolled fiercely by humorless security officials. Sex is a big no-no, as is sneaking onto the property after official business hours.

⊙ Solution

We'd opt for something a little less obvious than intercourse—like offering to trade hand jobs with a partner. You both arrive prepared, wearing loose-fitting, elastic-waisted pants with no underwear. Then you find a secluded corner from which to "admire the view." Your partner leans against the railing and you embrace her from behind, sneaking one hand down beneath her waistline. If anyone asks, you're just cuddling. When she's finished, you switch places. It might not be quite the same as sex, but at least you've both had orgasms.

On a Plane

⊙ Difficulties

There's hardly enough room to turn around in that restroom. But as long as you don't light up afterward, the airline probably won't nail you with a fine. "What people do in the bathrooms is their own business," says a Federal Aviation Administration spokesperson.

⊙ Solution

Book your flight on an airline that flies Boeing 777s—it's rumored they have larger handicapped bathrooms. Shortly after ascending, when there's no line and before any messy passengers have caused any turbulence-related spills, your partner casually enters the john. A minute later, you join her. Quickly execute rear-entry sex. You leave first. She leaves a few minutes later.

Coming soon: Airlines that will accommodate amorous passengers the same way trains and cruise ships do, with private sleeping quarters complete with hot tubs on certain trans-Atlantic flights. At least one airline has already come out in favor of the idea, and 49 percent of respondents to a recent *Prevention* magazine poll said that they support accommodations for in-flight sex.

SEX WARS

HELP ONLINE

THE LOVE DOCTOR

For online advice on relationships, take a look at the Web site
of psychologist and author Tracy Cabot, Ph.D. She's so cute, we'd like
her to take us on a personalized tour of her "Love Library."
www.loveadvice.com

BABIES AND BASEBALL

Want to guarantee that your mate won't talk to you—or make love to you—
for at least several weeks? Then miss the birth of your child
because it conflicts with the World Series, the Super Bowl, or some
other sports event you're dying to see. If, however, you'd like to keep
harmony in the house, check out BabyCenter's Web site, which has a
"Birth and Labor Conflict Catcher" that tells you when *not* to conceive in
order to avoid conflicts with your favorite sporting event.
www.babycenter.com/conflict

RELATIONSHIPS 'R' US

Links to discussion groups on subjects such as affairs, dating,
and breakups, plus other links to topics ranging from marriage
to divorce can be found on the Relationshipweb.
relationshipweb.com/index.shtml

MAN'S GUIDE INTERVIEW

Trouble in America's Bedrooms

An Interview with Edward O. Laumann, Ph.D.

If you think there is not much sex going on out there—or at least not nearly as much as the prime-time soap operas and R-rated movies would have you believe—you are probably right.

It turns out that we are a pretty dysfunctional lot. Most folks are having sex successfully, but a pretty large number of people are reporting serious sexual dysfunction that lasts for fairly long periods of time.

At least, that's what a statistically significant sampling of Americans reported to researchers who conducted a study titled "Sexual Dysfunction in the United States: Prevalence and Predictors."

And the researchers, God bless 'em, are sharing the dirt with the rest of us. In addition to coverage on television and in the press, the results of their study were published in the Journal of the American Medical Association.

One of the principal researchers for the study was Edward O. Laumann, Ph.D., professor of sociology at the University of Chicago and coauthor of the book The Social Organization of Sexuality. *In addition to working on the sexual dysfunction study, Dr. Laumann has contributed to such studies as "Private Sexual Opinion, Public Opinion, and Public Health Policy Related to Sexually Transmitted Diseases: A U.S.-British Comparison" and "Circumcision in the United States: Prevalence, Prophylactic Effects, and Sexual Practice."*

MAN'S GUIDE: Apparently, you and your compatriots discovered a pretty high rate of sexual dysfunction in the United States with your recent survey.

DR. LAUMANN: In fact, we found that 43 percent of women and about 32 percent of men who took part in the survey reported that they had experienced an episode of major sexual dysfunction within the previous 12 months. And mostly, these were not problems that came and went quickly, but that existed for at least 2 months during a 12-month period.

MAN'S GUIDE: What kind of sexual dysfunction did you look at? Were people just complaining about an inability to get aroused, or was it more like people could not function at all?

> **DR. LAUMANN:** We covered the full range. There are, essentially, three phases of sexual function and dysfunction.
>
> First, there is desire, or rather lack thereof if you are experiencing dysfunction. This is a lack of interest in sex.
>
> Second, there are problems of arousal, which express themselves in men as the inability to get or maintain an erection, and in women as lubrication problems.
>
> Third, there is dysfunction in climax, which in women is the inability to have orgasm and in men is often expressed as premature ejaculation.
>
> With any of these problems, we are talking about serious and persisting difficulties in being able to engage in sexual behavior.

MAN'S GUIDE: Is it just that the responses are being interpreted as problems? In other words, do the respondents see their dysfunctions as problems, or is it just that if they fall beneath a certain level of sexual activity, they get classified by the researchers as dysfunctional individuals? After all, some people may not consider a lack of desire for sex to be a problem.

> **DR. LAUMANN:** The responses are all self-reports by the people who took part in the survey. The people are basically saying, "Last year, I had such-and-such kind of problem for this many months."

MAN'S GUIDE: Did the prevalence of dysfunction surprise you?

> **DR. LAUMANN:** I think it surprised everybody, ha, ha.

MAN'S GUIDE: So I guess we have been so caught up in the work by Masters and Johnson that we all just assumed most of us were out there having lots of fun. Should we be worried that we as a society are not having as much fun in the bedroom as we originally thought?

> **DR. LAUMANN:** I think that this is a very sobering set of information. Erectile dysfunction—the inability to achieve or maintain

erection—is something we have often associated with older men, and rightly so. Men in their fifties are, in fact, 3½ times more likely to suffer erectile dysfunction than are men in their twenties.

But what is worth mentioning is that 7 percent of the men in their twenties who participated in our study reported that they have erectile dysfunction. And that is a pretty surprising admission. If I came up and asked you whether you were impotent or unable to have an erection, you probably would not want to fess up to that. This would be a fairly unlikely thing for a young man, in particular, to admit to. So our feeling is that this is an undercount. It is surprising enough that even 7 percent of men in their twenties experience erectile dysfunction. But if, as we suspect, that number is even higher, we have some significant problems out there.

MAN'S GUIDE: Is there anything that can be done to improve the situation, or is this basically something that we are going to have to accept and that we are going to have to deal with?

> **"** We found that 43 percent of women and about 32 percent of men . . . had experienced an episode of major sexual dysfunction within the previous 12 months. **"**

DR. LAUMANN: Well, you need to look at several parts of the story to answer that question. Sure, we have the sheer prevalence of sexual dysfunction, which is pretty high. But the next thing you have to ask is: What are the indications for these problems? What are the risk factors that elevate the likelihood that you will experience dysfunction?

One of the interesting things we found is that with women, the effect of age on dysfunction is not very strong. For example, 33 percent of women report that they experienced lack of interest in sex for 2 months or more in the past year. And that percentage is about the same whether the women are in their twenties or their fifties or somewhere in between.

It was pretty clear that, in general, two broad sets of factors tended to put people at risk for sexual dysfunction. One was poor health. The other major factor consisted of stress-related influences.

Among the women who reported, for example, that they lost a fifth or more of their income in the past 4 years, there was a doubling of the rates of sexual dysfunction in the desire, arousal, and orgasm phases.

For men, you double the rates for erectile dysfunction if you have lost your job or if you have had a substantial decline in income in the past 4 years. But it doesn't affect your interest in sex, nor does it affect your capacity to have orgasms.

MAN'S GUIDE: So women have problems across the board in all three phases of sexual functioning, whereas men almost invariably have problems in the arousal phase alone.

Any other interesting revelations?

> **" When things don't go well in the bedroom, they don't work well in the living room, either. "**
>
> —William H. Masters, NBC-TV, June 23, 1986

DR. LAUMANN: Men who have never been married or who are divorced, separated, or widowed have higher rates of dysfunction than do married men.

Men who have had a history of having sex with other men have twice the rate of sexual dysfunction as men who do not have same-gender experiences. Yet same-sex experiences have no impact on dysfunction among women.

And while it is no surprise that you see higher rates of sexual dysfunction in people who engaged in sex with adults before reaching puberty, we were somewhat startled by how many people had been sexually victimized. Roughly one in five women has been victimized in this way, and among men the rate is one in seven. So this is not as rare an event as we generally think.

MAN'S GUIDE: Because men are usually affected only in the arousal phase, it must be very frustrating for them to have sexual dysfunction. After all, they still want to have sex and they can have orgasms, but they cannot keep it up.

But given that women tend to be affected across the board, is sexual dysfunction less stressful for them? After all, if they lack the desire, it seems they wouldn't care that much about their inability to become aroused or have orgasms.

DR. LAUMANN: I don't know if they find dysfunction less bothersome, but certainly they can still engage in sex even if they are not interested. It won't be comfortable if they lack arousal, because the lubrication will not be there. But they can go through the motions. With a man, however, if he cannot become aroused, he simply cannot engage in any sexual intercourse.

MAN'S GUIDE: So a woman with dysfunction might just bite the bullet and say, "Come on in and get it over with." But for a man, the game is over before it even starts.

DR. LAUMANN: Right.

MAN'S GUIDE: Do you have any sense as to whether sexual dysfunction is worse than it used to be? Or was it always there and we just didn't notice it?

DR. LAUMANN: My suspicion is that it probably has not gotten worse or better over the years.

One of the points we are trying to make with the analysis of our survey data is that sexual dysfunction happens. People have to understand that these things happen sooner or later in life, and it is a mistake to think that it is just a matter of getting old.

These are clearly problems that can present themselves early in life. I have had a lot of phone calls from men who are in their twenties and have read about the survey results, and for the first time in their lives, they felt authorized to talk about their problems. All this time, they have been blaming themselves. And of course, that often makes the sexual dysfunction worse.

It is useful to simply know that this is something that can happen to you, and that when it does happen, it is probably because you are under stress. But you should not blame yourself or believe that something is wrong with you as a person. It is good to know that by trying to address some of your sources of stress, you may be able to deal with your problem better.

MAN'S GUIDE: So, you would say that we are better off knowing these things and accepting that they are facts of life so that we don't . . .

DR. LAUMANN: ... Blame ourselves.

MAN'S GUIDE: Which would only cause more stress.

DR. LAUMANN: Yes. That would make the problem worse. But by understanding the problem and some of the causes, you can do something. You can talk it through with your partner. You can try to figure out ways to accept your problem or get more social or emotional support. You can reduce the stresses that caused your problems to begin with.

Many times, people feel as though they are failing in a marriage because they can't perform like they want to sexually. But if you have this problem, you are far from alone. Sexual dysfunction is something that is quite likely to affect you sometime during your life. It may not appear until way down the road. It may come and go. But there is a good chance it will happen, so don't beat yourself up when it does.

Something else that is worth mentioning is this: If 43 percent of women have been dysfunctional sometime during the past year and roughly 30 percent of men have been dysfunctional in the past year, that means the chances of both partners in a relationship experiencing dysfunction is approximately 12 percent.

MAN'S GUIDE: So for one in eight couples, both partners are experiencing sexual dysfunction at around the same time?

DR. LAUMANN: Right. And that would put some really big stress on a relationship.

MAN'S GUIDE: What are some of the notable features of your study, compared to others that have been done before?

DR. LAUMANN: Well, our study is a true representative sample of men and women between the ages of 18 and 59 who are living in households in the continental United States. Many surveys of sex tend to use volunteer samples, such as questionnaires passed out to readers of *Playboy* magazine and things like that. So we are surveying people who truly represent the varied population of this country.

One of the important things to note is that we even included people who are not engaging in sex or who have not engaged in sex in years. Volunteer samples for sex surveys tend to pull in a very high percentage of sexually active people, which tends to lead to overestimation of the amount of sexual activity that is going on in the population.

Many other past studies of sexual dysfunction have involved clinical studies, in which the research is based on people who have come in to see doctors about certain problems. That does not give a good sense of how prevalent the problem is in society at large.

MAN'S GUIDE: What was the primary purpose of your survey?

DR. LAUMANN: It was initiated in part by the federal government and the National Institutes of Health, who asked the research community to evaluate the distribution of sexual practices in the United States.

We were really interested in the spread of sexually transmitted diseases. Sexual dysfunction is one of the other issues we have been involved in. We are also interested in how people make partner selections and whether they are married, cohabitating, dating, or just engaging in one-night stands. All of this was done to try to get more information as a basis for planning public-health interventions.

We originally released the information in a book titled *The Social Organization of Sexuality* and in another book that was more lay-oriented, which was called *Sex in America*. But those books were written very quickly to get the information out there as fast as possible and to try to cover a lot of the topics addressed in the survey. So the statistical analysis of our data was pretty limited.

When we began to look back at the data, one of the areas we really picked up on was sexual dysfunction. And that is where the article in the *Journal of the American Medical Association* comes in. That article was a much more elaborate data analysis of this material than were the two books.

MAN'S GUIDE: What has been the response to your study so far?

DR. LAUMANN: Our findings have attracted a huge amount of coverage. The findings have been talked about all over the world. Heck, I was just in China, and they were talking about our survey there.

Keeping Love Alive

An Interview with J. Dudley Chapman, M.D., D.O., Ph.D.

If your visions of aging and sex invariably include nightmare scenarios of a penis that would remain flaccid even in the presence of five buck-naked supermodels, you are not alone. Likewise, if you are afraid your wife will dry up like the Sahara long before you retire, you are not alone.

But there are ways to keep passion in our lives and to continue to have satisfying intimate relations with women, no matter how old we become. Rather than pronouncing the death of our private parts long before we actually perish, we should be trying to find ways to maintain the spark that we once swore we would never let sputter and die.

On the other hand, our bodies do begin to let us down with increasing frequency as we age. So what specifically can we do to keep passion alive?

J. Dudley Chapman, M.D., D.O., Ph.D., seemed a good candidate to answer this question. For one thing, he is trained in gynecology and obstetrics, so he knows women's anatomy. But even better, he is trained in psychiatry, so he has insight into their psyches. Although he is now retired from clinical practice, he continues to conduct research, and he currently serves as the academic dean of the Institute for Advanced Study of Human Sexuality in San Francisco.

We also figured that we should talk to Dr. Chapman because, against all societal expectations, he continues at the age of 71 to engage in sexual intercourse with his wife—and he has the nerve to enjoy it. God bless him.

MAN'S GUIDE: Because you have a background in gynecology as well as psychiatry, you obviously have seen more than a few female patients in your time. And I'm sure you have done your share of counseling regarding their sexual complaints. So what would you say is the biggest peeve that a lot of women express? In particular, what really bugs women in terms of what their husbands or boyfriends are doing or not doing, both romantically and sexually?

DR. CHAPMAN: Probably the most common complaint with women is: "That is all he ever thinks about." Of course, "that" translates as "sex."

She wouldn't mind just lying together and holding each other and being close, a lot of the time. Whereas he thinks that if he pats any part of her and she doesn't complain, that automatically opens up the door for full-fledged sexual escapades.

MAN'S GUIDE: I guess it's the age-old problem of trying to read each other's signals when we are speaking two different languages. So what is your advice? What is the best indication for a man to know when it's time to just be calm and stop at cuddling versus when it's time to move in and ravish her?

DR. CHAPMAN: Frankly, I don't think there's anything wrong with just asking her. Ask her what she wants. It's not so hard.

MAN'S GUIDE: The direct approach with a sensitive twist. That works.

DR. CHAPMAN: That can be a big turn-on to a woman. If the guy says, "Would you like to make love or just sit here and cuddle?" she may answer, "Let's just cuddle." But she's proud and happy as can be that he asked her. Because of that, a lot of times it may end up going all the way anyway.

MAN'S GUIDE: Because we are talking about keeping the passion alive in a marriage or other relationship, we clearly have to be thinking long-term. So let's address the more mature sexual partners.

Let's say you are approaching middle age, which means your wife or girl-friend is probably approaching middle age. That means that your performance may be in decline and the woman may be starting to enter menopause. What happens to the man's perception of romance and sex around this time?

DR. CHAPMAN: It gets overshadowed by fear. There's fear on the man's part that not only is his life going to come to an end, but perhaps more important, his sex life is going to come to an end.

The prospect of the death of sex is very, very scary to most men. At a certain point, many men start monitoring their penises. A guy gets very concerned about what it's doing, and he's very proud if he wakes up with an honest-to-God erection.

MAN'S GUIDE: But what about getting beyond the fear and actually doing something? What can he do from the standpoint of making sure that he's able to keep his wife happy? What sorts of things does he need to be aware of and sensitive to in terms of what she wants as the years go on?

> " At a certain point, many men start monitoring their penises. . . . He's very proud if he wakes up with an honest-to-God erection. "

DR. CHAPMAN: One of the big things he needs to be aware of is the differing nature of arousal. His manifestation of arousal is an erection. A woman's manifestation of arousal is lubrication. As the woman gets older, lubrication gets slower and it is not quite as copious, and this can cause both the man and the woman some concern. The perception might be: She's not interested in me. She's dry. I cannot really excite her anymore.

Well, that's not the issue. It's often a combination of declining hormone levels—particularly estrogen, which is a factor in lubricating the vagina—and adequate stimulation, or lack thereof.

The key word here, the operative term, is "adequate" stimulation. Some guys think if they kiss the woman one, two, three times, everything should be ready to go. There is a good chance that is not going to be adequate stimulation for his partner.

MAN'S GUIDE: So more foreplay may be necessary.

DR. CHAPMAN: Sure, more foreplay is important. But also, just make more time for sex and be more relaxed about it.

MAN'S GUIDE: You have a few years under your belt. And the last time we talked, you were still having fairly regular sex with your wife. So in your opinion, does sex get better, worse, or just different as you age?

DR. CHAPMAN: I think the word "different" is very provocative.

For one thing, sex is slower. Of course, everything in our bodies gets slower. It used to be that I would go to a hospital to make rounds, and I would take the steps in the stairway two or three at a time. Now, I clog along one step at a time. My body is doing everything slower. And so is my sexual apparatus. And my partner's. And I have to respect that.

If you start pushing or you start getting anxious, then you get into problems that magnify to terrible proportions.

MAN'S GUIDE: What are some of those problems?

DR. CHAPMAN: Failure to even begin to get aroused. Arousal comes more slowly as we get older. If you try to push it, the situation gets worse. That's the main problem that we're talking about.

MAN'S GUIDE: Obviously, the sexual act itself is only part of the picture. What about romance and passion in general? How do you keep them a vital and active part of your life throughout the years?

DR. CHAPMAN: First of all, don't be ashamed of sex. The greatest tragedy in our country is that we seem to think that sex is something that older people shouldn't enjoy. Or we think that it has to be as automatic as it was when we were teens.

It isn't automatic, and it takes a little investment. One of the great sources of sexual input is our eyeballs. Look at your partner. You don't have to hide behind piles of clothing because you're 50 or older. You can still read books that have sexual overtones and you can watch sexy videotapes, and you don't have to feel guilty for looking at something objectively sexual.

MAN'S GUIDE: But that still only goes so far if the body is not cooperating as well as it used to. What specific advice do you have regarding things like lubrication, or different positions that may help make sex in the later years more enjoyable?

DR. CHAPMAN: I'm a great believer in hormone replacement therapy. In the gynecologic world, physicians are still having trouble making hormonal replacement a complete process. Oh, we give women estrogen. We give them progesterone. But it's not nearly as common that women are given testosterone.

Testosterone in small doses raises sexual feelings in a woman. And the key thing is that we're replacing lost levels of testosterone. Women don't produce as much testosterone as men, but they do produce it, and it is an important part of sexual arousal. So if we administer small dosages of testosterone, we are not doing something different or ugly to the woman.

Doctors who do provide testosterone replacement therapy often worry about giving too much. They worry that they'll give her too much and suddenly she'll have all this hair on her face and she'll be growing a beard.

The fact is, the first symptom that a woman is getting too much testosterone is not facial hair, but a funny crick or frog in her throat. The larynx typically manifests testosterone-related changes first.

MAN'S GUIDE: What would you say to critics who would tell you that the loss of hormones is a natural part of the body winding down and that we should not be reversing nature?

DR. CHAPMAN: We're reversing nature in every other way possible. We do it in weight control. We do it in blood pressure reduction.

Hormone replacement is not a frivolous luxury. It doesn't just have to do with improving sex. It also helps prevent osteoporosis, heart disease, and stroke.

MAN'S GUIDE: Not to downplay the importance of hormone replacement, but what can men and women do in bed that doesn't have to involve a doctor? You don't have the time to go into a dissertation on the *Kama Sutra*, but what about some specific things, like artificial lubricants?

> **" Husbands are like fires. They go out when unattended. "**
>
> —Zsa Zsa Gabor, *Newsweek*, March 28, 1960

DR. CHAPMAN: Well, for one thing, the worst sexual lubricant in the world is Vaseline or any other brand of petroleum jelly. That just tears the vagina into unhealthiness.

The best lubricant is any of the many water-based products on the market today that are made and designed strictly for vaginal lubrication. If those are not available, a tube of K-Y jelly works very well.

But lubrication is not the only problem. The greatest thing to fight as we grow old is desire-phase problems.

MAN'S GUIDE: Can you explain that a bit more?

> **DR. CHAPMAN:** Desire comes before arousal. If I don't have the desire, I'm not going to get aroused. If you buy into the idea that you shouldn't be feeling or thinking sexual thoughts because you are older, that is one of the most destructive forces to desire.
>
> By the same token, people get into trouble when they think they still should be super sexual, because they listened to some quack on a talk show who said sex should get better as you get older. Well, it doesn't get better; it just gets different.
>
> We need to respect the fact that sex becomes different. Because if we try to push sex too hard to one side or the other, desire will walk right out the door.

MAN'S GUIDE: Now that you've mentioned quacks who insist that sex should get better, let's talk a little about performance anxiety. You keep trying to have more sex, and then you get frustrated because things aren't working like they used to, and you cannot get aroused properly. So you end up unable to have sex, your anxiety grows, and sexual frequency decreases because you pushed too hard.

Is the key really just to enjoy whatever amount of sex you are able to engage in, and to avoid setting some kind of sexual quota?

> **DR. CHAPMAN:** I think that any time we make sex subject to measurements, we have problems. We are obsessed with questions like: How long should sex last? How often should we have it? What's the best size for a penis?
>
> We too often treat life like golf scores. And if we keep score, then once again, we will have problems with both desire and arousal.
>
> It's awful how caught up we are in numbers and measurements in sex. For example, I won't answer questions like, "What is the time involved in premature ejaculation?" If we put a time limit on exactly what constitutes premature ejaculation, stopwatches will be running in every bedroom across the country. That image may sound funnier than hell, but it is closer to the truth than you may think.
>
> Sometimes guys don't know their shirt sizes, but they know the lengths of their penises. We step up to the urinal and some other guy is there, and our eyes move from side-to-side with the mental micrometer checking off how our lengths compare.

MAN'S GUIDE: Sounds like men can do plenty to disappoint themselves if they aren't careful. Is there anything they do that almost universally disappoints the women they are with?

DR. CHAPMAN: I think women are disappointed in general with ejaculation. I mean, they like for it to happen, but it is not nearly as big an event for them as it is for the guys.

MAN'S GUIDE: So it is climactic for the man, but anticlimactic for the woman. How do you bridge the gap? Should the man just put less emphasis on how much he enjoys blasting off, or should he show more affection after he has reached his end point?

DR. CHAPMAN: It think it's the second one. The guy needs to remember that he got there first, and he needs to at least stay close to her and cuddle her. He absolutely should not suddenly run to the john or turn over and go to sleep. That leaves her absolutely up in the air.

A man also needs to avoid rushing into the sexual act. The woman needs time for arousal, and that usually is a slower process for her than it is for him. A lot of times, women tell me, "All he thinks about is having an orgasm. And he doesn't understand that, many times, I'm just not ready right away, and I'm not relaxed enough for penetration."

Sometimes I tell the woman how to teach him a lesson. I tell her that the next time he has an orgasm, she should just look at him and say, "Honey, that was the greatest ever. You were so magnificent. I want more *right now!*"

That will be the one thing that brings a man into my office. Because he wants to know what the hell I did to his wife. And I tell him, "She says you don't worry about whether she is ready and willing. Why should she worry about whether you are?" It may sound silly, but I have found that to be a very effective therapeutic tool for many of my patients. Men do not think enough about arousal from the woman's perspective.

MAN'S GUIDE: On a less overtly sexual note, do you think it's possible to still be in your forties, sixties, eighties, whatever and still maintain that feeling of courtship?

DR. CHAPMAN: Oh, definitely. I think that when people capture that and hold on to it, they are the ones who have the most healthy and happy partnerships.

MAN'S GUIDE: So what is it that women want day-to-day from an intimacy standpoint? What makes most women feel happy, content, and warm and fuzzy toward their men?

DR. CHAPMAN: For him to come home and spend a little bit of each day sitting down and paying attention to her, which is manifested by actually listening to what she says. If guys would learn to just sit down and respect women by looking at them and listening to them, they'd learn a lot about women. They would be a lot more knowledgeable about what their wives and girlfriends want from them, and they wouldn't have to worry so much about trying to read signals.

QUICKIES

AFTERGLOW ETIQUETTE

By now, you'd think guys would have gotten the message that women don't appreciate it when their partners are deep in dreamland minutes after sex is finished. If you're among the guilty or you simply need a refresher course in post-sex behavior, read on.

● Stay awake.
Unless it's awfully late, fight the urge to snooze—at least for a few minutes. Staying awake for a while assures your partner that you value her and the relationship, not just the sex.

● Don't leave her side.
Staying awake doesn't mean you can go to the living room and start watching Letterman or Leno. And resist the urge to wash up or dispose of contraceptives—other than potentially leaky condoms—right away. Stay put for a few minutes.

● Cuddle.
Touch her, hold her, hug her, kiss her. Offer a massage.

● Talk to her.
Tell her how great she was. How sexy she is. How incredible she makes you feel. Telling her what part of the experience you most enjoyed makes her more willing to do it again next time.

● Bring her a beverage.
When you do get up, ask her what you can bring her. If you've had a vigorous workout together, she may be thirsty or hungry.

DRESSED TO THRILL

Readers of *Men's Health* magazine were asked, "What's the sexiest thing a woman can wear?" Here's what they said they'd most like clinging to their dream woman—other than themselves.

● Sexy lingerie
By far, the most common response, garnering 38 percent of the vote.

● **My shirt**
A distant second with 9 percent of the tally.

● **High heels and a summer dress**
Six percent of those responding cited this combo.

● **Food**
Some of those answering took "dressing" literally. Whipped cream and honey-mustard sauce were among the toppings suggested.

● **Body paint**
And we thought this died out with Goldie Hawn on *Laugh-In* a quarter-century ago.

● **Cellophane**
Sexier and not as noisy as tin foil.

LOVE NESTERS LUST FOR A RING

Researchers at Bowling Green State University in Ohio studied 398 unmarried people who had lived together for 1 month to 5 years and found that 75 percent of them—male or female—expect marriage after 2 years.

Waiting for that marriage proposal puts a strain on partners. Housemates scored higher on a depression test than a group of married people, according to Susan Brown, Ph.D., a Bowling Green sociologist and leader of the study. And if there is no proposal within 2 years, the relationship starts to hit the skids.

"Considering this evidence, I would think twice before cohabiting with someone I wasn't interested in marrying," says Dr. Brown.

GRANNY AND GRAMPS
ARE STILL GETTING IT ON

Good news for those who fear their sex lives will peter out as they grow older. A study commissioned by the National Council on the Aging found that nearly half of the 1,292 people interviewed who were age 60 or older had engaged in sex at least once a month in the past year. Among those with partners, 80 percent had been sexually active.

Of these older people with partners, nearly one in three said the physical part of sex is better than it used to be. One in four said sex is more emotionally satisfying than when they were in their forties. But men, by a margin of 31 percent to 17 percent, were much more likely to say the emotional benefits are better now.

Men surveyed said they appreciate partners who like sex and who are easy on the eyes. Women were turned on by a different asset—men's financial security.

BIRTHDAY CARD SERVICE FOR AMNESIACS

Finally, a company that will take care of everything in the event that you have more trouble remembering your mate's birthday than your high school SAT scores.

Simply Sign It lets you select from a catalog and a schedule of card-worthy events, then return the order form. The majority of cards cost roughly $3.50. A week before each noted day, you'll receive the card in the mail, along with a stamped envelope and a reminder. You simply address and mail it.

For a free catalog, write to Simply Sign It, 50 Lebanon Hills, Pittsburgh, PA 15228-1819. Or look them up on the Web at www.simplysignit.com.

DEAR DR. MANLY

Q: *I recently started seeing a wonderful woman. Everything is great, but I have a hard time reaching climax during intercourse. It's almost as if her vagina is too big and I can't get enough friction. I'm not a little guy, but I seem to get lost in there. Is this possible?*
— P. C., MANITOBA, CANADA

A: This is not meant as any kind of reflection on her character, but it sounds like you might be dealing with a "loose woman." It is likely that the muscles around her vagina have lost their tautness and tone. The good news is that she can pump them up with a simple, regular workout. More on that in a moment. First, though, let's get a mental picture of what's really going on here.

The vagina is not a hollow tube. The tissues of the vagina fold and collapse on one another. Obviously, they are pushed apart and separated when penetrated by a penis or when a baby pushes through. Because the tissues normally are folded, any vagina can accommodate nearly any size penis. But the feel from vagina to vagina may vary depending upon the vaginal musculature and life changes—like menopause and having babies. Having babies can do quite a bit of stretching. Imagine trying to pass a walnut through your urethra and you'll get the idea.

Kegel exercises—which are good for men's and women's sexual performance—can tighten up loose vaginal muscles. If the muscles are tight, the woman can grip your penis tightly with her vagina, intentionally or involuntarily, during the throes of passion.

To do Kegels, your new wonderful woman needs to identify the appropriate muscles. Just like you, she can do that by paying attention to the actions she uses to stop her flow of urine. Once she's found them, she can squeeze them several times a day, holding each contraction as long as possible.

Once she learns to do Kegels and can do them during intercourse, she will find it increases her sexual gratification as well as yours.

Q: *My wife had a baby 5 months ago and <u>we haven't had sex since a couple of months before the birth</u>. I can't hold out much longer. Is this normal? Is there anything I can do to change the situation?*
—C. T., LYTLE, OHIO

A: Welcome to daddyhood. You're feeling like you did what it took to get here and now you'll never get to do it again. It's part of the initiation, Pop. You need to realize that your wife's hormonal levels and sex drive have been changed substantially by pregnancy, delivery, and nursing. And she may still have physical discomfort from a painful delivery. All of this is temporary, if that's any solace. Actually, it may seem like eternity before her sex drive returns to normal. It takes some women a year to get their sexual selves back.

In the meantime, talk to her, nicely. Maybe she'll feel comfortable helping you masturbate or giving oral sex. Go ahead and get the relief you need—at home, buddy—even if she isn't ready to help.

Something else to consider is that your wife's body has changed a lot. She may not like how she looks and may think she's terribly unattractive. She may not feel comfortable having you see or touch her body. Some talk and reassurance and gentle understanding could help here. Then there's exhaustion. Giving birth takes a lot out of a woman. It takes some time for her to get the energy back. You know what happens to your libido when you're dog-tired. The same thing happens to her.

Complimenting her appearance and pitching in around the house may help alleviate her feelings of unattractiveness or exhaustion.

Be patient, be supportive, be loving, man.

When you do resume intercourse, take it slow and follow her lead. She may find some positions too strenuous or painful at first after the long hiatus.

Dr. Manly is a fictional character.
The actual advice was provided by a variety of
medical doctors and other qualified experts.

4

TUNE UP
YOUR
SEX MACHINE

It wasn't too long ago that a man expected his sex life to start fizzling like a soggy firecracker about the time of his 50th birthday. Most men now know better. And unlike our fathers or grandfathers, we aren't willing to accept a flagging sex life as an inevitable effect of growing older.

Nor do we have to. As you'll read in this section, guys can keep practicing their night moves well into their later years by paying attention to things like diet and exercise. And now we have Viagra (sildenafil) and other drugs coming down the pike to help us remain amorous longer.

This isn't to say that we'll be romping between the sheets as vigorously or as often at 60 as we did at 20. But with an enthusiastic partner, sex can continue to be very good—with luck, right up to the time we take our last breaths. That's good news for us and our women. Let the fireworks continue.

TOP TEN

Reasons to Do It

Sex is good for you. Really. Here are 10 ways that making love keeps you physically and mentally buff.

1 Love hates cholesterol. Sex is a form of exercise. Exercise helps lower cholesterol

2 Love is like oxygen. When you breathe fast and deep, your blood is enriched with oxygen, which nourishes organs and tissues

3 Sex raises your testosterone levels. Exercise boosts testosterone, which not only is important for sex but also fortifies bones and muscles and keeps your heart healthy

4 Amour is the ultimate analgesic. There is substantial evidence that endorphins released during sex are effective painkillers

5 Sex delivers DHEA (dehydroepiandrosterone). This hormone improves cognition, fortifies the immune system, and promotes bone growth, among other things

6 Sex pampers your prostate. Some pesky prostate problems that begin appearing in your late forties are caused or aggravated by fluids in the prostate gland not emptying out efficiently. Sex flushes the gland and helps keep it functioning smoothly

7 Sex soothes. Having sex produces feelings of well-being and relaxation

8 Sex equals love. Sex seems to make relationships more durable. A guy who has a vigorous sex life is more likely to be a loving husband and father

9 Sex burns fat. Having sex is a modest means of burning fat. If you have sex three times a week, you'll burn about 7,500 calories a year. That's the equivalent of jogging 75 miles

10 Lovemaking may help you live longer. Sex raises the substances that lengthen your life span—DHEA, a hormone called oxytocin, endorphins, and growth hormone—while decreasing those that may shorten life, such as cortisol and adrenaline

MUST READS

Exercise for Sex

Even if your sex life is as lusty as a porn star's, it can't hurt to have some strategies to keep it that way. And if your libido is lagging, all the more reason to read the following two chapters from Sex Secrets *by Brian Chichester and Kenton Robinson, which explain how certain exercises and foods can keep your sexual engine humming.*

Everyone has at least one Sexual Olympics story to tell. A story of gold-medal lovemaking so phenomenal you wouldn't believe it yourself if you weren't there. Maybe you were 17 and you'd bike 5 miles to sneak into your girlfriend's room and make love until dawn. Or maybe you were in college and you'd steal away from the dorm to a motel, where you'd rock the bed so hard you'd knock those cheesy paintings off the wall. Those are memories of a lifetime. But those days are gone—they're only for horny teens and carnal collegians.

Or are they?

After all, you're older now. Wiser. Worldlier. Wealthier. What's keeping you and your partner from going for the gold now? Could it be you have no energy from a nine-to-five job that runs eight-to-seven, a house where kids are running amok, and a spare tire in need of deflating? If you shed that tire, you may find yourself with energy to spare—enough to make it through the day, keep up with the kids until bedtime, and still have the gusto for Olympic sex at night. That's because, of all the natural aphrodisiacs in the world, fitness is one of the most potent around.

Fit for Sex

The basic benefits of fitness in the bedroom are clear: The fitter you are, the longer you live. The longer you live, the more sex you can have. Class dismissed. Thank you very much. Need we say more?

Maybe a little more. Consider these facts.

- One study of 78 sedentary men at the University of California, San Diego, found that after a 9-month exercise regimen, the men's sex lives soared. Their frequency of intercourse jumped 30 percent; orgasm, 26 percent; and masturbation, 50 percent.

- Exercise keeps your sperm healthier. That's really good news, considering the average guy produces little more than half the amount of whip-tail warriors his dad did 50 years ago.

● Exercise improves self-esteem. If you look better, you feel better about yourself. In an opinion poll of 2,500 readers of *Men's Health* magazine, 66 percent of the men who said their health was excellent ranked their sex lives as good to excellent. Of those who rated their health as fair, only 22 percent thought their sex lives were something to shout about.

● Exercise seems to enhance free-floating levels of testosterone, the hormone responsible for sex drive in men and women.

"A lot of guys expect to have sex like athletes, but they're not athletes—they're couch potatoes," says Barbara Keesling, Ph.D., a sex therapist in Newport Beach, California, and author of *How to Make Love All Night (and Drive a Woman Wild)* and *Sexual Pleasure*.

"There's nothing wrong with being a couch potato and wanting to enjoy sex, but if you want to last a long time and make love in a strenuous way, you need some level of conditioning," Dr. Keesling says. "Sex, in many ways, is like any other aerobic exercise."

Get Worked Up

Here's how to supercharge your sex life by starting down that road to fitness.

● **Arouse with a workout.**

A study of women at Chicago State University found that nearly one in four had been aroused—some even climaxed—while exercising. How's that for incentive to work out together?

● **Warm up.**

If it's been a while since you could see your toes, let alone touch them, then it's not a bad idea to warm up a bit before marathon lovemaking. There's nothing more unromantic than a pulled hamstring halfway through your best bedtime performance. Try some calisthenics and light stretching. "If you're exercising, you need a warmup period. You can't just build to a pitch right away," says Judy Kuriansky, Ph.D., sex educator, clinical psychologist, and host of the popular *LovePhones* call-in radio show in New York City. "I used to run in high

SEX TRENDS

BUSINESS PERKS UP

Operators of Nevada brothels reported an immediate bulge in business as soon as Viagra became available. The owner of two such establishments said business shot up 20 percent.

school—you can't just jump into exercise. Athletic sex is the same thing. It's a physical activity."

Too Much of a Good Thing

Exercise can be the cheapest, most effective libido pick-me-up this side of an all-you-can-eat oyster bar. But as with most things in life, there's always the risk of having too much of a good thing.

Overdoing exercise kills your sex drive. For starters, knocking yourself out for hours on end in the gym may mean you'll be so sore and stiff the next day you won't be able to move, let alone groove. But there's a more compelling, chemical reason to avoid excessive exercise: Too much exercise drives down your testosterone levels and, thus, your sex drive.

How much is too much? It's safe to assume that unless you're an ultramarathoner, you're probably okay. One researcher estimated that you'd have to run somewhere around 200 miles a week to seriously impair testosterone production. Nevertheless, keep your training down to the equivalent of running 30 miles a week or less, just to stay on the safe side.

And don't neglect the psychological traps some people fall into by working out too much.

"How you feel about your own body is certainly important, and you do want your body to function properly," says sexologist Ted McIlvenna, Ph.D., president and founder of the Institute for Advanced Study of Human Sexuality in San Francisco. "But don't kid yourself into thinking that you'll automatically be getting it more often and be a super stud."

● Run for it.
Aerobic conditioning should be high on your list of priorities. It gives you the stamina you need to last all night. Try low-impact aerobics at least 3 days a week for 20 to 30 minutes. Good choices include running, swimming, stairclimbing, and rowing.

Having trouble getting through that 2-mile run? Try not thinking about it. Researchers at the University of Alabama found that runners whose minds wandered felt more invigorated than those who concentrated on the running itself.

● Don't crimp your style.
During orgasm, guys tend to overflex their calf muscles, resulting in painful cramps. Maybe they're pushing off with their toes as they thrust, or perhaps they're curling their toes under too tightly in the midst of passion. Here's how to avoid such a crimp on your evening. It's called the runner's stretch: Stand about four steps from a wall, facing it with one leg forward about 8 inches and bent at the knee. Your back leg should be straight. Now reach out and

touch the wall at chest level and lean into it, keeping your heels on the floor. You should feel the stretch from your heel to the knee of your straight leg. Hold for 20 seconds, switch legs, and repeat.

Eat for Sex

This second excerpt from Sex Secrets *explores the link between food and your carnal appetite. Here's how to feed your woman's fantasies.*

The 1992 film *Like Water for Chocolate* is a delicious blend of romance, folk magic, and desire that highlights a sex secret lovers have known for years: the eroticizing power of food. In one scene, the main character, the youngest daughter of a Mexican family, bakes a wedding cake that mysteriously makes all who eat it long for their lost loves. In another scene, the bewitched baker cooks a steamy quail in rose petal sauce that literally turns the dinner table into an unbridled passion pit.

In ancient times, the food-mood connection enjoyed a colorful, albeit simplistic, history of sensuality, says George Armelagos, Ph.D., professor of anthropology at Emory University in Atlanta. This connection boiled down to what was called the Doctrine of Signatures, where people felt that the shape of things indicated their inherent preternatural powers. For example, the phallic form and size of a rhinoceros horn obviously meant it possessed the power of potency.

"Overall, though, the relationship between food and sex was that if you were well fed and healthy, you were more likely to think about sex," Dr. Armelagos says. "Even today, that's why nutrition and sex go together."

Food and Mood

Food continues to play a crucial role in love and lovemaking—and we're not talking only about the creative ways to use whipped cream.

Although we don't care much about the shape of our food these days, the link between the bedroom and the kitchen remains strong. Something as simple as your making dinner, washing the dishes, or using the right fork at her annual office party can be all the impetus your mate needs to make her simmer in bed. Ditto for more overtly sensual things, like playfully feeding her grapes or hors d'oeuvres.

"Everything is a prelude to a sexual encounter—we need not define sex as the minute we take our clothes off and are in bed," says Doreen Virtue, Ph.D., a psychologist and relationship counselor who blends spirituality into her practice in Orange County, California, and author of *Your Emotions, Yourself.* "Even what we do at the dinner table helps warm us up toward each other."

Finally, there's the chemical connection. The chemicals in food affect our moods and the way our bodies work, too. Researchers even think they've cracked that age-old sex/chocolate connection. It seems that chocolate contains plenty of phenylalanine, a type of amino acid that increases the body's level of endorphins, our natural painkillers and antidepressants.

Cheers to Your Sexual Health

A keen porter in Shakespeare's *Macbeth* has the definitive last word on alcohol and sex when he says that drinking "provokes the desire, but it takes away from the performance."

"Alcohol, which is a drug, can turn up the hypothalamus, the brain's sex center, and that's why many people find they're uninhibited and aroused when they're drinking," says Marilyn K. Volker, Ph.D., a sex therapist in private practice in Coral Gables, Florida. "But alcohol is also a depressant, and too much will have a real depressing effect on your sex drive and performance."

More than, say, two drinks in an hour is enough to send your libido packing. In one study, researchers found that men who had a blood alcohol level of .06 took significantly longer to ejaculate. Many men whose level was .09—nearly the level of impairment in many states—were unable to ejaculate at all. (For comparison's sake, to raise the blood alcohol level to .05, a 150-pound man would have to drink roughly three mixed drinks in 1 to 2 hours.)

Food for Two

Here's how to use the erotic power of food to supplement your romantic interludes. We don't promise it will have the same effect the quail and rose petal sauce did in *Like Water for Chocolate*, but it will point you, your stomach, and your libido in the right direction.

● **Think erotically.**
Any meal can be erotic. It's all attitude. Sometimes, just taking the initiative to prepare dinner or help in the kitchen is all that's needed to arouse your partner.

"The mind—and your imagination—is the greatest aphrodisiac around," says John Renner, M.D., president of the Consumer Health Information Research Institute in Independence, Montana.

The Revlon company surveyed more than 1,000 American adults on all things sensual. They found the following to be the most sensual foods around; add them to your menu of arousing vittles.

Champagne or wine (34 percent)

Strawberries (29 percent)

Chocolate (23 percent)

Whipped cream (19 percent)

Surprisingly, the least sensual foods were liquor, caviar, and beer.

● Add these to your list.
As we mentioned before, chocolate is rich in phenylalanine, a chemical found in food that researchers suspect causes a libido-lifting natural high. Here are other foods that make that list, too: almonds, apples, avocados, baked beans, beef, beets, carrots, chicken, cottage cheese, eggs, herring, milk, parsley, peanuts, pineapples, soybeans, spinach, and tomatoes.

● Make all foods erotic.
"Some people find the art of eating oysters erotic or sensuous, but eating almost any food with the right frame of mind can be just as erotic," says Marilyn K. Volker, Ph.D., a sex therapist in private practice in Coral Gables, Florida. "Try having your partner eat a hot dog or banana and then show her what you can do with your tongue and some ice cream.

"You'll be surprised at the results," Dr. Volker says, "because you're adding this sensual, visual element to eating."

● Keep up with the Joneses.
Remember that sumptuous and sensuous feast in the movie *Tom Jones*? (If not, run down to your local video store and check it out. We'll wait). Here's how to create your own, using some tips offered by Barbara Keesling, Ph.D., a sex therapist in Newport Beach, California, and author of *How to Make Love All Night (and Drive a Woman Wild)* and *Sexual Pleasure*.

Prepare a dinner for two, adhering to the following rules.

1. No feeding yourself, no utensils, and no talking.
Enjoy the strictly sensual facet of feeding time.

2. Serve only finger foods.
Good choices are sliced fruit, cheese and crackers, and meat that can be pulled from the bone.

3. Dine naked on the floor.
Cover the carpet with a sheet, if need be.

4. Feed and be fed.
Feed each other creatively. Eat off each others' bodies. Use your tongues instead of napkins.

Finish by toweling each other off with warm bath towels—or, better yet, take a warm bath together.

Preserve Your Sexual Anatomy

You change the oil, rotate the tires, and get the occasional tune-up to ensure that your car runs well and will last long, don't you? Well, you should be the doing the same thing with your sex machinery, according to the editors of Sex and Health. *Read on to learn the basics for keeping your private parts performing at their best.*

We're going to give it to you straight: The chances that you'll have great sex every time you want it for the rest of your life are not good. Even if you're burning with desire and your partner is willing and able, there can be some basic, physical stumbling blocks.

Almost one out of five men over age 40 rarely gets an erection hard enough for penetration. That number rises to 74 percent by the time they hit their eighties. Eighty percent of all guys will eventually develop enlarged prostates, and of those, sexual difficulties will afflict 58 percent, according to their partners. Thirty percent of all men develop a testicle disease known as a varicocele. And that's just the beginning of a long list of potential afflictions.

You can sit back and hope that luck will carry you over the major hurdles that threaten your sex life. Or you can opt for action. "For the vast majority of men, the ability to remain sexually active into their eighties is under their own control," says Irwin Goldstein, M.D., professor of urology at Boston University Medical School.

What causes sexual anatomy to stop functioning? Preventable injuries are one major cause. Poor diet, lack of exercise, and penile disuse are also major sex busters. But each organ you need for good sex and peak fertility has its own quirks. Each has certain weaknesses and susceptibilities, whether from disease, injury, or misuses. Simple steps you can take, from protecting your testicles during racquetball to downing a daily herbal supplement for your prostate to keeping your penis well-lubricated during sex, can all help preserve your sexual parts.

Keep them healthy today and they'll be ready to serve you well into the future. Here's our part-by-part guide to the care and preventive maintenance of those organs most critical to your sexual function.

Part: Prostate

HAZARDS

Cancerous tumors, noncancerous enlargement, infection. Anything that's bad for your prostate is bad for your sex life. Researchers estimate that as many as half of all men with slowed urination and other symptoms of prostate diseases have a related interference in their sex lives, including problems with erections and orgasms.

INSURANCE

● Cut back on fat.

Researchers now have evidence that as many as one in every three 30-year-olds already has the beginnings of prostate cancer. While studying 525 men, William R. Fair, M.D., of Memorial Sloan-Kettering Cancer Center in New York City, found that 30 percent of the men ages 30 to 39 had microscopic prostate cancer. "Diet probably prevents the cancer from growing," he says.

Many experts believe that fat helps "wake up" sleeping cancer cells, and studies show that men who say they eat foods high in saturated fat (such as red meat, mayonnaise, and butter) are three times more likely to be diagnosed with prostate cancer than men who avoid such fare. Instead of rich and meaty meals, aim to get more soy and bean products in your diet. Scientists report that, in human studies, compounds known as phytoestrogens (found in beans and in soy products like tofu and tempeh) can cut the rate of cancer cell growth nearly in half. If you're new to tofu, let a good Chinese restaurant hook you. Our local place puts together a garlic-eggplant-tofu dish that's become our favorite takeout.

● See more red.

Any excuse to eat tomato sauce is an excuse to improve your prostate. One study showed that men who consumed 10 or more servings of cooked tomato products a week were 45 percent less likely to develop prostate cancer than men who ate fewer than 2 servings. Pasta sauce makes an especially good choice because it provides the perfect opportunity to combine cooked, concentrated tomatoes (which yield the most concentrated amounts of the active ingredient, lycopene) with fresh garlic. Compounds in raw garlic have been shown to slow prostate cancer cell growth by more than 50 percent in test tube studies.

● **Think zinc.**

While a healthy prostate is loaded with zinc, researchers have discovered that infected prostates tend to be low on the essential mineral. Although they haven't quite confirmed the importance of the connection, many doctors believe zinc to be essential to a healthy gland. If you eat two servings a day of lean meat or fish, you're probably fine. If not, consider supplementing with no more than 50 milligrams of zinc daily.

● **Have sex.**

Urologists believe that ejaculating at least every other day helps keep the prostate clear of bacterial agents and prostate secretions that eventually can cause blockage or lead to irritation or infections.

● **Keep things flowing.**

The best way to keep acid in urine from back washing into your prostate (and potentially irritating it) is to keep your pee dilute. A good rule of thumb: Drink enough water or clear liquid every day until you pee clear. Waking up at night to pee is no excuse to cut back; just make sure you get all your liquids before dinner. Also, be wary of spicy foods, caffeine, and acidic citrus beverages that can make your urine more irritating.

● **Consider herbal help.**

The two best herbs that have been studied: saw palmetto and *Pygeum africanum*. "I'm taking saw palmetto as a preventive measure, and I'd recommend the same to anyone with a family history of prostate enlarge-

ment," says Steven Margolis, M.D., clinical instructor at Wayne State University in Detroit and an alternative family physician practicing in Sterling Heights, Michigan. For prevention, he recommends a half-dose: 160 milligrams a day of saw palmetto and 50 to 100 milligrams of *Pygeum africanum*.

● **Schedule a checkup.**
Because the earliest stages of prostate cancer are often symptomless, the only way for doctors to catch it are with prostate-specific antigen (PSA) blood tests and digital rectal exams. We know they're no fun, but if you're over 50 (over 40 for African-Americans or those who have had a father or brother battle the disease), they're simply a fact of life.

Part: Testicles
HAZARDS
These dangling external organs are especially vulnerable to injury, and they're also prone to a number of diseases. Testicular cancer is the most common cancer in men under age 40.

INSURANCE

● **Wear a cup.**
Every year, about 250,000 American men suffer sports-related groin injuries. The consequences? In one study, researchers found that 17 percent of infertile men owed their substandard sperm to past testicular trauma. And one nasty mishap could leave you impotent. "These statistics are no reason to avoid your favorite activities, but they are an argument for proper protection," says Wolfram E. Nolten, M.D., associate professor of medicine at the University of Wisconsin in Madison. If there's any chance you could be hit by a stray ball, kicked, kneed, or tackled, wear a high-quality athletic cup made from molded plastic.

● **Soften the jostles.**
In addition to a cup, experts recommend a little extra support for your scrotum if you'll be running, mountain biking, or doing anything else that may cause your testicles to jiggle around. "Many men, especially those with looser scrotums, need extra support to prevent the tissue loss that causes sagging. It's the same reason women wear sports bras," says Bruce R. Gilbert, M.D., Ph.D., assistant clinical professor of urology at the State University of New York at Stony Brook. Worse, too much jostling could bruise your testicles or epididymis, the tube that carries your sperm. The solution? Your pick: A jockstrap, a pair of snug cotton briefs, or spandex bike shorts.

● **Screen monthly.**

Once a month, after a warm shower, slowly roll each testicle between your thumb and fingers, applying slight pressure. Feel carefully for any lumps or odd shapes that could indicate the beginnings of a tumor. If you find anything, have your doctor check it out. Ninety-five percent of testicle cancer cases are curable if they're found and treated early enough.

Once you've checked for cancer, stand and strain your pelvic muscles as though you were trying to have a bowel movement. While you're straining, examine your scrotum (use a handheld mirror if it helps) for any bluish veins that show up just underneath the skin. Such veins, which are often described as looking like a bag of worms, could indicate a varicocele, a varicose vein in the scrotum. Varicoceles afflict 30 percent of men and raise testicular temperatures by as much as 4°F, an increase that hampers sperm production. "Left unchecked, varicoceles can also result in flagging libido and decreased potency," says Marc Goldstein, M.D., director of the Center for Male Reproductive Medicine and Microsurgery at the New York Hospital-Cornell Medical Center in New York City. Doctors can repair the leaky veins with a microsurgical operation.

● **Learn the emergency drill.**

If you do get injured in the groin—and sooner or later you will— the proper first-aid can help prevent serious damage. First, lie on your back and support your testicles by putting a rolled-up towel or shirt underneath them, with one end of the roll resting on each thigh. Take an acetaminophen pain reliever (such as Tylenol) and apply ice to reduce swelling. If you're bruised, swollen, or in pain for more than 10 minutes, find your way to the emergency room. Request the urologist on call and ask for a scrotal ultrasound, the best way to diagnose a testicle injury.

hot **TIP!**

To improve your ability to delay ejaculating and have stronger sensation when you do climax, do your Kegels. Flex your PC (pubococcygeal) muscles, which are in the genital area. These are the same muscles that control the flow of urine. Tighten and release them several times a day—anywhere, anytime. Work up to doing Kegel exercises 10 times a day, for a total of at least 100 repetitions.

Part: Penis
HAZARDS

You name it. Freak injuries can cause fractures, bumps, or bends to the shaft. Sexually transmitted diseases or poor hygiene can result in outbreaks of rash. And any number of poor dietary and lifestyle habits can leave its hydraulics impaired. Researchers who measured how much blood travels how fast into the penises of men in their thirties, forties, and fifties found that the greatest slowdown occurs in men as they turn 40.

INSURANCE

● **Keep your body fit.**
Exercise boosts levels of "good" high-density lipoprotein (HDL) cholesterol—in one study, researchers found that they climbed three points for each 6.2 miles jogged. And HDL cholesterol helps maintain clear arteries throughout your body, ensuring that plenty of blood can enter your penis during an erection.

The probability of developing impotence soars from 6 to 25 percent as HDL levels drop from 90 to 30.

Exercise also boosts testosterone output, improving erections and boosting libido. In one study, men who exercised three times a week had sex more, masturbated more, and had more frequent orgasms than their couch potato counterparts.

Exercise also helps keep your stomach flat and trim. If layers of fat and skin in the lower abdomen are allowed to expand and succumb to gravity, they can slowly engulf the penis in excess tissue, making it appear shorter and eventually interfering with upward-pointing erections.

● **Keep your penis fit.**
Strong pelvic muscles (pubococcygeal, or PC, muscles) can help drive more erection-nourishing blood into your penis—and help keep it there. In one Belgian study of 179 impotent men, 43 reported being cured after an intensive 4-month-long rehabilitation program of Kegel exercises.

Sit on It

Yet another way an unsuspecting guy can become impotent: riding a bicycle. It's true. Bicycle saddles can crush arteries that deliver blood to the penis, leaving you as limp as last week's excuse for coming home late.

The cycling industry has taken notice of the problem by designing safer saddles less likely to rob you of erections. One of the best is something called the Specialized Body Geometry Comp. Its design shifts weight to the pelvic bones and reduces compression of nerves and arteries.

You can find the Comp seat in most bike shops, or you can write to Specialized at 15130 Concord Circle, Morgan Hill, CA 95037. You may want to get one for your honey, too. Many female cyclists complain of clitoral numbness after riding a bike.

◉ Select seafood.

Eating seafood once or twice a week has a twofold effect on penile health. First, fish is a great source of arginine, an amino acid that is an important component of nitric oxide, a gas produced in the penis that relaxes the penile muscles, allowing even more bloodflow to the penis. And fatty fishes, like salmon and tuna, are a great way to stock up on heart-healthy omega-3 fatty acids, which researchers believe help to widen and protect arteries.

◉ Stay slippery.

Make all your sexual experiences more penis-friendly by keeping a bottle of high-quality lubricant handy.

If you thrust without lubrication and your penis meets with even slight resistance, tiny tears may develop along the blood-filled cylinders inside the penis. As these tears heal, they may form scar tissue, causing a sometimes painful curvature of the penis known as Peyronie's disease.

Keep a spray bottle of warm tap water nearby to refresh the lube as it starts to dry out.

◉ Stay focused.

Being interrupted during sex isn't just annoying, it's dangerous. Sudden or unexpected movements during penetration can result in a painful penile fracture, which occurs when the blood-filled cylinders rupture.

"Between three million and four million American men are impotent today because of an injury they sustained to their penis during masturbation or intercourse," says Dr. Goldstein.

◉ Protect and preserve.

For the same reason that some men get dry, chapped hands during the winter, others end up with scaly patches on their penises. These rough spots aren't just unsightly; they can actually toughen and reduce sensitivity.

To keep dry skin at bay, use a mild, moisturizing bath bar (like Dove) during every shower, and rinse and dry your

This Just In

If you value preserving your sexual health, don't try this at home: A man in New Jersey seeking a sexual thrill with a vacuum cleaner nearly bled to death when the machine cut off a fraction of his penis.

The drunken man hoped to get gratification from the appliance's suction. He didn't realize there was a blade under where the hose attaches that pushes dust into the collection bag. When the man turned on the vacuum, the vacuum did not turn him on. Instead, the blade chopped and diced.

penis thoroughly after washing. Stick to absorbent, all-cotton underwear, and if you need to, apply a mild skin moisturizer formulated for sensitive skin (avoid fragrances, preservatives, and products containing any ingredient that ends in "-ol").

● Keep it busy.

After studying dozens of samples of penis tissue, a team of urologists concluded that guys who have more frequent erections also have more erection-nourishing arteries in the spongy chambers of their penises. In other words, the more you use your penis, the healthier it becomes.

SEX WARS

HELP ONLINE

FROM PENIS TO PROSTATE

The Male Health Center Internet Education Site provides online medical
help just for men. The site provides answers to questions and concerns
about everything from enlarged prostate to painful ejaculation
and testicular problems, plus other health matters. The site is operated by
Kenneth A. Goldberg, M.D., a Dallas urologist and author.
www.malehealthcenter.com

THE FIRST CUT IS THE DEEPEST

Not sure whether to have your son circumcised?
Wondering what all the foreskin flap is about?
Check out the Circumcision Information and Resource Pages.
www.cirp.org

MEN'S HEALTH ISSUES

For medical information of interest to men, click on
HealthNet Connection's Men's Health Issues.
Topics include prostate cancer, hernias, and sports medicine.
www.healthnetconnect.net/men.html

MEN'S HEALTH

Men's Health magazine gives you the scoop on everything from
weight lifting to nutrition. The magazine's online site also has a sex-and-
relationships section where you click on categories that include things like
giving a sensual massage and a test to gauge your condom I.Q.
www.menshealth.com

MAN'S GUIDE INTERVIEW

Holding Back the Years

An Interview with Ronald Klatz, M.D., D.O.

Just as nobody wants to fade away unremembered, no one wants a marriage or other long-term relationship to simply die a slow death. Sadly, though, that is what many of us seem to anticipate from the very moment we start a relationship.

We assume that as we grow older with the women we love, the feelings of passion will, over time, inevitably change to deep, mostly platonic friendship. Of course, we should be friends with our partners in life, but why do we assume that sex has to fade into the background?

As a form of intimacy and a way to maintain feelings of romance and vitality, sex has few rivals. So it seems to be in our best interests to keep sex alive, to nurture it and cherish it—if we want to have satisfying relationships with the women in our lives.

It is often noted that sex is a team sport. In that spirit, it should also be remembered that in the world of sports, a team is only as strong as its weakest player. So both partners need to be in shape.

To gain some insight into the fitness, nutritional, and medical options for maintaining peak performance in our relationships, particularly in the bedroom, we consulted with family physician and anti-aging specialist Ronald Klatz, M.D., D.O., of Chicago.

Dr. Klatz is the president and cofounder of the American Academy of Anti-Aging Medicine, which, with 7,000 members in 50 countries, is reportedly the largest medical society focused on the issue of slowing the effects of aging.

He also has authored or coauthored several books, including Stopping the Clock, Grow Young with HGH, Advances in Anti-Aging Medicine *and* Death in the Locker Room II: Drugs and Sports in the Locker Room.

MAN'S GUIDE: Everybody knows that exercise and nutrition are good for a healthy heart. But do they also have a role in getting your heart rate up in the bedroom?

    DR. KLATZ: Acrobatic sex is quite aerobic in nature, and it can be quite a strain on the man's heart if he is going to take a dominant and assertive role in the sexual act. So it is to his benefit to be in reasonably good shape.

MAN'S GUIDE: So it's not just that good nutrition and regular exercise help you look sexier. They also help keep up your endurance for sex.

> **DR. KLATZ:** Well, certainly, sex is often an endurance activity when performed properly, and regular exercise can help you stay in the game.
>
> But beyond that, there is another sexual benefit of regular aerobic exercise. It maintains the small-vessel, peripheral vascular system—the small capillaries that are so critical to the maintenance of a turgid member.
>
> The inability to maintain that turgid penis is the root of many male sexual dysfunctions. Men with sexual dysfunction have difficulty achieving or keeping their erections, and many times, those problems are due to peripheral vascular disease.
>
> Insofar as cardiovascular conditioning and exercise in general are protective against peripheral vascular disease, they are also protective against male sexual dysfunction.

MAN'S GUIDE: So you would say that exercise and good eating habits are an important part of maintaining a healthy relationship and long-term sexual gratification?

> **DR. KLATZ:** It is a critical issue because sexual attraction throughout life is multidimensional. Sexual attraction is a combination of all those things that cause us to find our partners alluring and sexually interesting. Both sexual attraction and sexual attractiveness rely heavily on perceptions of physical beauty, physical health, youthful energy, mental attractiveness, psychological attraction, and physical power.
>
> Sexual attraction and sexual satisfaction cut across many strata. But two of the strongest factors involved in sex are one's physical health and the perception of vitality. There is no substitute for proper nutrition and exercise in maximizing both factors.

MAN'S GUIDE: What sort of bad habits are pretty much guaranteed to slow us down in our relationships with women?

> **DR. KLATZ:** Poor hygiene.

MAN'S GUIDE: Nice general term.

DR. KLATZ: Dirty underwear always killed it for me.

But poor hygiene, poor grooming, signs of disease, physical illness, missing teeth—those are big turnoffs. One of the biggest turnoffs for women that I know about is obesity.

For some women, the mood killer can be poorly groomed facial hair or the presence of facial hair at all. Some women actually find facial hair to be a turn-on, but the majority of women find it to be something of a negative.

MAN'S GUIDE: Some of the herbal products on drugstore shelves scream about how they improve sexual potency, give you increased energy, and so on. I know you have written and lectured a lot on vitamin and herbal supplements. So how much of this is snake-oil salesmanship and how much is true?

DR. KLATZ: If you have poor nutrition, you will suffer in many ways, mentally and physically, and that includes sexual performance. So from that standpoint, the vitamins and herbs in stores may help you.

But if you have adequate nutrition in your diet, these claims that the manufacturers make about their products become much less significant.

As far as increasing stamina, sexual ability, and so on in a person who has good nutritional habits, there are a few products in stores that can make an impact.

One of those products is yohimbine, but some of the B vitamins also can help. Any of the products that are specifically designed to increase endurance and aerobic performance in general, or that increase nitric oxide (NO) levels in the male member, can be helpful. NO is a compound that is necessary for engorgement, for the purposes of erectile stimulation. L-Glutamine and lysine can help stimulate it.

> " Men have a much better time of it than women. For one thing, they marry later; for another thing, they die earlier. "
>
> —H. L. Mencken, *A Mencken Chrestomathy*, 1949

MAN'S GUIDE: One of the things we adults always complain about is that teens are nothing but raging hormones with legs, while our hormones are on their last legs. What role are hormones going to play in making us healthy and happy with our spouses or other partners?

> **DR. KLATZ:** Hormone levels are quite important in both men and women. Testosterone, for example, is a wonder drug for enhancing sexual interest and sexual performance in men and women. Interestingly enough, a number of over-the-counter products are proving to be quite effective in raising natural levels of testosterone.

MAN'S GUIDE: Such as?

> **DR. KLATZ:** Dehydroepiandrosterone (DHEA) and androstenedione supplements. They don't call Mark McGwire "slugger" just because he hits the balls out of the park.

MAN'S GUIDE: So, as a physician, is this something you would say is safe for people to take without guidance, or should they consult their physicians first?

> **DR. KLATZ:** Well, hormone replacement therapy is a big thing, and even over-the-counter hormones are powerful substances. If you are going to use these substances routinely, even the very safe over-the-counter hormones such as melatonin, you should definitely inform your doctor.
>
> Ideally, you should obtain blood tests to measure the effective levels of these hormones to make sure you are not overdosing yourself. Because there is a downside to hormone replacement therapy. Vitamins are generally very safe. With most of them, if you put too much into your body, you will just pee it away. But not so with hormones.
>
> Hormones have a much more pharmacologic-like activity to them. And over a long period of time, the side effects can be such that taking the hormones becomes a negative.

MAN'S GUIDE: I have to ask about Viagra (sildenafil). Now that is has enjoyed its 15 minutes of possibly overblown fame . . .

DR. KLATZ: More than 15 minutes of fame, I should say.

MAN'S GUIDE: Well, maybe 15 months then, if we want to paraphrase Andy Warhol. Viagra is no doubt an effective medication, because it gives men erections who otherwise have problems getting erections. But now that the dust has settled, is it a wonder drug or was it mostly hype?

DR. KLATZ: Well, I have to say that in people I have spoken with, in the patients I have interacted with, and in my own personal clinical testing, the substance performed as advertised. Knock on wood, ha, ha.

> **"** One of the biggest turnoffs for women that I know about is obesity. **"**

MAN'S GUIDE: Pun intended?

DR. KLATZ: So I'm being a little cute.

Seriously, though, there is a caveat to using Viagra. As with most performance-enhancing drugs, there is an acclimation to the drug, a diminution in its effectiveness over time. So the first brush with using it gives you the best result. People who use this drug need to use it sparingly because the dramatic effect is lost over a period of time. Men with erectile dysfunction should probably save Viagra for special occasions.

MAN'S GUIDE: With Viagra, Vasomax, and whatever other medications may come along, do you think this is the beginning of the end for penile pumps and penile implants, or are bionic penises and the like always going to be part of the sex lives of some men as they get older and less responsive?

DR. KLATZ: Well, the thing we are doing with Viagra and other performance-enhancing drugs is truly producing anti-aging effects. That is, they allow a 50- or 60-year-old man to perform as well as a 20- or 30-year-old. How long they will allow that performance level to continue is anyone's guess right now. What we are seeing with these and other forms of anti-aging medicine is that we are rolling back the pages of the calendar so that people can act, think, feel, and perform at roughly 20 years younger than their chronological age. That is something we are quite proud of in the field of anti-aging medicine, and our goal is to keep pushing the limit further and further.

But people eventually will grow old. It's just that, instead of growing old at 55 or 60, like people did when I was a kid, or growing old at 70, like a lot of folks do now, people will not start feeling old or acting old until they are well into their seventies or eighties. Maybe one day soon we can push that back to the 100-year mark.

However, no matter what we achieve in medical science, people will eventually succumb to aging. Therefore, there will always be a need for a variety of products to assist in sexual functioning.

So maybe Viagra is great for somebody who is 65 or 70, but maybe it will stop working when the guy approaches his nineties, and he will need some other product. The more options we have, the better.

MAN'S GUIDE: A urologist once told me in an interview that he could achieve erection in any man with erectile dysfunction by using some form of medication or surgery, but it was pointless if the man's wife or girlfriend wasn't enjoying sex to begin with.

DR. KLATZ: Maybe he should ask the guy whether he is enjoying sex.

MAN'S GUIDE: Well, are there things the guy should be doing on the home front to make sure that his artificially induced erections aren't just a big waste of blood that could have been coursing through his brain instead?

DR. KLATZ: Ha, ha. What should he be doing? Well, maybe he should be looking for someone who is a little more appreciative of his efforts, ha, ha.

MAN'S GUIDE: Seriously, though, do some men look at getting the erections as the primary goal, instead of thinking about whether they were ever doing things right in the bedroom to begin with?

DR. KLATZ: Well, yeah, that does happen. But on the other hand, aren't you just sick to death of all this sensitive-male stuff?

MAN'S GUIDE: Actually, sometimes, yes. I guess your point is that if the man doesn't have the means to achieve an erection in the first place, he certainly is going to fare badly in bed. So get the erection first, and work on the finesse later.

DR. KLATZ: That's about right. Sex is . . . well, let's put it this way: Good sex is a team activity. It is a couples' sport. Typically, the man is the one who is expected to make the initial effort, so he has to be able to perform. But the activity should ultimately be for the mutual satisfaction of both parties.

MAN'S GUIDE: So we have oral medication, penile injections, pumps, implants—is there anything else for men to use?

DR. KLATZ: There are a number of herbal Viagra-like substances that work rather well.

MAN'S GUIDE: Such as? I know you mentioned yohimbine before.

DR. KLATZ: Yohimbine is one. But there are also products that work on increasing NO levels, such as glutamine and lysine.

MAN'S GUIDE: So we have all of these options. But can sexual spontaneity survive when men are waiting for their pills to kick in or running off for a needle to inject their penises, or grabbing hydraulic tubes and pumping up their privates?

DR. KLATZ: Well, I don't know how much sex you have had in recent years, but there is a hell of a lot less sexual spontaneity in general than when I was growing up.

MAN'S GUIDE: Fair enough. You've got me there.

DR. KLATZ: Can sexual spontaneity survive? Unfortunately, I mourn the death of sexual spontaneity as much as the next man. But we live in an age of rampant sexually transmitted disease and quite reasonable concern over unwanted pregnancy, so sexual spontaneity is becoming a lost art anyway.

MAN'S GUIDE: So what can we do? Oysters and Spanish fly don't work as aphrodisiacs, despite rumors to the contrary. What is the real aphrodisiac that we men have been overlooking all these years?

> **DR. KLATZ:** Well, it is really simple. All you need to do is look like Brad Pitt, wear an Armani suit, have a $150,000 limo with a chauffeur, and wait outside the woman's place with a dozen roses and an 8-carat diamond ring. Then you whisk her away on a Caribbean vacation, where you will stay in a five-star resort.

" Early to rise and early to bed makes a male healthy and wealthy and dead. **"**

—James Thurber, "The Shrike and the Chipmunks," *Fables for Our Time*, 1940

MAN'S GUIDE: What about us mere mortals? What can we do?

DR. KLATZ: I'm still trying to figure that out.

But if the woman legitimately needs performance enhancement because of arousal problems, testosterone can be an incredibly effective sexual tonic, particularly if her levels of the hormone are very low.

MAN'S GUIDE: Well, now that you've taken us back to the realm of hormones, let's continue in that vein. Testosterone plays a huge role in arousal for men and women. What other hormones play a role in ensuring that the woman is ready to rock when the sex begins? What hormonal concerns should we have from the female end of things, especially as a couple gets into middle age and menopause gets closer?

> **DR. KLATZ:** Sexual dysfunction in women is very common post-menopausally, and estrogen replacement can be very effective in maintaining sexual functioning.
>
> Estrogen replacement therapy is turning out to be an incredible preventive health measure in general for women who are past menopause, protecting them from heart disease, diabetes, osteo-porosis, and Alzheimer's disease.
>
> Beyond that, though, maintaining the proper estrogen balance after menopause also maintains a woman's appearance. It keeps her skin plump and hydrated and moisturized, which reduces the appear-

ance of wrinkles. And it also maintains vaginal moisture. That is very important because you need good lubrication for good sex.

MAN'S GUIDE: So we have had an increased focus on fitness and nutrition in the past couple of decades; we now have herbal products that weren't on the shelves 10 years ago; and advances in medicine are increasing our ability to be sexually active as we age. Are men better off now than their dads and their grandfathers were when it comes to maintaining happier, more vibrant, and more sexually active lives?

DR. KLATZ: Oh, I think so. Effective options that allow men to perform late in life are there. Technology is giving men almost mythic performance capabilities. And not only are we living 20 years longer on average than our grandfathers did, but we are able to perform 20 years longer.

For the latest information about anti-aging, visit the official Web site of the American Academy of Anti-Aging Medicine at www.worldhealth.net/a4m, or contact them at 2415 North Greenview, Chicago, IL 60614.

QUICKIES

THOUSANDS THRONG FOR LEGENDARY LOVE POTION

More than 14,000 people flocked to the western Turkish town of Manisa, where local authorities tossed hundreds of pounds of a mysterious paste, said to be a potent aphrodisiac, from the top of a mosque in the main square.

The paste, known as Mesur Macunu, is made up of 41 different spices and is said to have been concocted in 1540 by a prominent medicine man in the Ottoman Empire. The recipe has been secretly transferred from generation to generation among the town's ruling class. Every year, the town throws a special festival to distribute the potion to the masses.

The latest festival was marked by the announcement that the formula has been officially approved by the Turkish Pharmaceutical Standards Institute. Manisa authorities say almost 40 tons of the paste will be produced, with a quarter of it exported to European countries.

SEX MAY STAVE OFF COLDS

People who have sex once or twice a week give their immune systems a boost in fighting colds and flu, psychologists at Wilkes University in Wilkes-Barre, Pennsylvania, concluded.

The scientists measured the amount of an antigen in immune systems of 111 undergraduate students. Those who had sex less than once a week over the previous month had a tiny increase in the antigen over those who abstained completely. Participants who had one or two sexual encounters each week had a 30 percent rise in the levels of the antigen.

The news wasn't good, however, for the most sexually active of the participants. Those who had sex three times a week or more had lower levels of the antigen than those who abstained from sex.

LATEST SKINNY ON SKIN FLAP FLAP

Circumcision opponents gained an ally when the American Academy of Pediatrics ended its position of neutrality and said the surgery is "not essential to the child's current well-being."

The academy also advised that "parents should not be coerced by medical professionals to make this choice." The surgery should only be done on babies who have been given analgesic pain relief, the organization added.

Potential benefits of circumcision, such as a reduced risk of urinary tract infections during the first year and lower risk of rare penile cancer, don't warrant routine circumcision. But doctors should respect the religious and cultural customs of groups favoring circumcision, the pediatricians' group said.

NEW PRODUCTS
PRODUCE ERECTION DETECTION

Alternatives to Viagra may soon be coming to the aid of men with erection difficulties. Among them is Topiglan, a gel that contains alprostadil, an impotence drug that has long been used in injectables such as Caverject. A patented hydrocarbon in Topiglan helps the alprostadil penetrate skins cells to reach the corpus cavernosum—the tissue that traps blood to form an erection.

Also on the erection horizon is Melanotan-II. When injected, this drug stimulates the brain in a way that often produces erections.

Topiglan and Melanotan-II must still undergo clinical trials before getting Food and Drug Administration approval.

SEX SO GOOD
THEY FORGOT THEIR OWN NAMES

Doctors at Johns Hopkins Hospital in Baltimore reported on the cases of two men in their seventies who developed amnesia immediately after having sex. The first man regained his bearings about 12 hours later. The second man needed 15 hours, but even then he could recall nothing of the first 6 hours after intercourse.

Doctors attributed the phenomenon to a Valsalva maneuver—a bearing down hard that can occur during bowel movements, childbirth, and sexual intercourse. This may have created intense pressure in the men's blood vessels, resulting in a temporary lack of blood flow to the central part of the brain. In short, amnesia.

GENDER BENDERS

Men who want sons may do well to marry younger women, while women who want daughters may do best with younger men, a study suggests.

A study of 301 British families concluded that when men married women at least 5 years younger than they, firstborn sons outnumbered firstborn daughters nearly two to one. And when women married younger men, they produced baby girls by about the same ratio.

The age differences had no bearing on second-born children. Researchers are at a loss to explain the gender ratios for firstborns or whether they are significant.

DADDY WAS A DEAD MAN

In the first known case of its kind in the United States, a dead man became a daddy. A California woman gave birth to a daughter after being impregnated with sperm extracted from her husband 30 hours after he died suddenly of an allergic reaction.

Sperm has been removed from other dead men, but the California case is the first publicly acknowledged case in America in which a birth resulted. Sperm can live in a dead man for around 12 hours in a warm climate, longer in a cool setting. The dead man in California—who was in his early thirties—was in a refrigerated morgue.

OOH, BABY

A British researcher found that giving your sex partner an orgasm may help conceive a baby. Women with little enjoyment of their most recent sexual experience had almost no sperm in their cervical mucus, while 90 percent of the women with the highest enjoyment did have sperm in their mucus.

Women needn't have orgasms, of course, to get pregnant. But the findings suggest that it may help them conceive if they do climax.

IT'S BIGGER THAN YOU THOUGHT

A woman's clitoris is bigger than we—or anybody else—realized. An Australian urology surgeon dissected the bodies of 10 women and concluded that the clitoris's total size is at least twice as large as most anatomy texts show and considerably larger than everybody else thinks.

Don't feel bad if you have more trouble locating your squeeze's love bud than finding a lost contact lens. Most of the clitoris is inside a woman, concealed by fat and bone. It's now estimated that about 3½ inches of organ extends inside a woman, above the roof of her vagina.

DEAR DR. MANLY

Q: *I've started using one of those <u>rings that are advertised to enhance erections</u>. Is there anything I should know to avoid damaging my penis?*
—D. A., FLAGSTAFF, ARIZONA

A: Absolutely. Don't let it park on your penis for more than 30 minutes. Rings tend to do what they're made to do—trap blood in the penis to keep it erect. However, without an inflow of fresh, oxygenated blood and an outflow of old, stagnant blood, after a while your penis starts to strangle. Cells die. In my professional opinion, this is not a good thing.

If you do use a ring, find one made of rubber rather than metal, so it's easier to snip off if you encounter pain or swelling. You don't want firefighters coming in with bolt cutters, believe me. And remember, remove the thing before you fall asleep. Those are the rules of the ring.

Q: *I just got blood work results back from my doctor, and they showed that <u>my testosterone levels are down</u> slightly. Do I have any options besides supplemental shots and patches?*
—L. D., BIRMINGHAM, ALABAMA

A: Prescription-grade testosterone supplements are often helpful for men with very low testosterone levels. But for most middle-aged guys whose levels are just "down slightly," simple lifestyle changes can yield many of the same benefits with none of the risks.

● Exercise.
In one study, researchers found that men who ran for 30 minutes on treadmills boosted their testosterone levels 27 percent. Strength training can also up levels. Just be sure not to overdo it.

● Compete.
In a study of tennis players, researchers at Pennsylvania State University in University Park found that testosterone levels rose just before

and during matches and stayed with the players for longer than a day after the competition. If you can, win: The effect was more pronounced in the winners.

● **Have sex and go to bed.**
Simply having sex and orgasms stimulates testosterone production. That's my favorite way. Then drift off into sweet, peaceful dreamland. A good, full night's sleep helps hold down stress. Keeping stress in check is considered by some researchers to be the very best way to boost testosterone levels.

Q: _My wife claims she's allergic to semen._ *Is this just another variation of the "headache"?*
—R. L., SEATTLE

A: Researchers from the University of Cincinnati College of Medicine report that as many as 12 percent of women have this unfortunate allergy. Their symptoms range from a mild itching or burning to wheezing, hives, nausea, and fainting. The reaction may be the result of a hypersensitive immune system response to a common protein found in all semen. It's not a case of her being allergic to your semen, but not to the milkman's.

Take your wife to an allergist. An allergy specialist can use the proteins found in your semen to create a desensitizing compound. In the meantime, bag it, bud. Wear a condom.

Dr. Manly is a fictional character.
The actual advice was provided by a variety of
medical doctors and other qualified experts.

5

ORCHESTRATE
SIZZLING
DATES

It was so much easier being a guy and dating in our teens. Before they began to vanish like carhops and tabletop jukeboxes, drive-in movie theaters were the dependable staples of teen dating. They were cheap, and you could talk and make out during the movie without disturbing some 300-pound gorilla in the seat behind you.

Alas, now we're older and expected to show more creativity—and cash—whether our dates are our girlfriends or our wives. Here, we offer advice on everything from cooking a romantic meal to planning a romantic getaway. We even provide tips on how to merge smoothly into the singles' scene if you are reentering after a lengthy time away. Regardless of your marital status, a date is a date, and a date is supposed to be hot. So turn up the sizzle.

Pickup Tips

Bartenders know what women like. After all, from where they stand, they've witnessed more blowouts than a pit crew. They know what strategies work and what lines send women searching for their pepper spray. Here are their suggestions for success.

❶ Find a quiet bar. If a bar is so loud you can't talk, looks become the only criteria. And not every place is as dimly lit as your basement

❷ Go in early. "The bar is more relaxed early in the evening, and conversation takes on a more casual tone," says veteran bartender John Doyle, of the American Beverage Institute. You'll beat the crowd; and since everyone's guard is down, you're seen as less of a sleazeball. Nurse that martini; if you're lucky, it may be a long night

❸ Bring someone along. "You look more appealing," says Jimmy G., bartender at Raoul's in New York City, "even if it's your sister." (Don't stretch this by necking)

❹ Observe from afar. You can learn a lot about women by the men they blow off, says another veteran bartender. If they blow off losers, that's a good sign. If they blow off every man, they're obviously with the LPGA tour

5 Fish for the flawed. "Find a knockout with a minor flaw—a slight lisp or an overbite," says Doyle. "If you act like it doesn't exist, or even compliment it, it's disarming." Don't say, "I have a friend who can get rid of that for you"

6 Approach them yourself. Never get a waitress or your mother to do your dirty work. "Women will label you a wimp," says bartender Troy Straker of the Marlin Bar in South Beach, Miami

7 Don't buy her a drink. "It's too obvious," says Irene Davis of the National Hotel in South Beach. Spend your money on something helpful, like a Mercedes key chain (actual Mercedes optional)

8 Use the bartender. Let him join the conversation. He'll banter with you, which makes you look good. Just don't take it personally if she goes home with him instead

9 Talk to the "smart" one. When attracted to one woman among a giggling throng, you have no choice but to approach them all. And now you're risking the scrutiny of a dozen female eyes—a more unsettling experience than hot-tubbing with your parents. But here's a tip: "Focus on the plainest one in the group," says Doyle. "Her friends will think highly of you, and you'll have the opportunity to talk to all of them." Then you have your pick (and who knows, the plain one may be the coolest, and maybe she'll help you with your taxes)

10 Be interested in your job. "Some guys apologize for wearing their suits to the bar," says Jimmy G. "That's ridiculous. I knew a guy who was a mouse wrangler—he handled rodents on movie sets. He got women because he loved his job." And his rodents (some say too much)

MUST READS

Get Back in the Game

The sad truth is, despite our best efforts, a lot of us are going to end up divorced. Maybe even more than once. Trying to maneuver through the daunting world of being single again isn't like riding a bike—you can forget what to do. Maybe you never really learned during the first go-round. Writers Larry Keller and Christian Millman help you make the transition in this chapter from Guy Knowledge.

It's been a while. Flustered, timid, tongue-tied, and unsure sum up how you're feeling. And you haven't even talked to a woman yet.

If eight-track tapes were the hottest thing on the market the last time you were on a date, this chapter is for you. But take heart—you're not alone. About half of us get another go at being single, thrown back into the whirling waters of unwed women. Consider this an opportunity to get it right.

The first thing you should know is that women's attitudes toward men with a courtly eye have changed. Today's women have heard it all before, says Lila Gruzen, Ph.D., a Sherman Oaks, California, relationship, marriage, and family therapist and coauthor of *Ten Foolish Dating Mistakes*. They're more worldly, more egalitarian, and less inclined to be forgiving of a man with awkward overtures.

That said, the basic emotional plumbing of women (and men, for that matter) remains the same, untouched by shades of Gloria Steinem. "Men and women are more alike than different," Dr. Gruzen says. "We all want the same things." That includes love, respect, a bite of the kids' Happy Meals, and, yes, even sex.

The New Rules

Gone are the days when you sidled up to a woman at a club, ogled her from Birkenstocks to beret, and invited her to come inspect the shag in your van.

"I know of so many women who say, 'I just wish he'd move his eyes up 10 inches,'" says Wendy Maltz, a certified sex therapist and counselor in Eugene, Oregon, and author of *Passionate Hearts: The Poetry of Sexual Love*.

So here are a few important pointers to get you back into the swing of things.

❶ Be light of heart.

A sense of humor is often the most underused item in a man's chest of wooing tools, says Dr. Gruzen. "When men lose their sense of humor, it's a really fatal foolish dating mistake," she says. Women truly appreciate a man who can laugh and not take himself too seriously. How else can a short, fuzzy-headed guy like Billy Crystal get to hang out with Meg Ryan and Debra Winger?

◎ Keep first dates short.

In the initial stages, meeting for a cup of coffee is a great way to avoid investing too much time with someone who just isn't going to work out, says Dr. Gruzen. "If you go on long dinner dates and you end up hating the person who is sitting across from you, you get turned off to dating altogether," she says.

◎ Don't give too much too soon.

This can be money, gifts, information, whatever. People have a tendency to want to skip over the creepy, awkward stages of getting to know someone and develop intimacy as quickly as possible. "If you skip over that part, then you don't get to know them," Dr. Gruzen says. "You just get to know the fantasy, who you think they are."

◎ Dodge the bullet.

If, in the initial stages of dating, she asks you to tell her about your ex, Dr. Gruzen has one emphatic word of advice—don't. "It's a trick question. If you hate her, you're not over her. If you like her, you're not over her either," she

Stranger Than Fiction

There are a lot of men out there with the pattern of a barroom floor imprinted squarely across their faces. This comes from falling flat on their faces after delivering a hopelessly bad pickup line.

While writing his book *How to "Pick Up" Beautiful Women*, former bartender John Eagan interviewed more than 2,000 women whom he considered beautiful, trying to discover what they look for in a man they are meeting for the first time. One of the questions he asked each woman was, What was the nicest, most unusual, or funniest line a man ever said to you? Here are some of the answers.

● "Wow! Great job, God."

● "My Jaguar needs an oil change. You want it?"

● "You remind me of my mother."

● "I would take you out for dinner, but I don't have any money."

● "Well, now you've done it. I'll have to dismiss my whole harem now that I met you."

● "I wish I had a higher IQ so I could enjoy your company."

● "Four out of five voices in my head recommended I come over and talk to you."

● "I'd take my pants off over my head for you."

perfect figures

The average man has had 13 sex partners, according to a worldwide study.

. . . .

warns. Say something vague, like it just didn't work out, and move on.

● **Forget that she's a woman.**
Well, at least once you've established that she *is* a woman. "Put blinders on. Block out the person's genitals, their sexuality, and listen to what they have to say," Maltz suggests. You want to find out her hopes, her dreams, her beliefs. Let her tell you. Funny thing is, the best conversationalists are those who are the best listeners, Maltz says. "You can be aware of your sexual attraction, but just enjoy it on your own for a while." The best part is that she'll love you for it. After years of fending off crude sexual advances, she'll find you to be a breath of welcome spring air. And you know what happens in spring. . . .

● **Postpone the sex.**
Yeah, right, you say. We're serious here. It's not a moral or physical thing, although the specter of AIDS should have you thinking carefully before you hop into anyone's bed. "Sex allows you to fall asleep for about a year in a relationship, and then you wake up and realize that you know nothing about this person," Dr. Gruzen says. The connection in the bedroom can mask the fact that you're largely incompatible in every other way. And by the time you realize that she's definitely not the one for you, she is wearing your clothes, has joined your health club, and is playing cards with your sister-in-law. It gets messy.

Man Shortage

If you're getting back into the singles' scene rather late in life, take heart in the fact that the older you are, the less competition you'll have for the ladies.

Between ages 40 and 49, men make up 49.4 percent of the U.S. population. Between 60 and 69, we comprise just 46.5 percent of the total, and from 70 to 79, only 42.8 percent of the population. And if we make into our nineties, three-fourths of the people in our age group will be women.

So, how long should you wait? "It's psychologically not in a man's best interest to have sex until at least 3 to 4 months into the relationship," says Dr. Gruzen. You'll know by then if you want to give her some space in your sock drawer.

● **Fix her an old-fashioned.**
If your last dates were, say, 15 to 20 years ago, you probably know some things that younger men find totally foreign. "I firmly believe that the old-fashioned manners, grace, and

charm have never gone out of style," says Susan G. Rabin, a New York City relationship therapist, director of The School of Flirting, and author of *101 Ways to Flirt*. "Women still very much appreciate that." Younger men, she adds, have few of the social skills that their older counterparts have. Use that to your advantage. And as for that modern dilemma: "Picking up the check is never a turnoff to a woman," she says. There you have it.

You've heard a lot here about patience and taking it slow. For a reason. As in sex, women take longer to warm up to a relationship, says Maltz. But once they do, look out. "Men would score a lot more if they just learned the art of patience," she says. "Once a woman feels safe, she's pretty open. She's going to start moving on you."

Cook a Romantic Meal

If you want to turn up the heat with your woman, get in the kitchen and prepare a meal for the two of you. She'll be impressed. You may get lucky. Here's how to proceed, according to Larry Keller and Christian Millman, the authors of Guy Knowledge.

If you labor under the misconception that the culinary arts are only for women and wimps, meet Biker Billy.

As comfortable on his Harley police bike as he is in the kitchen, Bill Hufnagle, host of the TV cooking show *Biker Billy Cooks with Fire* and author of a cookbook by the same name, scoffs at the idea that cooking is unmanly. "It's one of those myths," he says. "It's like the one that says all bikers are mean, evil people. It's not true."

So dust off your chopper and wipe the counter clean, it's time to learn the essence of creating a romantic meal for the apple of your eye. Because, as Hufnagle so eloquently puts it, "food is edible love."

Secrets of a Sensual Meal

The first secret of a romantic repast is simplicity. "A man needs to remember not to overdo it," says Martha Hopkins, coauthor of *InterCourses: An Aphrodisiac Cookbook*. "Anybody who thinks he's going to cook a five-course meal from scratch is out of his brain." Here's what you need to know if you want passionate sex on tonight's dessert menu.

◉ Surprise her.

Invite her over for, say, a movie. Or, if it's your wife, suggest a quiet game of cards in the evening. Then, when she walks in, she'll see that you've really been a cooking Casanova. "She'll love it," promises Hopkins. And you, too.

◉ Plan ahead.

The focus should be on your lady love, not the food. Cook what you can ahead of time, even the day before, says Hopkins. Don't try to do it all while she sits in the living room with a warming glass of wine, listening to your muffled curses.

◉ Know what she likes.

You may think your hot dog and peanut butter stew is the best dish since Betty Grable, but what if she doesn't like soup? Make a mental note of her favorites and also any allergies she has, Hufnagle suggests.

◉ Choose a few choice dishes.

Once you've established what she likes, select one or two dishes that you're going to make. Ideally, they are ones you've made before or ones that stand a reasonable chance of turning out on the first try. "You don't have to make a leg of lamb or some fancy French dish," Hufnagle says.

Augment your choices with premade dishes. "That's what the gourmet section in the grocery store is for," adds Hopkins. Get a dessert from a local bakery, appetizers from the Piggly Wiggly, and you're all set.

◉ Set the mood.

As important as the food you cook is the atmosphere you create. Candles or a crackling fireplace are always appropriate. "Fire captures the heat of the moment," says Hopkins. Appropriate music is another good bet. Even your clothes matter. If you're striving for a more formal meal, put a tie on under your apron.

perfect figures

Thirty-one percent of people surveyed by the Travel Industry Association of America said they traveled at least 100 miles for a romantic getaway in the previous 12 months.

One-tenth of those questioned said they took five or much such journeys in the prior year.

Nearly 75 percent of the respondents said they visited a city. The second most popular choice, at 44 percent, was beaches or lakes.

Three-fourths of the romantic travelers were married, and their average annual income was $67,000. Men, more than women, viewed these trips as romantic getaways, by a margin of 54 percent to 46 percent.

◉ **Think presentation.**

Sorry, but a book *is* judged by its cover, and a Cornish hen by its glaze. Be artful in the way you serve the food, says Hufnagle. It doesn't matter how delightful your peppercorn sauce is if you serve it out of something from your army mess kit. If you make a salad, choose colorful vegetables. Nachos look wonderful with red bell peppers diced on top. Use parsley, kale, even wildflowers to garnish plates. Lay a breadstick on the side of the plate. Use your imagination, or steal some ideas from a magazine in the checkout line of the grocery store.

◉ **Go for aroma.**

Just like presentation, the way food smells is crucial to how she perceives it. When she walks in, the first thing that should greet her is a kiss from you. The second should be the smell of your cooking. Buy yourself some partially baked rolls at the grocery store, suggests Hufnagle. Throw them in the oven for a few minutes before she gets there. Consider choosing other foods that are as pleasing to the nose as they are tantalizing to the tongue. Baked Brie cheese, fresh spices, even crushed garlic scent the air wonderfully, he adds.

◉ **Be flexible.**

"A romantic meal can be so many things," says Hopkins. "Sometimes you feel really loving, sometimes you feel really playful, and sometimes you feel really horny. Pick the foods and moods to match." A picnic spread out on the living room floor, an impromptu breakfast in bed, take-out food served with a candle and a glass of wine. They're all meals, they're all romantic.

 "It's all about saying, 'I love you' with an act that includes food," Hufnagle says.

◉ **Wine and dine her.**

"Alcohol, if appropriate, is a good addition to almost any meal," says Hopkins. It relaxes the mood and adds to the ambiance. Choose the booze to suit the situation. Wine is almost always a good choice, as are after-dinner

SEX ✲ TRENDS

TASTY DATE

An increasing number of restaurants are creating "tasting menus" that allow diners to sample from five to a dozen courses prepared personally by the chef. Each night's menus are created afresh and often spontaneously. The 1999 Zagat guide to New York restaurants reportedly lists more than 80 restaurants that offer tasting menus. It may be a nice way to impress the woman you're with, but know that it won't be cheap. Prices in the Zagat guide range from $27 to $120 per person.

liqueurs. Don't overdo it, though. "If you have too much, the machinery isn't going to function," reminds Hopkins.

● Forget about the dishes.

Don't don your rubber gloves and leave her after a great meal. Forget about cleaning up and just concentrate on her, says Hopkins. The Joy you're looking for is not in a dish detergent bottle. There is a statute of limitations on this advice, however. Eventually, it's your job to clean up. Don't leave the mess for her to do later.

Eating for Pleasure

What makes a particular food sexy? Why are mangoes equated with lovers while corned beef hash just doesn't register on the lust-o-meter?

Martha Hopkins, coauthor of *InterCourses: An Aphrodisiac Cookbook*, has an interesting theory. Sensual foods, she says, should generally work as well on the body as they do on the plate. Here, then, are some of the foods she considers sexiest.

● Honey
"The word rolls off your tongue," Hopkins says. "It's sticky, it's sweet. Picture the way it drips. You just keep drizzling it to wherever you want." But be cautioned—honey is not a lubricant, she stresses. It can gum up the works in a hurry if it's used that way.

● Nutella
You know the stuff. It's a chocolate-hazelnut spread usually found in the peanut butter aisle. "We're all convinced it's just sex in a can," Hopkins says.

● Grapes
Since the days of ancient Rome when Mark Antony fed grapes to Cleopatra, the juicy fruit has been associated with lovers. "The way they burst in your mouth is definitely sensual," she notes.

● Oysters
What list of sexy foods would be complete without oysters?

● Chocolate
"You can't mess up with chocolate," she says. But if you do, oh, what fun it is to clean up.

● Asparagus
"A phallic symbol, albeit slender." Feed your lover steamed stalks of asparagus and watch her devour them.

● Strawberries
Enough said.

'A' for Effort

There are many ways to make your meal memorable, but remember one thing—the fact that you're doing it at all is significant. Don't sweat it if your cooking skills aren't completely up to par. "Women just love the fact that they're being cooked for," says Hufnagle. "It's really something they adore."

So much so, adds Hopkins, that you may not make it to the end of the meal before she decides to put that strawberry sauce to another use. No problem. "Many meals taste better the next day," she says.

How to Date out of Your League

Most guys are intimidated at the prospect of asking out a particularly beautiful woman. This Men's Health *magazine article by Matt Fitzgerald tells you how to succeed.*

You see them everywhere: chatting, smiling, quietly contemplating world peace as they suck on the ends of their Ray-Bans. You want to talk to them, but you wonder if there's any point. After all, you aren't a billionaire. You don't model underwear. You aren't even an actor in rehab.

We are speaking, of course, about the universal beauties you've always assumed were beyond your grasp. Well, you're wrong. In reality, great-looking women fall for nice guys like you, guys who have only one thing you lack: a strategy.

To this end, we have probed the minds of leading relationship experts and the lives of regular guys who have taken their modest, farm-team talent to the Big Show. From the evidence gathered, we have compiled a definitive, eight-point plan to help you attract and keep all those women you've been fantasizing about.

The really good news? None of our steps requires mail-order aphrodisiacs.

❶ Show her you're a gutsy guy.

Because most men are intimidated by overwhelming looks, the amount of competition for beautiful women is much smaller than you may think. In fact, the reason many unassuming guys are with knockouts is simple: They were the only ones who took the risk.

"Two of the main traits beautiful women are attracted to in men are power and self-confidence," says Warren Farrell, Ph.D., author of *The Myth of*

Male Power and an expert on man-woman relations. "If a man is intimidated by a woman's looks, she assumes he's going to be intimidated by the world in general."

A guy who takes a risk, however, exudes power by overcoming the initial desire to run when he comes face-to-face with stunning beauty. And while perfect 10s get zillions of propositions from newly brave yokels soaked with alcohol, they encounter comparatively few serious (and sober) suitors. You can score big points with a beautiful woman simply by making a mature, confident approach and by treating her like a normal person—which is probably what she is, underneath that leather mini and skimpy halter top.

❷ Worship at the altar of Larry King.

The talk-show host and serial husband is living proof that you can't predict what women will find attractive. "Sometimes beautiful women prefer a handsome man, and sometimes they don't; sometimes they prefer a wealthy man, and sometimes they don't," observes David Deida, a lecturer on the sexes and author of *The Way of the Superior Man.*

Although you may not need extraordinary looks or money to attract a ravishing woman, you do need *something*. So use your best social selling points when you approach her.

My buddy, an ad sales representative in San Diego, says humor works well for him. "If you can make a woman laugh, you can probably make her do anything," he says. He recounts one occasion when he approached a woman at a club and offered to buy her a drink. She curtly refused. He then asked her to dance and received the same response. He finally asked, "Well, can I just stand here?" She laughed despite herself, and within minutes he had her name and phone number.

❸ Don't hit on her; talk to her.

The problem with an opening line is that it's just that—one sentence that seldom leads to anything.

hot **TIP!**

If your condom breaks at a critical moment, do the following: Wash immediately with soap and water. Ask your partner to inspect herself for condom bits and refrain from douching, which can push in microbes. Also ask her to see her doctor to inquire about the "morning-after pill." Rehash histories about previous sexual partners and diseases, and if you're concerned about sexually transmitted diseases, get tested within a few days. Finally, try to learn why the condom broke, so you can avoid a repeat. Was it an expired condom? Did you use an oil-based rather than a water-based lubricant?

HIM: Hey, you come here a lot?
HER: No.
HIM: Oh.

Besides, most good-looking women have had more lines tossed their way than the entire Wallenda family put together.

You'll fare better by starting a real conversation. Dr. Farrell recommends hunting for something the two of you have in common, no matter how small. Asking her advice on the relative ripeness of melons in the produce aisle just might punch your ticket. It's been done before, but it demonstrates that you value her opinion.

Another guy I know, a software entrepreneur in San Francisco, made eye contact with Ellen one morning on his commuter bus. She was a knockout; he's an average guy with a big nose. "When I saw her on the same bus a couple of weeks later," he says, "I told her, 'I was hoping to see you here again. Do you work downtown?'" She responded, and they were off.

> **"** Forget lines. You'll fare better by starting a real conversation. Ask her advice. Then, think about follow-up questions, not about her breasts. **"**

❹ Don't intimidate her.
What? *You* intimidate *her*? You bet. Most guys fail to appreciate that romantic approaches make even the prettiest of women just as nervous as they make you. Making her feel comfortable will calm you both down and improve your odds of success. Smiling, asking for advice ("My parents are coming to town—what show should I take them to?"), and listening attentively (think about follow-up questions, not about her breasts) are proven ways to put her at ease. "Even the way you breathe makes a difference," adds Deida. (Think slow and deep. And don't drool.)

❺ Focus on something other than her looks.
"Beautiful women are like a second-term president: insecure," says Dr. Farrell. "They know their powers are ephemeral, and that one day, inevitably, someone will replace them." (Pray it's not Gore!)

So, even at the height of their radiance, women like to be appreciated. When courting her, catalog her subtler virtues and let her know you admire them. Also, compliment her appearance at the moments when she feels least beautiful—when she's sweaty, tired, or just waking up.

6 **But don't ignore her looks.**

A lot of men believe you should never let a woman know you think she's beautiful because it puts you in a "vulnerable" position. That's a load of bull. Gorgeous women know they're beautiful, and they know you know it. If you try too hard to play it cool, they simply see you for what you are: a phony. But while you don't want to mask your attraction, neither do you want to express it lewdly ("Nice rack") or in a manner that fails to distinguish you from the scores of other guys who compliment her ("Gee, you're pretty").

Instead, focus on the quieter aspects of her loveliness. "Beautiful women are suspicious of the grand compliment." says Dr. Farrell. Tell her you like the way she wrinkles her nose when she smiles or the way she tilts her head when

How to Wake Up to a One-Night Stand

Last night, you couldn't be honest with her and you couldn't be honest with yourself. Now it's daylight, and you have two choices: (1) Creep away like a . . . well, like a creep; or (2) face the music. Like a man.

● **Listen.**

Birds, traffic, dogs barking, her talking. Listen to what she's saying. She may be saying something like, "This was an awful mistake." If that's the case, agree. But not while you're yanking on your pants and heading toward the door. Reflect for a moment on human weakness. Then yank on your pants.

● **Talk.**

Be completely honest, but also be completely tactful. Her biggest risk, aside from an unwanted pregnancy, is damage to her ego. Your biggest risk is that she will turn into a lethal, pathological stalker, waiting to jump out of your shower.

● **Leave nothing behind.**

Including doubts. Make it clear that you enjoyed meeting her but that there is no relationship to end. There is nothing to end, except last night. Don't tell her you'll call. Don't say you'll see her around. Treat her like a grown-up. She may return the favor.

● **Don't do it again.**

You see a sign on a fence above a hole. It says, "Stick your willy in here because it feels real good." No way? So why push yourself into strange, dark places? You could get sick or sued. Besides, sex is better when you know a woman well enough to know what she wouldn't dream of . . . then persuade her to do it.

she talks to you. Notice things that only women notice amongst themselves—how well her scarf matches her eyes—and you'll impress her with your sensitivity and powers of observation. Either that or she'll think you're a closet Elsa Klensch fan.

7 Use your brain, not your wallet.
If your intended is as great-looking as you think she is, she'll still have plenty of opportunities to date other men—rich men, actually, with silvery hair and tight little convertibles. That's just something you have to accept.

Because men tend to associate female beauty with sex, we often mistakenly assume that a beautiful girlfriend is a sex object waiting to be bought by a higher bidder. In the rare case that it's true, say good riddance to the superficial bimbo.

Otherwise, advises Deida, "the best way to encourage fidelity is to show her what she would be missing if she weren't with you. Challenge her beyond her expectations." Does she like to dance? Sign up for ballroom lessons. Does she like to paint? Keep her in brushes. If a woman recognizes that you not only make her happy but also help her grow, she won't want to lose you.

8 Don't tie her down.
A ravishing woman has too much beauty for you to hog. Grow up and let her share it with the world. "When a woman realizes that her beauty is a gift, that it can bring joy to other people, then her beauty deepens and she becomes radiant," says Deida.

By encouraging her to smile, strut, and show off, you won't lose a piece of her beauty; you'll gain a grateful chunk of her

perfect figures

According to a survey of 2,315 single men and women conducted by the Chicago-based dating service It's Just Lunch, men and women approach dating at different speeds. Such as:

Average length of time it takes a woman to decide if a man is worth dating a second time: 1 hour

Average length of time it takes a man to decide if a woman is worth dating a second time: 15 minutes

Percentage of women who say a man's income is an important dating criterion: 90

Percentage of men who say a woman's income is an important dating criterion: 51

Percentage of women who date for more than 6 months before having sex: 17

Percentage of men who date for more than 6 months before having sex: 7.5

heart—a chunk she has probably never shared with a guy before. What about other guys, who *will* try to steal her?

Your extreme options are to fight or flee, but both choices are foolish. Instead, says my software-selling buddy, "steal the guy's attention yourself and strike up a conversation. When he finds out you're a nice guy, he won't want to disrespect you." If he does, that's where a martial-arts background really comes in handy.

SEX WARS

"THIS IS FUN. CAN I CALL YOU AGAIN?"

HELP ONLINE

MIDDLE-AGED AND SEARCHING

Now there's a dating service for people age 45 and up. Called Dating
Connections, members can fill out a variety of profile topics,
such as music, family, religion, and politics. Members are able to control
who can see their profile as well as who can contact them.
www.thirdage.com/romance/dating/

CUPID, PLEASE HEAR MY CRY

At Cupid's Network, you'll find links to singles' services, magazines,
organizations, travel clubs, and personal ad services.
www.cupidnet.com

UPSCALE AND SEARCHING

Match.Com offers upscale professional singles a means of meeting
similar people. The majority are 21 to 49 years old, and half of the
users are women. Matches are two-way, and e-mail alerts tell you when
potentially suitable members register. There's a registration fee, but you
can get a free 7-day trial membership or explore as a guest.
www.match.com

MAN'S GUIDE INTERVIEW

Planning
Romantic Getaways

An Interview with Larry Fox

To hear travel writer Larry Fox tell it, planning a romantic getaway can be a minefield of potential arguments, regrets, and recriminations.

It's not that such emotionally charged trips are very difficult to plan—just that, frankly, many men are not willing to do their homework beforehand. Or worse yet, they plan a getaway around activities or events that they like, instead of thinking about mutual likes and considering the pastimes that would make their girlfriends or wives happy.

Plan too haphazardly, and you risk staging your own remake of The Out-of-Towners *or* Planes, Trains and Automobiles *or any other movie about a trip gone terribly awry.*

On the other hand, micromanage your trip, and you risk reaping nothing but disappointment.

But romantic getaways can be pulled off, Fox says, and they can be carried out superbly—if men will think about comfort, convenience, and beauty first and foremost when they make the plans.

Because after all, if the woman is happy during the getaway, that's more than half the journey to making sure the man is happy.

As a staff writer for the Washington Post*'s weekend section, Fox's job duties include writing articles on entertainment and travel in the Mid-Atlantic states.*

He also has coauthored several travel books with his wife, Barbara Radin-Fox, including Romantic Weekend Getaways: The Mid-Atlantic States, *in its third edition. Their other books are* Romantic Island Getaways: The Caribbean, Bahamas and Bermuda, Romantic California Getaways, Romantic Hawaiian Getaways, *and* Romantic Getaways in the Pacific Northwest and Western Canada.

In addition, the Foxes maintain a Web site called Cruise News, which is a monthly e-magazine that features articles, columns, and advice on taking cruises. You'll find it at www.romanticgetaways.com.

MAN'S GUIDE: What is the key element of any romantic getaway, whether it's a long vacation or a short weekend trip?

FOX: First off, let me talk about when you *shouldn't* go on a romantic getaway. My wife and I have made some of these mistakes, and we have heard other people's horror stories.

Don't go on a trip when you are tired. If you're stressed out at work, don't think that a romantic weekend away is going to happen. You cannot switch from one mode to the other just like that.

Don't go when one of you is sick. Romance just isn't going to happen then, either.

And don't go when you're fighting, because it's not going to get any better. Travel really is stressful, and you don't want to do it when things are going badly in life.

Too many people think, "Ahhhh, vacations are relaxing." But just get to the airport and start dealing with all the problems involved with lines, late flights, and baggage problems, and a lot of the romance goes right out the window. So first off, you have to understand that travel in general is stressful.

Now, when you are talking about weekend getaways, one of the main things to keep in mind is not to overplan the trip. You don't come in with a script that says this and that and the other thing will happen, and then at 9:00 P.M., she'll throw off her clothes and we'll have wild sex. That is not going to happen, you know? You have this script, but she hasn't read the play yet. And probably, if you do tell her you have a script, she's going to walk out. So you cannot afford to overplan.

> **"** Growing up tends not to cure Americans of the notion that the number of miles covered is an important gauge to the success of pleasure travel. **"**
>
> —Calvin Trillin,
> *Travels with Alice*, 1989

MAN'S GUIDE: So that's what you shouldn't do. What *should* you do?

FOX: When my wife and I are asked what makes a trip romantic, we don't really have any one theme. But at some point, you have to surround each other with beauty. You know, a beautiful inn, a beautiful resort, beautiful countryside, whatever.

When the man is planning a romantic getaway, a lot of it comes down to how well he knows the woman in his life. What are her likes and dislikes? What really turns her on? What relaxes her? A lot of men don't know the answers to these questions.

And often the man and the woman don't see eye to eye on what to do. Women call me all the time and ask for advice on romantic getaways. They want to know about the inns across the country, and they want to know what there is to do during the daytime near the inn.

Whereas the man may think, "Well, let's stay in bed until 4:00 P.M., get up, and have a meal." That's not going to happen.

Women want to do things during the day that are enjoyable to them and that allow for time to communicate and to share feelings and experiences with their partners.

Also, the women want to know the details about an inn. What are the rooms like? What are the beds like? What restaurants are nearby? Are they romantic? Are they noisy? Do many couples go to them?

MAN'S GUIDE: Would you say that while a man can't afford to overplan things, he does need to pay attention to the details?

FOX: Yeah. Just don't have a schedule. And if you call an inn to make reservations, don't just say, "Give me any room." Ask what the differences are between the types of rooms. And you definitely want a room with a private bath. Forget going for the "down the hallway" setup so that you can save $20.

Don't get a room that's tiny either. You need space.

And it's always good, if you don't know about restaurants in an area, to ask the innkeeper about places to eat when you make the inn reservations. Then, make some restaurant reservations right away. You can change your mind later on. But the worst thing you can do is to be somewhere and have to scramble around for something to eat.

MAN'S GUIDE: So while you shouldn't overplan, you also shouldn't just fly by the seat of your pants.

FOX: No. You need a room, and you need to eat.

As far as activities, you can do some research on some of the towns nearby. A lot of the states have very good travel guides. If you don't want to pop for the cost of a guide, then go to the library.

And if you are driving, I have one key suggestion to make the journey as pleasant as possible: Get off the interstate. Nothing is less romantic than driving at 70 miles per hour down two lanes of straight concrete. You don't see anything except gas stations. If you get off the interstate, you end up on the old state highways, and you find some quaint towns. We always say, "Never take the bypass; always go through the towns."

You never know what you might find in these towns. There might be antique shops there. There might be wonderful, quaint restaurants. We've discovered festivals going on when we've driven into some towns. You don't find out this stuff by driving down the interstate. Interstates are fine if you need to make time. But for romance, they're deadly. They are mind-numbing for both the driver and the passenger.

Make sure you have a good set of maps if you are driving. There are many good map companies out there, but I think that maps from the American Automobile Association stink. You want decent maps that will show you how to get to some of these little towns and how to get off the interstates and so forth without getting lost.

> **"** Local radio stations dissolve in static every 5 miles; insects detonate against the windshield. He stops and has the oil checked. The American is in his seasonal migration. **"**
>
> —James Thurber, quoted in *Time*, July 20, 1970

But as far as that goes, don't worry too much about getting lost. You're not going to wind up getting eaten by dinosaurs someplace. The worst thing that can happen is that you drive for an hour, and then you eventually run into the main road. You'll probably see a sign there pointing you back to the highway.

Sometimes, the most wonderful things we've ever seen we found when we thought we were lost. You have no clue where you are, which adds a bit of tension, and then suddenly you come to a town that's just charming, or maybe you drive up on some fantastic scenery. And there's nobody else there to create crowds and spoil it for you because nobody wants to get lost, so everybody else is on the interstate.

MAN'S GUIDE: What else can you do to make things special?

FOX: This is a special occasion, so why not have flowers delivered to the inn and tell the innkeeper that they're coming. The innkeeper can make sure the flowers are waiting in the room for your wife or girl-friend.

You can pack chocolate and champagne. Some innkeepers will even have the champagne ready in an ice bucket if you just let them know in advance. There are a lot of things you can do to surprise her when the two of you arrive.

MAN'S GUIDE: What about taking a day or a weekend to spend in a hotel in your own city or town? What if all you want to do is get out of your house or apartment for a little while? Is that cheap?

> **"** Thanks to the interstate highway system, it is now possible to travel across the country from coast to coast without seeing anything. **"**
>
> —Charles Kuralt,
> *On the Road*, 1985

FOX: My wife and I do that. It can be great, and it is a great way to get rid of the kids for a little while. You are within a half-hour of home, so the baby-sitter or grandparents or whoever is taking care of the kids can easily call you over if there's a major emergency. But you can get away.

We generally do it when we have a play or concert we want to see downtown. We check into the hotel in the afternoon, and then we hit the play after we've had dinner. Then maybe we go to some late-night music place.

But regardless of the specific plans, we tend to dump the car as soon as we can. Once we get to the hotel, there is no more driving until we leave to go home. We take cabs. It's a little bit of added expense, but it makes the evening so much more pleasant. You don't have to worry about parking, for one thing.

A lot of the hotels have great weekend packages that you can take advantage of for these mini-getaways. Sometimes they include meals or Sunday brunch or other amenities, such as wine. Getting away in our own area is something my wife and I do often, at least three or four times a year.

MAN'S GUIDE: **We certainly don't want to advocate cheapness, but what about the husband or boyfriend who wants to do something nice for his partner but doesn't have a lot of money? What advice can you offer about how to be cost-effective and still have a romantic getaway? Or are the two concepts like oil and water?**

FOX: No. You can have a cost-effective getaway. I'll give you an example. Where do you live?

MAN'S GUIDE: Chicago.

FOX: The Outer Banks in North Carolina are a very popular destination. You can get there pretty easily from Chicago. You can stay in a room on the beach, and it will probably cost you $125 to $200 a night for a room, depending on the time of year. It will be a nice place, but nothing special. Just a room.

> " A lot of men think of a romantic weekend as wild, nonstop sex. . . . Well, chances are, that's not her idea of a romantic weekend. "

Me? I'll be spending time on the same beach. But because I've done my research, I'll stay somewhere in Nag's Head, about 5 minutes from the beach, whereas you're 2 minutes away from the beach. I will stay at an inn that is filled with old antiques and stuff salvaged from shipwrecks. I'll chat with the innkeepers, whose families have lived in the region for eight generations and who know all the people and all the stories and all the history. I'll pay $55 a night.

Now, what's the difference here? The difference is that I did some research. And if you do some research, you can find these places. Many guidebooks have this information.

I know a lot of people don't like to do research for a trip, but $100 a night is a big savings. And rather than getting a chain hotel room, I'll get someplace where I can sit on the porch, and the innkeepers can tell me stories of the Outer Banks back before there were bridges.

Another thing you can do to keep getaways cost-effective is to go to smaller towns. Go to places where the attractions are maybe a bit more scenic than anything else. Some of the state park systems have very good deals, for example. But if your girlfriend hates the woods—and all the ticks, deer, and bears that come with them—then that's the wrong place to go. As I said before, you have to know what she likes.

MAN'S GUIDE: Travel sections in bookstores tend to have a lot of offerings. What about the Internet? Is the World Wide Web a good place to do research on travel?

FOX: I use the Web every day. It's a good resource, but you have to really refine your search parameters.

Some of the state tourism Web sites have links to bed-and-breakfasts and resorts, and those are usable, though I frequently find that they tend to be overly complex and very frustrating.

Yahoo! has directories for a lot of the major cities, and Sidewalk also has such directories. These directories tend to focus on bigger business-type hotels, downtown places, chain places—much like Fodor's and Frommer's do.

MAN'S GUIDE: I want to briefly get back to a point you alluded to earlier regarding talking to the locals to find things out. My wife and I recently went to New Orleans. We had horrible luck with the food. There are so many restaurants, and you figure you'll get great Cajun and Creole cooking. Instead, I found that the Louisiana-style cuisine I have eaten in several other cities in the country was far superior.

After several days of this, my wife asked a local where to eat and we finally got a good meal. Should it become your standard operating procedure to ask the locals about where to eat and where to go, even when you are in big cities?

FOX: It doesn't hurt. Ask the concierge at the front desk. Dancing is one activity you may have to ask around about. Since the hotels began dropping their nightclubs that had dancing, it's hard to find a place to dance at when you are traveling.

But the biggest thing to remember in any getaway is to just go with the flow and enjoy the subtle things. I know a couple who celebrated their 20th anniversary by going to one of the finest inns in America. It cost them $1,000 for this one night of celebration.

Afterwards, I asked them how it was, and they told me the whole affair was miserable. When I asked what went wrong, they told me their expectations were too high. There was no way they could make that $1,000 worthwhile. They had placed too much of a burden on themselves.

A lot of men, for example, think of a romantic weekend as wild, nonstop sex, during which the woman does things he's never even heard of before. Well, chances are, that's not her idea of a romantic weekend. And if your expectation is continuous sexual activity, you are going to be disappointed because it isn't going to happen.

If you keep your expectations well-grounded and just think of the weekend as a way to get closer to the woman you love and share some good times together, it may turn out to be one of the best weekends of your life.

MAN'S GUIDE: And if she's content and comfortable, you just may get that wild sex, too.

FOX: Right. But if you plan the wild sex into the itinerary, it's not going to happen. You can't schedule it. The best thing is to just let the romance and intimacy happen.

QUICKIES

HOW TO SCORE PRIME CONCERT TICKETS

You're outnumbered 50,000 to 1. Here's a way to improve your chances of catching some front-and-center sweat.

Getting the best seats in the house, even when the house is the size of Madison Square Garden, is nothing you leave to luck. We're not talking about the kind of bonehead craziness that makes guys spend the night on cold concrete down at the Camp Box Office. We're talking about a savvy craziness, the sort of nutty stuff that just might work.

● Submit to the TicketMaster.

If you're not a member of the Roadies' Union, the only way in is through the country's biggest ticket distributor. To find that great seat, escape from New York, Los Angeles, and any other metro area and go to a suburban outlet. Why be 150th in line when you could be second? TicketMaster has an online site (www.ticketmaster.com) that will help you find the location of each ticket center in your area.

● Show your face.

Go to your nearest mom-and-pop ticket outlet, and you'll avoid the delays of trying to get through on the phone, especially if it's a local concert. And pay cash; you'll speed up the process because you won't have to hassle with your credit card numbers.

● Call long distance.

If you have to use the phone, don't scrimp. If you're in Boston, then call the TicketMaster outlet in Hartford, Connecticut, or someplace like that (just stay within your region of the country). The more out of the way, the better—you won't have as much direct competition on the phone lines.

● Never say die.

If the "Sold Out" signs are everywhere you turn, just keep calling back. Previously unavailable sections can suddenly go on sale. Also, concert venues that reserve seats without making you pay up-front will sell unclaimed tickets hours or days before the concert.

CHICK FLICKS AND MANLY MOVIES

Editors at *Men's Health* and *New Woman* magazines asked their readers to name their favorite sexy movies. There wasn't so much a gender gap as a chasm. The results:

Women's Favorite Sexy Movies	Men's Favorite Sex Movies
Titanic	Body Heat
Top Gun	Basic Instinct
Dirty Dancing	Wild Things
Ghost	Sliver
The Big Easy	9½ Weeks

FIRST DATE DO'S AND DON'TS

Here are some of the best and worst places to take somebody on a first date.

Best	Worst
A coffee shop	A bar
Brunch	A movie
A walk on the beach, in a park, or through a historic or interesting part of town	A concert
	Your place
The zoo	Her place
A museum or gallery	

HOW TO GET INTO A TRENDY NIGHTCLUB

Tickets aren't a problem when you're trying to get into a nightclub. The problem is that you're a nobody, or at least that's what you believe. To get past Mr. Biceps and that long line of pathetic schmucks, you need to convince yourself and everyone else that you're "someone," and that no one who is anyone would think of turning you away.

Start by skipping the line. Instead, walk a few blocks until you find an expensive hotel. Hang out until a limousine pulls up. (If your wait is more than a half-hour, you didn't pick the right hotel.) After the driver lets the passengers out, offer him $20 to give you a ride around the corner to the nightclub. Hesitate for a few minutes before you make your exit. (Humming the theme to *The Godfather* will help put you in the mood.)

When you make your exit from the limo, just walk toward the door as if there's no question that you'll be let in. If there is a question, answer in French.

CHEAP AND PROUD OF IT

Want to save some dough on those romantic getaways? Spend $60 on the annual membership fee for the Travelers Advantage Discount Travel Club, and you can stay in about 4,000 hotels nationwide—including Radisson, Best Western, and Days Inn—for half the regular price.

Plus, you can book car rentals, air and train tickets, resorts, and cruises at a guaranteed low price. If you find a lower published fare for the same reservation, Travelers Advantage will refund the difference plus 5 percent on *all* the trip reservations made through the club—even if only one price was beaten by another advertisement. For more information, look up the club on the World Wide Web at www.travelersadvantage.com.

AND YOU THOUGHT
LEONA HELMSLEY WAS GRUMPY

Innkeeper Clifford Shattuck provided service with a snarl. The 66-year-old was barred from having dealings with guests of the Lighthouse Motel in Lincolnville, Maine, and fined $15,000 after a judge found that Shattuck verbally abused people. The judge said Shattuck was abusive toward people who asked to see the rooms before they registered and toward those who used the motel driveway to turn around. He had been fined in the past for rude behavior, but this was the first time he was ordered to stay away from guests.

DOLDRUMS DRAG DOWN
DATING SERVICES INDUSTRY

The total market for dating services has fallen 27 percent from its 1994 peak of $784 million, according to Marketdata Enterprises in Tampa, Florida. The dating services industry serves about 4 percent of the singles market—more than three million people—mostly between the ages of 25 and 44.

Some reasons why: The personal ads market has declined, dating service franchises have withered due to negative publicity, and the Internet has hundreds of dating sites.

TENNIS, SWIMMING, AND KIDNAPPING ON TAP AT RESORT

Some 373 guests were held hostage by striking workers who were irate over working conditions at Club Med's Sainte-Anne Resort in Martinique. The guests were freed with no significant injuries after gun-wielding commandos stormed the resort. Tourism officials began a program of especially warm welcomes at the airport to subsequent incoming tourists in an effort to assuage their fears.

DEAR DR. MANLY

Q: *It doesn't matter how many bucks I drop and how great of a date I create if <u>my lady thinks I'm a lousy kisser</u>. My ex-wife used those exact words. Any tips?*
—K. H., Moscow, Idaho

A: While I know just about all there is to know about kissing, I thought I'd solicit a female response to your question. I referred it to Patrizia DiLucchio, who writes the "Sexpert" column on the Women's Wire Web site (www.womenswire.com). Here's some of her thinking and a little of mine mixed in.

"Some guys approach a kiss like it's an invasion, but it's not erotic when somebody attempts to annex your tonsils with his tongue," DiLucchio says. Probably the most common mistake a guy can make is sticking his tongue out too soon. (Don't worry—she'll let you know when she's ready.)

Try varying the speed of your kisses (shorter and longer periods of mouth contact) and pressure (softer and harder). Throw in a few timid, tender kisses among some more brazen, forceful ones. But don't be scientific about it. Do what feels right and let nature take its course.

And once you've done the mouth thing, don't forget that there's plenty of other stuff you can kiss. Slide your lips down her body, stopping at her throat, her fingers, the nape of her neck. If she likes it, move on to soft biting, and pay particular attention to any move that elicits happy noises. In my professional opinion, happy noises are a *good* thing.

Q: *Especially after a special evening out, <u>my wife asks me to massage her</u>. She says it will make her hot, hot, hot. Problem is, doc, I am no masseur. What can I do? And why would* massage *make her hot?*
—A. S., Omaha, Nebraska

A: In a word, foreplay. Massage is sensuous, relaxing, and arousing. A well-orchestrated erotic massage can be nearly as intense a sexual experience as intercourse itself. You don't have to be a pro to seduce the tens of thousands of nerve endings that most lovers never think to look for. Just do this:

● Her face

Kneel above your partner with her head between your knees. Keeping your touch light, caress her cheeks, ears, and temples with the pads of your fingers, using circular motions. Use your thumbs to gently massage the center of her forehead and the bridge of her nose. Finish by raking your fingers gently across her entire face, finishing well above her hairline.

● Her back

The key word here is "kneading." Say, "I knead you, I knead you." And use deep, firm strokes to work not just the skin but also the underlying muscles of her upper and lower back and shoulders. For best results, squeeze with one hand as you release with the other to establish a rhythm.

Use plenty of massage oil to keep everything slippery (be sure to warm it in your hands before working it into her skin). Or, for less mess, you can use cornstarch. It's dry, powdery, and really satiny and slippery.

● Her arms and legs

With your palms open, grip each limb—one at a time—with your hands side-by-side. Pull on her skin and musculature in one direction with one hand and in the opposite direction with the other, twisting the same way you'd wring out a wet washcloth. Work your way slowly up and down each limb.

● Her chest

When you get close to delicate areas (such as her breasts), or in places where the bone is close to her skin, you'll want to use a lighter touch, gently caressing her body with just your fingertips. In many cases, a light, electrifying touch can actually be more erotic than deep-muscle kneading.

● Her feet

Feet are packed with many nerve endings. Some women can have orgasms just from having them rubbed.

Take one of her feet in your hand and gently knead it, using your entire hand, from her ankle to her toes. Stroke hard enough to avoid tickling but not so hard as to make her grimace. One by one, give each toe a slow, delicate tug, paying special attention to the middle toe, which some people believe has a direct nerve connection to the genitals.

Dr. Manly is a fictional character.
The actual advice was provided by a variety of
medical doctors and other qualified experts.

6

SEX
IN THE
PUBLIC EYE

 Actors and politicians tend to enjoy sex as much as the rest of us. The big difference between us and them, besides the fact that they are rich and famous, is that sometimes they wind up having sex in public. Not intentionally, of course. But because they are public figures, their every twitch and twinkle makes the news, from the nightly network feed to tabloid headlines.

Were we surprised to hear about Bill and Monica? Not really. Peccadilloes by presidents and prominent others were around long before our current president from Hope, Arkansas, gave middle-aged men hope that big-breasted 20-year-olds might find them irresistible. Need a history lesson?

James Buchanan, our only bachelor president, was rumored to be gay. A controversial new book contends that Honest Abe may have swung both ways. Warren Harding rendezvoused in a White House closet with a woman other than his wife. More recently, John F. Kennedy apparently mistook the White House for the Playboy mansion. And we've long known of Prince Charles's love affair with a woman almost as attractive as he is himself.

Sexual shenanigans have always been part of the social fabric. We aren't betting the farm that it's likely to change.

TOP TEN

Influential Folks

The Sexuality Information and Education Council of the United States (SIECUS) asked visitors to its Web site to pick up to 10 people from a list of 100 who have made "a positive change in the way America understands and affirms sexuality as a natural and healthy part of life" in the past 35 years. Here are the top 10, in no particular order.

1 Playboy magazine founder Hugh Hefner

2 Comedienne/actress Ellen DeGeneres

3 Singer/actress Madonna

4 Former basketball star Magic Johnson

5 Dr. Ruth Westheimer

6 Writer Judy Blume

7 Former surgeon general Joycelyn Elders

8 Law school professor Anita Hill

9 Feminist Gloria Steinem

10 SIECUS co-founder Mary Calderone

MUST READS

Grover Cleveland:
"Ma! Ma! Where's My Pa?"
"Gone to the White House,
Ha! Ha! Ha!"

With all the hue and cry over Bill Clinton and Monica Lewinsky, one would think no other president had ever had sex with anyone other than his bride. Not the case. But never have so many media exhausted so many resources covering extramarital grappling and groping. And this was the first presidential sex scandal to hit the World Wide Web.

The fact is, many other presidents have been plagued by questions of sexual improprieties. Among them was Grover Cleveland. In this chapter from Presidential Sex: From the Founding Fathers to Bill Clinton, *author Wesley O. Hagood tells how, more than a century ago, Cleveland successfully responded to stories that he fathered a child out of wedlock.*

It was their turn now! They had enough of the malicious attacks against the upright moral character of their candidate, James G. Blaine, the Republican nominee for president of the United States. It was time for them to get even. They made their final preparations. It took a lot of work to round up all of the equipment and props needed for the publicity stunt they were about to unveil. Revenge would be sweet. The men had all reached the rallying point. The leader blew the mouth harp to sound a distinct note that could be heard throughout the room. All of the men began to hum in unison. The doors of the building were flung open.

The smartly dressed businessmen, adorned in their top hats, vested suits, ties, and polished shoes paraded into the darkness carrying burning torches. They marched down Main Street pushing tiny baby carriages, while singing, "Ma! Ma! Where's my Pa?" in voices of high diminuendo. They were mimicking the voices of the small children supposedly coming from within the carriages. All the children were crying out for their "Pa," Grover Cleveland, the Democratic party's nominee for president of the United States. Some angry Democrats began shouting out, "Gone to the White House, ha! ha! ha!" after each Republican chorus.

The election of 1884 is often considered one of the dirtiest in American political history. Grover Cleveland's political fortune had taken him from the obscurity of mayor of Buffalo, New York, to governor of that state to Democratic candidate for president in less than 3 years. The Republicans were "pulling out all stops" trying to exploit a recently discovered sex scandal soon after Cleveland was selected as his party's nominee.

Stephen Grover Cleveland, the fifth of nine children, was born on March 18, 1837, in Caldwell, New Jersey. He was named after his paternal grandfather. His father, a Congregational Presbyterian minister, earned a meager annual salary of $600 to support his large family. Eventually, he became district secretary for the American Home Missionary Society, which provided a little more income. On Sundays, Grover was expected to attend church twice, both in the morning and early evening, as well as Sunday school. He also went to regular midweek prayer meetings with his father. As he grew older, he became less observant of church, and no longer attended until he became president.

After his father's death, Grover, at age 16, was on his own. Too poor to attend nearby Hamilton College in Clinton, New York, he traveled to New York City in search of work and found a job assisting his brother, a teacher in the New York Institution for the Blind. Later, Grover's uncle helped him get a job as a law clerk in the Buffalo law offices of Rogers, Bowen, and Rogers. He clerked during the day and began studying Blackstone's Commentaries about the law at night, often going without any sleep. Grover was admitted to the New York bar in May 1858 at the age of 22. He was drafted in 1863 during the Civil War but selected a legal option available to him under the Conscription Act of 1863 and paid $150 to a young Polish immigrant, George Benninsky, to fight in his place.

In 1870, Grover ran for sheriff of Erie County, New York, and won by a margin of only 303 votes. He served for 3 years, then joined Bass and Bissel, to practice law full-time again. He became a partner in 1878.

Grover established a reputation as one of the most respected attorneys in Buffalo. He would often work through the night until early the next morning memorizing the legal arguments he would present during trial. He was very thrifty and considered extravagance sinful. By 1881, he had amassed nearly $75,000 in a savings account.

He sought solace from the monotonous practice of the law in male companionship, poker games, and ribaldry he found in several of Buffalo's local saloon-restaurants and German beer gardens, especially the Shades, Bass's Saloon, Louis Goetz's restaurant, and Schenkelberger's. He loved to eat German food and beer, sausages, and sauerkraut and soon his weight doubled to 250 pounds. Relatives began to call him Uncle Jumbo.

Grover was a short, stocky man with a portly figure. He had a prominent nose, a bushy walrus mustache, and steely blue eyes. A wisp of gray hair adorned his balding pate. His official presidential portraits show a stout, fleshy man with great jowls. Two different pictures of his character emerge. Some thought Grover to be a coarse, humorless, and uneducated roisterer. Others considered him an honest and responsible lawyer.

In 1881, Big Steve, as he was known to his close friends, ran for mayor of Buffalo as a reformer against Republican corruption and won. A year later, he was elected governor of New York. He was selected as the presidential nominee in 1884 when the Democrats were looking for some new blood to invigorate their national campaign.

Occasionally, he paid a visit to a brothel, but his love life remained relatively lackluster. It was in Buffalo, during 1873, that he met and had a brief affair with a young widow named Maria Crofts Halpin. Although there was some talk about his scurrilous behavior at the time, the local scandal soon died down.

Maria was a 35-year-old widow who had left her two children behind in New Jersey to

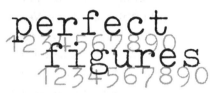

perfect figures

Number of sexual encounters President Clinton had with Monica Lewinsky: nine

start a new life in Buffalo. She was described as attractive and amusing. She "never swore" and "seldom drank except at meals." First, she found work as a collar maker; later, as a clerk in a local department store. She worked hard and eventually became the director of the cloak and lace department.

In 1884, 10 days after Grover Cleveland won the Democratic party's nomination for the presidency, Maria Crofts Halpin made newspaper headlines when she declared that Grover was the father of her illegitimate 10-year-old son, Oscar Folsom Cleveland. On July 21, 1884, the *Buffalo Evening Telegraph* printed a front-page news article about Grover's past liaison with Halpin headlined by: "A Terrible Tale—A Dark Chapter in a Public Man's History." The article said in part: "A child was born out of holy wedlock. Now 10 years of age, this sturdy lad is named Oscar Folsom Cleveland. He and his mother have been supported in part by our ex-mayor who now aspires to the White House. Astute readers may put the facts together and draw their own conclusions."

The chief source of this sensational journalism was the Reverend George

H. Ball, pastor of the Hudson Street Baptist Church and a loyal Republican. He characterized the story as the sexual liaison of "Grover the Good" and Mrs. Maria Halpin. Since Cleveland was running against Blaine as a spotless reformer, this juicy bit of salacious gossip emboldened the Republicans. Reverend Ball characterized Grover's bachelor quarters as "a harem" and said he sought out victims "in the city and surrounding villages."

The paper also published a political cartoon showing a disheveled Grover Cleveland attempting to cover his ears while a young baby with outstretched arms held by a crying woman wails, "I want my Pa!" The baby in the cartoon is reaching out toward Cleveland. The cartoon is captioned "Another voice for Cleveland."

Soon other newspapers jumped on the bandwagon. Charles Dana, editor and publisher of the *New York Sun*, wrote: "We do not believe the American people will knowingly elect to the Presidency a coarse debauchee who would bring his harlots with him to Washington and hire lodgings for them convenient to the White House."

The Republicans had a field day. They also subsidized the mass distribution of a song published by the National Music Company of Chicago entitled "Ma! Ma! Where's My Pa?"

Other clergy rallied around Cleveland after the shock of the story died down. The Reverend Kinsley Twining, a highly respected minister at the time, was sent to Buffalo to investigate the reports of the local clergymen. He wrote the following words in Cleveland's defense, published in the *New York Times* on August 12, 1884: "The kernel of truth in the various charges against Mr. Cleveland is this, that when he was younger he was guilty of an illicit connection; but the charge brought against him lacks the elements of truth in these substantial points; there was no seduction, no adultery, no breach of promise, no obligation of marriage; his conduct was singularly honorable, showing no attempt to evade responsibility, and doing all he could to meet his duties involved, of which marriage was certainly not one."

Another clergyman, the Reverend Henry Ward Beecher, who was having his own struggle with moral probity and adultery, said, "If every New Yorker who had broken the Seventh Commandment were to vote for Cleveland, he would carry the state by a large majority."

The issue had been raised by the Republican opposition. After this story was revealed in the newspapers and his panicked campaign staff wired

hot TIP!

From Kris Kristofferson: "The number one rule of the road is never go to bed with anyone crazier than yourself. You will break this rule, and you will be sorry."

him for instructions, Grover advised them by telegraph, "Above all, tell the truth." Although Grover heard similar smutty accusations against his Republican opponent, James G. Blaine, he chose not to use them. For example, the Democratic camp learned that Mrs. Blaine had given birth to their first child just 3 months after their wedding, technically making Blaine a fornicator, too. Instead of using this bit of sensitive information, Cleveland tore up the report and burned it in the fireplace. He said, "The other side can have a monopoly on all the dirt in this campaign." However, word did leak out, and the *Democratic Sentinel* published an account of Blaine's shotgun wedding. Instead of admitting the truth, Blaine concocted a story about having had two wedding ceremonies 6 months apart. His explanation was sketchy and had few details. No witnesses to the earlier ceremony were ever identified. Needless to say, no one believed him.

perfect figures

Number of times
Monica Lewinsky
performed oral sex on
President Clinton: eight

Grover did admit that as a bachelor he, and some of his friends, had kept company with Mrs. Halpin. "The boy could be mine, I do not know," he confessed. This young widow had given birth to a son in September 1874, claimed Cleveland was the father, and tried to pressure him into marrying her. When Grover refused, Maria began to drink heavily. Fearing for the child's safety, Grover had his friend, Judge Roswell L. Burrows, commit Maria to an asylum for 5 days and place the child in an orphanage until suitable parents could be found. Grover regularly paid the orphanage's costs of $5 a week. After Maria was released from the asylum, Grover gave her enough money to start a small business in Niagara Falls, New York. Eventually, she became angry and pursued legal custody of her child. After getting nowhere with the courts, Maria kidnapped Oscar in 1876. The boy was quickly found and brought back to the orphanage 3 months later. Grover paid her $500 to leave town, drop the lawsuit, and allow the boy to be placed for adoption. Eventually, Grover found a prominent, wealthy New York couple living in the western part of the state to adopt young Oscar. He received a good education and eventually become a respected medical doctor. Maria moved to New Rochelle, New York, and later married.

Grover never denied he was the child's father. But he couldn't be sure, since Maria also shared her pleasures with many men. Grover could have easily pushed Maria aside, claiming he was but one of many men who had slept with her. However, he reasoned that since he was a bachelor and all of his other friends and her suitors were married, it would be the least damaging for him to respond to her claims of paternity and agreed to give the child his last name. Maria named the boy Oscar Folsom Cleveland after Grover and Oscar Folsom, his friend and law-firm partner. Perhaps Maria was trying to imply that his partner was twice as likely to be the child's father, since the boy's first and middle names pointed not to Grover but to his friend.

Grover decided to do the responsible thing. He placed young Oscar in an orphanage until he found suitable parents and provided assistance to the couple. The presidential campaign of 1884 could have devolved into mud-slinging, but he refused to yield to this temptation. Grover may also have felt that his chances of being elected would be greater if he were candid with the American people rather than trying to cover up his past mistakes. He told his close friends and campaign workers that there should be absolutely "no cringing" from the truth.

Grover's chances of winning the presidential election soon looked bleak. The Democrats knew that capturing New York State was pivotal to winning the national election, but Cleveland's scandal threatened to destroy any victory they had hoped for there. But a last minute attempt by Republican presidential nominee Blaine to milk this scandal one last time apparently backfired and very probably cost him the election. Just a week before the election, on October 29, 1884, at the Fifth Avenue Hotel in New York City, Blaine met with a group of 500 clergyman who were upset that someone with such loose morals as Cleveland could possibly become the next president. Members of the press were present at this meeting and were jotting down notes from this lively discussion for another feature story. The Reverend S. D. Burchard, pastor of the Murray Hill Presbyterian Church, a good Republican, and spokesman for the group of clergymen, referred to Cleveland's Democrats as "the party of Rum, Romanism, and Rebellion." Blaine did not object to this description. Irish Catholics, deeply offended by the religious slur, turned out at the polls in record numbers to vote against Blaine. They helped Cleveland carry New York State by a mere 1,150 popular votes and, consequently, win the presidential election.

Cleveland's gambit paid off. The electorate decided to forgive his philandering, or rather fornicating, since he was not married at the time of his sexual indiscretion, and elected him 22nd president of the United States. The Democrats had the last laugh. After their victory, they responded to the Republican-backed song "Ma! Ma! Where's My Pa?" with "Gone to the White House, Ha! Ha! Ha!"

In 1886, 2 years after the election, Grover married Frances Folsom. She was the daughter of Grover's law partner, Oscar Folsom. He had been her unofficial guardian and looked after her since her father's untimely death when she was only 11 years old. Frances was only 21 at the time of their marriage. Grover was 49. Grover first met Frances soon after her birth when he was 27 and she just an infant. A regular visitor at the Folsoms' house, Grover bought Frances toys, her first baby carriage, and even a pet terrier.

Tall, charming, and graceful, Frances was very beautiful. She had dark brown hair and delicate features. She graduated from Buffalo's Central High School and then attended Wells College in Aurora, New York. Grover once confessed to his sister that he was "waiting for his wife to grow up," referring to young Frances. During her college days, Grover's interest took on a more romantic quality. Her dorm room was often decorated with flowers sent by her ever-so-considerate "Uncle Cleve." Soon after Frances graduated, in August 1885, Grover proposed by letter. One can imagine what this young woman must have thought when she received a marriage proposal by letter from the president of the United States.

She immediately accepted. Their engagement was kept secret until just 5 days before the wedding, no doubt to prevent gossip and to spare her from the media's curiosity and prying.

The wedding ceremony took place in the flower-filled Blue Room of the White House on June 2, 1886, at 7:00 P.M. The wedding was attended by 31 close friends, relatives, and cabinet members and their wives. Theirs was the first wedding to take place inside the White House. As president, Cleveland had to work on the wedding day but managed to set aside 5 days for their honeymoon. The location of the honeymoon cottage was a heavily guarded secret. The press, however, dis-

Vital Stats

GROVER CLEVELAND

Twenty-second President of the United States (1885–89)

Twenty-fourth President of the United States (1893–97)

BIOGRAPHICAL INFORMATION

Born: March 18, 1837

Died: June 24, 1908

Wife: Frances Folsom

Children: Two boys; three girls

EXTRAMARITAL SEXUAL PARTNER

Maria Crofts Halpin, 1873–74, Buffalo, N.Y.

ALLEGED ILLEGITIMATE CHILDREN

Oscar Folsom Cleveland

covered its location in the Cumberland Mountains near Deer Park, Maryland. The new couple awoke to find the cabin surrounded by reporters equipped with high-powered binoculars, ready to snap photographs when the happy couple emerged. Infuriated, Cleveland called the press "professional gossips" and accused them of "doing their utmost to make American journalism contemptible." Subsequent newspaper reports conjectured about the dangers slim young Frances faced on her honeymoon because of the president's size and weight.

Frances enlivened the dreary atmosphere that prevailed at many official White House events during the first 2 years of Grover's term as president. She liked parties; and her receptions brought youth and culture into the White House. Happily married, she was Grover's constant companion. She convinced him to work a little less hard, to take longer vacations, and in general to enjoy life more.

Their first child was born between Cleveland's two terms. The second child, Esther, arriving during Cleveland's second term, was the first baby to be born in the White House.

After the Republicans' muckraking strategy failed to doom Grover's first presidential campaign, one might think they would have developed a new plan of attack. But his Republican opponents did not change their tack. They continued to spread rumors, saying Cleveland often flew into drunken rages and beat his young wife. William A. White, presidential biographer and newspaperman, interviewed Cleveland and asked him, "Is it true what the papers say about your kicking your wife down stairs?"

"I never laid a hand on her" was Cleveland's reply. Although Frances repeatedly denied such rumors, they persisted nonetheless. Both Grover and Frances were wounded by the baseless accusations, but for the most part they suffered together in silence.

Grover lost his bid for reelection in 1888 to Benjamin Harrison. Frances told the back-stairs staff at the White House not to worry; she and Grover would be returning in 4 years. Her forecast proved to be correct. Cleveland was elected to a second term in

SEX TRENDS

PORN PRODUCTION IS HOT

The United States is easily the world leader in the production of hard-core adult videos, cranking out perhaps 150 new titles a week. An estimated 75 percent of all such videos made in the United States come from Los Angeles County.

1892, the only president to serve two nonconsecutive terms. After his second term ended in 1897, Grover and Frances moved to Princeton. Grover lectured at the university there and eventually became a trustee. They had two more children, born in Princeton. The Clevelands lived in Princeton until Grover's death in June 1908.

After Grover's death, Frances married a professor of archaeology at Princeton University, Thomas J. Preston, making her the first presidential widow ever to remarry. Frances died in October 1947. She was buried in Princeton, next to her beloved Grover.

Endless Exposure

From the tabloids to talk radio to the Internet, you can find celebrity gossip everywhere. Writer Gail Collins traces the evolution of no-holds-barred journalism in this chapter from her book Scorpion Tongues: Gossip, Celebrity, and American Politics.

"If Someone's in Rehab, the Tabloids Will Find Out"

By the mid-1990s, the technology that transmitted the assaults on officials' personal integrity, rumors about their sexuality, and allegations about their mental health created a whole new pattern on the kaleidoscope. Besides inventions like the Internet and cable TV, old forms of communication were re-creating themselves. Radio had become talk radio, and the scandal magazines of the 1950s morphed into supermarket tabloids like the *National Enquirer* and the *Star*. The tabloids used many of the old techniques—checking police records and bribing servants, greedy spouses, low-level studio employees, and mistresses. When the *Star* admitted it had paid a woman to tape-record her pillow talk with former football star Frank Gifford, it was a throwback to the days when *Confidential* had printed an informant's stories about sex with Desi Arnaz. In a new wrinkle, the tabloids also recruited former patients who spent some time in group therapy with a famous alcoholic or addict. "If someone's in rehab, the tabloids will find out," said entertainment-industry journalist Nancy Griffin. "You can't even go and dry yourself out without having somebody at your group meeting sell the story to the tabs. I'd hate to be a celebrity today."

There were limits to the power and influence of the tabloids. Many of the stories they published, particularly those relating to celebrities' sexual orientation or possible drug use, were not picked up by the mainstream media. And like their scandal magazine ancestors, they had very little interest in politics.

The *Star*, which had published Gennifer Flower's story, also paid a Washington prostitute for a first-person account of her ongoing relationship with presidential adviser Dick Morris that made a huge sensation when it appeared on the stands during the 1996 Democratic national convention. But the attention those exposés attracted gave the impression that the tabloids were far more concerned with governmental figures than they really were. A politician, to be worth exposing, had to be at the highest level of national fame. Governors, congressmen, and even senators who were not part of the Kennedy family would have to misbehave in a spectacular manner to draw the tabloids' attention. But the papers happily covered the misfortunes of all entertainers, large and small, down to the sins and embarrassments of the most obscure former actors from long-dead TV sitcoms ("'Webster' Ex-Star Selling Car Wax from His Van").

perfect figures

Number of times
President Clinton ejaculated
during oral sex with
Monica Lewinsky: two

The one medium that really preferred political gossip was talk radio, where viewers need a topic with a little more meat than Hollywood rumors are likely to carry. "The key is entertaining conversation rooted in something important," said Michael Harrison, the editor of *Talkers Magazine*. "If it seems frivolous or shallow, it doesn't work." On talk radio, President Clinton has always been a far bigger draw than Tom Cruise. "Bill Clinton has been a boon to talk radio," Harrison enthused. "He's just a guy that has—I could go on for hours. Bill Clinton is a package with lots to talk about. He embodied people's hopes. Brought them down. Raised them up. Down. Up. The man's whole way of governing is similar to a talk-radio program." Even the Clintons' uneventful vacation to the Massachusetts coast in the summer of 1997 gave the radio audiences something to chew over. Callers traded rumors that the First Family would be guests at a secret wedding of Barbra Streisand and her boyfriend, argued about how Clinton's sexual harassment defense would play when he got home, and speculated that the president would be playing golf with Tiger Woods. "That had it all," Harrison said with a sigh. "Show business, politics, sports, personalities."

Talk radio really came to life after 1987, when deregulation made it easier for stations to broadcast political opinion without worrying about offering equal time to the other side. "The late 1980s was a cold and lonely place. People didn't know their neighbors. Talk radio created an electronic community, a backyard fence," said Harrison. Ten years later, there were more than 1,200 stations doing talk-radio programs. But there was also a general suspicion that the form had peaked. Like newspapers at the start of the century, radio stations were being grouped into chains and media conglomerates that were less friendly to the more outrageous forms of programming. "There's a new corporate culture, and it doesn't have the same stomach for controversy," said Harrison sadly.

The Internet: "A Vanity Press for the Demented"

Gossip on the Internet really is like a transcribed version of careless back-fence chatter or barroom meanderings:

"My guess is there is significantly less evidence of Kemp having a gay encounter than there is that Bill and Hillary had Vince Foster bumped off," mutters one "chatter."

"Many gays I have talked to say that Kemp's homosexuality is known in the gay community," chimes in another, in the age-old tradition of "everybody says" gossip.

Another chatter throws in his 2 cents' worth on the ongoing Internet speculation about Bill Clinton using drugs, and sounds remarkably like the country club Republicans of the New Deal era, passing around stories about the president's supposedly insane behavior: "When he burst into endless laughter during Yeltsin's visit, I knew he had inhaled something."

The Internet, which Lars Nelson of the *Daily News* calls "a vanity press for the demented," breeds a strange lack of accountability. We don't think of gossip as something that involves much responsibility to begin with—think of all those generations of dinner party conversationalists who passed on stories about Grover Cleveland's wife-beating or George Bush's mistress. Still, the other dinner party guests knew who the gossip was coming from. But on the Internet, other users cannot even tell whether the person they're talking with on a Republican chat line (say, the one who informs them that "Liddy Dole has her lesbian problem licked" or that Bob Dole is joining a professional wrestling league), is really a fellow partisan, or a Democratic mole, or a pair of giggling 12-year-olds.

Even gossip you hear from a stranger at a bar comes from a person about whom you can make a few general assumptions based on age, appearance, and the general rationality of his or her conversation. But a posting on the Internet comes bearing no hints at all. "Anita Hill was trained as a teenager to be a sleeper agent in the service of a lesbian wicca coven operating out of a NAACP chapter in the Deep South," announces a correspondent in a chat line devoted to people who follow the doings of white witchery. "She was brainwashed into Marxist-Communism and left to sleep as she pursued a career in Republican circles." Is this a joke, or the product of a right-wing conspiracy group, or some new strain of conservative witchcraft aficionado? Is it someone who wants to make the wicca movement look silly, or to discredit Anita Hill's detractors? Gossip, it becomes clear, really does need some kind of context to give it meaning.

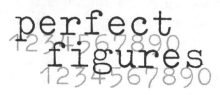

perfect figures

Amount of money that actor Charlie Sheen estimates he spent on women in Hollywood madam Heidi Fleiss's call-girl ring: at least $50,000

The anonymity of the Internet, however, is perpetually at war with the national urge for recognition. Matt Drudge, a Los Angeles gift-shop worker, transformed himself into a celebrity with his Internet Web site featuring gossip about politics and Hollywood. Drudge, who fancied himself a cybernetic Walter Winchell and disdained the rules of traditional journalism, made a splash with dramatic revelations such as his reports that Hillary Clinton would be indicted by the end of 1996, and that it would be revealed that the president had an American eagle tattooed on a hidden part of his anatomy. None of these things happened to be true, but they created quite a buzz.

But by making himself known, Drudge became accountable. Late in the summer of 1997, former journalist Sidney Blumenthal began his first day in the White House as a special adviser to the president, and discovered that Drudge had sent out a bulletin quoting unnamed Republicans as saying that "court records" showed Blumenthal was a wife-beater. But Blumenthal knew there were no such court papers about him, and he was further incensed by Drudge's quotes from unnamed Democrats debunking the wife-beating charges and saying: "This story about Blumenthal has been in circulation for years."

Vanity Fair's Jennet Conant called the story about Blumenthal "stale gossip" in conservative circles that had been passed around by a *Wall Street Journal* editorial writer. But Blumenthal claimed he had never heard of such talk until the Drudge bulletin hit, and his acquaintances started asking, in tones of deepest sympathy: "There aren't really any *court records*, are there?" Within an hour after he started his new job, Blumenthal had hired a lawyer and directed him to file a libel suit. His co-workers joked that in the frequently investigated Clinton White House, Blumenthal was the first plaintiff.

"I Heard the First Lady Say, 'Oh, My God'"

Don Imus had begun incorporating political comment into his radio show even before he had his famous encounters with Bill Clinton. It was a move not unlike the one gossip columnist Walter Winchell had made decades earlier when he found the dwindling Broadway scene too feeble for a daily column and started cultivating Franklin Roosevelt and J. Edgar Hoover as subjects. Imus turned out to have a knack for forcing politicians to talk in ways that his politics-hating listeners found interesting. "You get an opportunity to see a different side of these people. It loosens them up when we get them to try to humiliate themselves and reveal some embarrassing aspect of their lives," he explained.

Elected officials lined up to be humiliated. Americans' dislike of politics, which was already founded on a too-intimate knowledge of their human frailties, forced the politicians to expose themselves more and more. They needed to make connection with the voters, and they knew that irreverent media stars like Imus could serve as intermediaries. The producers of David Letterman's late-night talk show complained that after Vice President Al Gore was invited to come on and recite the top 10 reasons why he liked his job, they were besieged with calls from senators and congressmen begging to appear on the program too, promising to make themselves as ridiculous as necessary. (Gore's staff, in an effort to maintain dignity, did reject the suggestion that he say being vice president was fun because "chicks dig it when I break a tie vote in the Senate.")

In 1996, the Radio and Television Correspondents Association recognized Imus's new position in the world of politics by inviting him to be featured speaker at their annual dinner in Washington, where the Clintons sat on the dais as guests of honor, and most of the top politicians and television journalists in the country were part of the audience. The result was a really spectacular example of what happens when the barriers of decorum collapse. "You know, I think it would be fair to say that back when the Clintons took office, if we had placed them all in a lineup . . . ," the host began, in a long joke about Hillary Clinton's recent appearance before a grand jury. There was nothing in his performance that was different from his normal radio patter.

(*continued on page 188*)

Who's Who

Think your knowledge of presidential sex scandals rivals Bill Gates' expertise in computers? Then take the following quiz from *Presidential Sex: From the Founding Fathers to Bill Clinton* by Wesley O. Hagood:

1. Which president repeatedly made love to a young girl from his hometown in a White House coat closet when, on at least one occasion, his wife was prevented from beating down the closet door by a Secret Service agent?

2. Which president married a woman who was not yet divorced from her first husband and was later labeled an "adulterer" during his reelection campaign?

3. Which future president wrote love letters to his neighbor's wife while he was engaged to another woman?

4. Which had numerous caustic and politically damaging poems written about his sexual dalliance and published in the major newspapers of the day?

5. Which president called his mistress "Pookie"?

6. Which one allegedly smoked marijuana in the nude with a naked, nubile young playgirl and joked about being incapacitated when it came time to push "the button" in the event of a nuclear attack?

7. Which two presidents had their former lovers die under mysterious circumstances? (Name the lovers, too.)

8. Which president said, "What a way to end the day!" when anticipating a rendezvous that was about to take place with a young playgirl?

9. Which presidents allegedly fathered illegitimate children?

10. Which vice president became angry because he felt that his record of actual sexual conquests was far greater than the then-president's existing reputation for such conquests?

11. Which presidents called upon visits from young women in the White House secretarial pool for recreational sex?

12. Which had an alleged affair that lasted for decades with a slave who was also his wife's half-sister?

13 Which president had a torrid love affair with the first lady's personal secretary?

14 Which president had sex with one of his secretaries stretched out on top of a desk in the White House?

15 Which two presidents had rendezvous with their mistresses at the Mayflower Hotel in Washington, D.C.?

16 Which future president never married because his fiancée broke off their engagement because of his reputation as a "man about town" and her death (which was rumored to be a suicide) occurred shortly thereafter?

17 Which president allegedly had an affair with one winner and one finalist in the Miss America Pageant?

18 Which president's wife was labeled an adulteress during his election campaign?

19 Which president had an affair with his driver?

20 Which president had a song written about his alleged illegitimate child that was often chanted at parades and political rallies?

21 Which president's campaign train made a layover so he could visit his mistress?

22 Which president lined up all the women willing to sleep with him at a private party on the eve of his inauguration and selected two with whom he would have sex?

23 Which president hid in his mistress's wardrobe when he thought a police raid was occurring?

QUIZ ANSWERS

1. Warren G. Harding; 2. Andrew Jackson; 3. George Washington; 4. Thomas Jefferson; 5. Bill Clinton; 6. John F. Kennedy; 7. James Buchanan (Anne Coleman) and John F. Kennedy (Mary Pinchot Meyers); 8. John F. Kennedy; 9. Thomas Jefferson and Grover Cleveland; 10. Lyndon B. Johnson; 11. John F. Kennedy and Lyndon B. Johnson; 12. Thomas Jefferson; 13. Franklin D. Roosevelt; 14. Lyndon B. Johnson; 15. John F. Kennedy and Lyndon B. Johnson; 16. James Buchanan; 17. Bill Clinton; 18. Andrew Jackson; 19. Dwight D. Eisenhower; 20. Grover Cleveland; 21. Grover Cleveland; 22. John F. Kennedy; 23. Warren G. Harding

But this time, Imus was talking about important people's personal lives while they were sitting behind him, being watched by all the other most important people in Washington, and being broadcast live by C-SPAN.

Imus reminisced about a day when Clinton was watching a baseball game in Baltimore and being interviewed on the radio. "Bobby Bonilla hit a double, and we all heard the President, in his obvious excitement, holler 'Go, baby.' And I remember commenting at the time, 'I bet that's not the first time he said that.'" Looking over at the Clintons' table, Imus realized things were not necessarily going well. "I can't even describe his face," he told Maureen Dowd later. "If he'd had a gun, he'da shot me."

> " Looking over at the Clintons' table, Imus realized things were not necessarily going well. "I can't even describe his face," he told Maureen Dowd later. "If he'd had a gun, he'da shot me. "

Moving on to the media celebrities in the audience, Imus began to make fun of anchorman Peter Jennings's sex life. "Here's Peter Jennings, sitting there each evening, elegant, erudite, refined, and I'm wondering, what's under his desk. I mean besides an intern. The first place the telecommunications bill should have mandated that a V-chip be placed was in Mr. Jennings's shorts." It was somewhere during this section, Imus said later, that "I heard the First Lady say, 'Oh, my God.'" Imus finished his monologue, joking about newsman Sam Donaldson and Senator Joseph Biden for their hair-replacement techniques, claiming that when Tim Russert of NBC worked as an aide to New York politicians earlier in his career, his "duties included hiding the bottles for Pat [Moynihan] and the bodies for Mario [Cuomo]."

Official Washington was left reeling. Bernard Kalb of CNN said he walked out of the dinner at the point where Imus "poked fun at marital problems of correspondents who were there, by name." (That was several minutes after the disc jockey had poked fun at the marital problems of the president and the legal problems of the First Lady, by name.) Presidential spokesman Mike McCurry unsuccessfully tried to get C-SPAN to cancel the scheduled rebroadcast. The Correspondents Association sent the president an apology. The president ended all relations with Imus, and many of the disc jockey's Washington guests backed away, at least temporarily. "You can't make fun of the President when he's sitting right there," said Cokie Roberts, declaring a boycott.

But to the public, the real boundary line had never been what you could say about the president in his presence and out. It was between what could be said in private conversation, in political pamphlets, or even in supermarket tabloids, and what got said on television and in family newspapers. A sense of respect for the nation's highest elected officials—in particular the president— had been one of the restraints on the publication of gossip about politicians' private lives. But as new media entrants like cable TV channels and Internet Web sites popped up everywhere, the traditional media was less able to dictate the rules of the game. And the politicians were making it even more difficult by failing to draw any line themselves.

SEX WARS

" WHAT'S BETWEEN US, MELANIE, STAYS BETWEEN US, OUR AGENTS, MANAGERS, PUBLICISTS AND ATTORNEYS. "

MAN'S GUIDE INTERVIEW

Bill, Monica, Teen Prostitutes, and Oral Sex

An Interview with Ted McIlvenna, Ph.D.

With each passing day, the United States seems to become more and more a society of couch-potato voyeurs.

If that were not true, The Jerry Springer Show and all of its low-rent talk show kin could not survive. We have to keep our eyes glued to the TV so that we won't miss the point at which the two inner-city monster mommas start to duke it out over their bigamist, transvestite, codependent stripper husband. And then we have to keep watching for a few minutes more, waiting for the guy to trot out his hermaphroditic, nymphomaniacal lover, for whom he is leaving both of his wives.

So it was only a matter of time until we turned the sex lives of our political figures into a spectator sport. President William Jefferson Clinton—"Bill" to his 200-something million friends out there in the 50 states—was just the most high-profile victim of our crazed need for fresh sexual scandal.

In almost any other country in the world, an affair between a high-ranking political figure and a relatively insignificant political lackey would have passed virtually unnoticed. But here, we have to turn it into an event. And we also cannot stop at merely chiding the man for his moral and ethical missteps. We have to turn the whole affair into an excuse for impeachment.

To get some perspective on what, if anything, the public debate over the president's deeds means for us as a society, we have chosen to consult with sexologist Ted McIlvenna, Ph.D., president and founder of the Institute for Advanced Study of Human Sexuality in San Francisco.

The institute, a fully approved graduate school that awards master's- and doctoral-level degrees in sexuality studies, focuses on training people to be sexologists. To this end, curricular studies cover such areas as sex research, sex counseling, sex and society, and sex education.

MAN'S GUIDE: Bill Clinton gets some oral sex periodically from a White House intern, he only completes the act a handful of times, and suddenly we have a huge public debate over what constitutes sex. As an expert on human sexuality, you settle the argument. Is oral sex a form of sexual intercourse?

DR. MCILVENNA: As a sexologist, the idea that someone would call oral sex anything but sex is a joke. It's definitely a sociosexual activity, and oral sex is something that people engage in as part of the activity of sex. Various religious groups and cultures have identified oral sex as something that has to do with leading up to the sex act of penetration, which is designed to bring about procreation. Of course, that doesn't always happen, and oral sex in fact has been considered a sex act that is an alternative to other forms of sex because it acts as a form of birth control.

It also has been perceived as a way to have sexual contact and avoid contracting sexually transmitted diseases. That is not true, but it is a less risky activity than is genital-to-genital contact.

Oral sex has been defined as foreplay. In some cultures, it is even a form of ritual contact.

As sex outlets go, oral sex has had a very active existence. It is one of the major sexual outlets for men and for women. So I find it hilarious that we could consider oral sex to be nonsexual. On the other hand, oral sex has for many people been a way to protect virginity. Some religious denominations, in fact, implicitly tell their young people that it's okay so long as they don't give away access to the genitals. Many people who come up in Southern Baptist or Jewish communities take this approach. As long as the women have only engaged in oral sex, they are still virgins.

Clinton came up through the Southern Baptist belief system, and whether we like it or not, his justification of oral sex as something other than intercourse is probably completely defensible in his mind.

What I find interesting is that in all this debate, very few people have asked if he went down on Monica Lewinsky. Was he giving, or was he just receiving? Was he giving her any pleasure, or was this strictly a one-way activity? Some people argue that for her to give him pleasure was enough to give her pleasure, even if she didn't receive any direct sexual gratification. But that's bull.

Granted, Monica may have been getting something other than sexual gratification out of giving Clinton oral sex. This may have been a way for her to exert some control over a powerful man, in which case she got some kind of satisfaction from the act.

From that standpoint, if the act of sexual gratification is only going in one direction, it could be perceived as something less than sexual because it was not a form of two-way intercourse.

I once talked to 14- and 15-year-old prostitutes for a study I was conducting, and I was amazed at how many of these prostitutes considered themselves virgins because they only offered their mouths. Oral sex was just a business to them, and they performed that activity because they could do it much more frequently and much more quickly than if they were performing sexual intercourse. But I found it amazing how they justified their virginity on the basis on having given only oral sex, even though they had done it hundreds of times.

MAN'S GUIDE: To some extent, women have bought into this notion of oral sex as something less sexual than coitus. Teenage girls sometimes maintain their virginity, or at least their perception of virginity, by consenting only to oral sex. So when does this shift suddenly take place, where women grow up and get incensed at men for engaging in an activity that they themselves once considered somewhat nonsexual?

DR. MCILVENNA: It's a double standard, plain and simple. But that's not what I find interesting about oral sex among young women. What I find interesting is that women are much more concerned about performance than we think they are.

I conducted a study in the Sacramento Valley area to find out what the major sexual issues and concerns were among teenagers and young women. I wanted to talk to teens, in particular, to get their views because teens tend to signal what the future holds for us. Their opinions and outlooks are going to shape the future.

I figured that they would be concerned about sexually transmitted diseases, pregnancy, and all the other issues that we expect them to be worried about. But they weren't primarily concerned with those issues. Their biggest sexual concern was how to learn to be a good lay. They wanted to be good at what they were doing in bed. The perception of how to be good at sex has really taken over many of the other sexual concerns that we assume are more important.

Part of the reason that being good at sex is such a concern is that being good is a way to effectively manage men. It's similar in some ways to the thinking of a prostitute. You want to be good at giving pleasure so that you can manage men and get money out of them consistently. For most women, the issue of managing men is a bit more complex because it isn't a simple business transaction. But much of women's pleasure is connected to how well they can manage their men. If they can give their men pleasure, they can manage them better, and they concern themselves with their own pleasure secondarily. Otherwise, the men may not stick around.

There's a book called *The Hunting Hypothesis*, by Robert Ardrey, that describes human females as the most amazing creatures ever developed in nature because they are always in heat or capable of performing as if they were in heat. And because of this, the men stick around. Otherwise, they'd almost always be off hunting. Women know how to get men off, and they know how to get what they want from men by getting them off.

> **" I conducted a focus group with five women. . . . Three of the women said they would not hesitate to engage in full-fledged sexual intercourse with (Clinton). All five of the women were willing to give him oral sex. "**

Nobody really dealt with that issue in the instance of Bill Clinton and Monica Lewinsky. For the president, he seemed to want some kind of release. And for Monica Lewinsky, the issue seemed to be more about finding ways to please him because it gave her influence over him. It was not so much his power over her but rather her power over him, in my view.

I conducted a focus group with five women, and at one point I asked them about Clinton, and whether they would have sex with him. Three of the women said they would not hesitate to engage in full-fledged sexual intercourse with him. Two of them would not go that far. But all five of the women were willing to give him oral sex.

For some, it was the idea of being intimate with a president that worked for them. But there was also an element of having had some influence and power over a powerful man. Yet somehow in all this debate over Clinton's behavior, the focus has been on him as the predator.

We sexologists look at people's activities and what they engage in to get off. And it looks to me like Monica was enjoying a power trip, and for Clinton, it was more of a release.

MAN'S GUIDE: Within Clinton's mindset and that of many men, do they honestly think that oral sex is not really cheating?

> **❝** It's a good thing that I am not a woman. I would always be pregnant. I just can't say no. **❞**
>
> —President Warren Harding, talking to friends, 1919

DR. MCILVENNA: Within his belief system, I think he honestly did not perceive oral sex as sexual intercourse. If Clinton had wanted to have some down-and-dirty intercourse, I think he and Monica would have done so. But they defined their relationship in a very specific way.

Having done many sex histories and sexual profiles, I don't find Clinton's actions all that odd. About 50 percent of all males engage in sociosexual activity of some sort outside of their primary relationship. And when you get into the men who have wealth, power, and influence, like Clinton, the figure is more like 90 percent.

MAN'S GUIDE: The rich and powerful can get more because they can afford it, then?

DR. MCILVENNA: Let's be honest here. The people who are most knowledgeable about sex have the best sex lives. Socioeconomic status and education play huge roles in sexual behavior. It's not the poor people or the uneducated people who are engaging in a wide range of sexual activities, oral or otherwise.

MAN'S GUIDE: So do a lot of issues regarding oral sex and other forms of sex break down along cultural, ethnic, and racial lines?

DR. MCILVENNA: Absolutely. Black and Hispanic women generally do not like to perform oral sex. To some extent, with higher educational levels, you see fewer racial differences. But they still exist.

If you are engaging in oral sex, you are generally using it as a form of foreplay. The goal is pleasure, and to some extent, you must delay the gratification. In people who belong to lower socioeconomic classes, concepts like foreplay often do not exist, and they are much less likely to engage in things like oral sex. In fact, they are often very uptight about the subject.

If you are a woman in a higher socioeconomic class, you probably have career goals and educational goals, and something like pregnancy can stop you dead in your tracks. It's hard to go to college if you have a kid to raise. So engaging in oral sex and finding other ways to derive sexual pleasure without genital-to-genital intercourse is much more important. It's a freedom issue.

MAN'S GUIDE: President Clinton enjoys some extramarital oral sex, and the public cannot get enough of it. Eddie Murphy and other actors are caught with transvestites and prostitutes, and we have to know all about it. Has this country gotten to the point where our most famous and popular people define our sexual agendas? Are we a bunch of hormonal lemmings?

DR. MCILVENNA: We have always had heroes of entertainment and sex. We have always been fascinated by the sex lives of those people who are cultural heroes. And we are always trying to pump up our heroes and manufacture new heroes. John Wayne was portrayed in movies as a war hero, so we all think of him as a war hero. But he was never in a war.

We exaggerate things and make people more than they are because the boy next door is much less interesting by comparison. But in actuality, everyone is pretty much the same when it comes to sex. There are only so many openings on our bodies and only so many things we can do with those openings.

I have spent much of my life doing sexual profiles, and people in Africa tend to bump and grind in much the same way as the people in France. Minor cultural differences aside, people are doing pretty much the same thing. The human body tends to respond in the same way for everyone, so we are driven to do pretty much the same things as everyone else to derive sexual gratification. Testosterone pretty much has the same effect in everyone's bodies—both men and women—and so the urges are the same.

Some people have made the claim that we would never see Clinton's kind of atrocious sexual behavior in a female president. Well, they're wrong. These people haven't conducted sex histories of women like I have. There are things that women feel and do sexually that men couldn't keep up with in a thousand years.

Sociologists try to say that sexual behavior is socially prescribed, but that is mostly a pack of lies. People are still doing things the way they always have.

Frankly, it's amazing how similar it all is. And as far as oral sex goes, more than 50 percent of people worldwide engage in some form of oral-genital sex. It may not be a major sexual outlet for all of them, but it is still an outlet to some degree.

MAN'S GUIDE: Does all this media attention to oral sex and sex in general have an upside?

DR. MCILVENNA: No. In fact, it has had an incredible downside. Suddenly, everyone in the media is a self-proclaimed sex expert, even though most people know little about human sexuality. All this attention has hurt sexology, I think, and there is already too little money going into research on human sexuality.

Worse yet, the people who are spending so much time commenting on Clinton's sexual peccadilloes aren't even asking the right questions. They focus only on the issue of values. Nobody has really explored what the president and Monica Lewinsky really got out of this relationship. No one has asked if they used the proper protection. No one has asked if the oral sex was any good. There are more important issues in sex than just the value judgments.

> " Modern men and women are obsessed with the sexual; it is the only realm of primordial adventure still left to most of us. "
>
> —Edward Abbey,
> "Down the River
> with Henry Thoreau,"
> *Words from the Land*, 1981

MAN'S GUIDE: So what do we say to our children now that "oral sex," "phone sex," and "semen-stained dress" are terms that have dominated the airwaves for so long?

DR. MCILVENNA: That's a crazy question. The kids don't give a hoot. They only care about their peers and what their peers think of them. To imagine that kids haven't already picked up on references to oral sex on TV and in the movies is absurd. Find me a teenage boy who hasn't gotten into his dad's collection of sex magazines.

Also, they can find sexual images on the Internet much better than we can hide them from them. In fact, they're just better at finding things on the Internet in general. I was trying to search for some information on the Internet recently and just couldn't locate it. My grandson found it almost immediately. I'm 67 and he's 7, and he knows more about the Internet than I do.

So one way or another, the kids find out about all these sexual activities anyway. Honestly, I suspect that the more our kids learn about sex, the better off they are. My son and daughter have both worked for me at the Institute for Advanced Study of Human Sexuality, so they have been exposed to many sexual issues, some of them pretty racy. Yet my children and grandchildren are among the straightest people in the world, sexually speaking. You'd think they would have turned out to be sexual maniacs. I probably would have, had the roles been reversed.

We should just be honest with our kids that people do these things. The world is not going to end because someone diddled someone else. We have much more important issues to address.

> **" Granted, the sexual revolution went too far, information-wise. When you find phrases like 'suck face' as a euphemism for 'kiss,' it sort of takes the zing out of intimate personal contact. "**
>
> —Ian Shoales,
> "Single in the '80s," *I Gotta Go*

The important issues are not the sex lives of our presidents and our entertainers. The important issue is not who is diddling whom. What is tremendously important is the quality of the sex that people are having.

No one seems to care about whether the sexual activity between this president and this intern was any good. And that's not a good sign. A lot of people have sexual dysfunction, and that worries me. I would rather see everyone having enjoyable sex. I'm worried about the people who have sexual dysfunction and act out their problems on themselves and other people in negative ways.

The fact that our president can get it up actually makes me feel good in one respect. I would rather know that the president can and does get off than to worry that he has pent-up frustrations and hostility that are going to propel him to push the wrong button someday.

QUICKIES

DOCTORS LOSE THEIR HEADS OVER ORAL SEX

Add the longtime editor of the *Journal of the American Medical Association* (*JAMA*) to the list of those ensnared by the Clinton sex scandal. George Lundberg, M.D., was fired after 17 years as *JAMA*'s editor because he published an article about a survey of college students' opinions of oral sex.

The article featured the results of an 8-year-old survey in which 60 percent of college students questioned said they did not consider oral sex the same as "having sex." Dr. Lundberg was canned, the journal said, because he inappropriately dragged the publication into the presidential impeachment debate, threatening the integrity of *JAMA*.

THE UNHAPPY HOOKERS

Film depictions of prostitutes—think Julia Roberts in *Pretty Woman*—often show working girls as not only beautiful but also amazingly well-adjusted. Researchers who interviewed nearly 500 prostitutes from around the world, however, found something else: two-thirds suffered from post-traumatic stress disorder. The nationality or place where the prostitutes worked appeared to have no bearing on the frequency with which they suffered the condition.

Post-traumatic stress disorder is found in less than 5 percent of the general population. About 20 to 30 percent of Vietnam War combat veterans are estimated to have the condition—still less than half the ratio of the prostitutes surveyed.

BODY ENGLISH BARED IN ITALY

A British Airways flight attendant who stripped to her underwear after losing a bet was given a dressing down by the airline but allowed to keep her job.

Andrea O'Neill, 31, stripped at the airport in the Italian city of Genoa after losing a bet that her flight from London would not land on time. Male airport staff happily watched O'Neill peel off her uniform.

The airline allowed O'Neill to keep her job after concluding that her stunt had given the company valuable publicity about the promptness of its flights.

PUBLIC WON'T BE PRIVY TO PAM'S PARTS

Hoping to keep abreast of developments in public taste, *Ripley's Believe It or Not!* reportedly tried to buy Pamela Anderson Lee's breast implants for display after she had them removed.

Ripley's had hoped to display the implants in an exhibit in its Hollywood museum alongside corsets, body-piercing paraphernalia, and ancient Chinese foot-binding instruments.

Lee, who gained notoriety from a video in which she had sex with her husband, said she wasn't interested in selling the implants.

ONLY IN SAN FRANCISCO

Political campaign strategist Jack Davis held a 50th birthday bash in San Francisco that raised eyebrows even in that tolerant city.

With Mayor Willie Brown and other city and county officials attending, Davis's party featured live sex and bondage acts, male and female strippers, and a glory-hole near the stage, through which the men could receive anonymously performed oral sex. As if that weren't enough, a woman carved a pentagram into the back of a satanic priest, then urinated on the bleeding design and sodomized him with a bottle of whiskey.

Kind of makes you wonder what Davis will do for his 60th birthday party, doesn't it?

R-RATED COMIC STRIP

President Clinton's affair with Monica Lewinsky even shook things up on the comics pages of American newspapers.

When Garry Trudeau's *Doonesbury* featured a strip in which a "scandal facilitator" spoke to an elementary school class about the scandal, several newspapers declined to publish the strip that day. The panels included language such as "oral sex" and references to sexual fluids.

DEAR DR. MANLY

Q: *I have this fantasy of <u>making it with my wife in a department store</u> <u>dressing room</u>. Doc, is this feasible?*
—T. R., Tulsa, Oklahoma

A: A little adventurous, are we? There's a lot to be said for sex in a dressing room, what with all those mirrors. And of course, there's no better aphrodisiac for your partner than letting her spend your money. Unfortunately, most department stores frown on dressing room sex. So, if you're intent on doing this, it's best not to tell them or ask if it's okay.

My professional advice: Pick a large dressing room with a securely closing door, preferably one that extends all the way to the floor. Your partner goes in first, taking enough clothes with her to justify how long she's going to be. Then you go in to provide a "second opinion." Standing rear-entry sex will likely be your best bet unless there's enough space to be more creative.

Now the fun part: Try not to make noise, even if your salesperson comes by to ask you about the fit. "Silent sex can be very encouraging. Remember that every orgasm discharges tension. The more tension you can build first, emotionally and physically, the more powerful the orgasm will be," says Phillip Hodson, a fellow of the British Association for Counseling and a sex therapist and marriage counselor in London.

And afterwards? Buy the dress.

Q: *I have an unusual problem. <u>Whenever I drive my car, I get an erec-</u> <u>tion.</u> Not only is it a distraction but sometimes my penis gets so hard that it's downright uncomfortable. What to do?*
—C. C., Manitoba, Canada

A: You've heard guys say they "love" their cars? Now you've got me wondering. . . .
You've heard the phrase "It's a hard road"? What's that all about?

Seriously, your problem isn't as unusual as you think: An informal office poll here at *Man's Guide* revealed that one staffer gets an erection every time he climbs aboard his riding mower and another once had an embarrassing incident on a city bus.

I checked in with the author of *Superpotency*, Dudley Seth Danoff, M.D. He's senior attending urologist at Cedars Sinai Medical Center in Los Angeles. Dr. Danoff says he's been down this road before. "Road erections," he says, "are a combination of two factors: vibrations from the vehicle that provide stimulation and send blood into the penis; and the fact that sitting on a car seat puts pressure on the veins that shunt blood out of the penis, blocking them off and trapping the blood inside."

The erections won't do you any harm, especially if your trousers are roomy enough for your penis to comfortably expand. If the unwelcome hitchhiker becomes an annoyance, try slipping a doughnut-style seat cushion under your bottom, the kind of cushion used by people with hemorrhoids. That will lighten pressure on the key veins and may help reduce the unwanted erections.

Dr. Manly is a fictional character.
The actual advice was provided by a variety of
medical doctors and other qualified experts.

7

SIDESTEP
THE SEX POLICE

 Love is a battlefield, the song goes, and often the skirmishes are in courts of law. One day, it's an attempt to censor an adult video or magazine. Another day, it's a challenge to an illegal sex act between two consenting adults.

Much of the sex-related litigiousness today revolves around sexual harassment in the workplace. Plenty of guys are wondering if they could lose their jobs for simply complimenting or flirting with a coworker.

Almost makes you want to join a monastery, doesn't it? Well, that's not necessary. This is one battlefield on which you needn't get bloodied. You do, however, need to use some common sense and self-defense. This section will bring you up to speed on the latest legal lashes in the sexual arena.

So read on. After all, if love is a battlefield, you need to arm yourself with knowledge.

TOP TEN

Silly Laws

Various communities all over the United States have found certain sex acts just too despicable for their citizenry to tolerate, so they've outlawed them. Does this mean that these acts were commonly taking place before the laws were enacted? That, we don't know. Some of these sex laws are forgotten or rarely enforced and seem too weird to be true. Among those cited on a Web site and attributed to The Odd Index: The Ultimate Compendium of Bizarre and Unusual Facts *by Stephen J. Spignesi are:*

❶ Harrisburg, Pennsylvania: Forbids sex with a truck driver in a tollbooth

❷ Willowdale, Oregon: Prohibits a husband to talk dirty in his wife's ear during sex

❸ Tremonton, Utah: Outlaws sex in an ambulance

❹ Newcastle, Wyoming: Sex is not allowed in a butcher shop meat freezer

❺ Alexandria, Minnesota: Illegal for a man to have sex with his wife with the stench of onions, sardines, or garlic on his breath

❻ Ames, Iowa: Unlawful to drink more than three slugs of beer while lying in bed with a woman

❼ Washington, D.C.: Mandates the missionary position: only face-to-face sex is legal

8 Clinton, Oklahoma: Prohibits masturbating while watching people in a car engage in sex

9 Kingsville, Texas: Pigs may not mate on Kingsville Airport property

10 Fairbanks, Alaska: Unlawful for two moose to engage in sex on city sidewalks. Don't you have to wonder what symbol they use to depict this on the warning sign?

MUST READS

Flirt with Flair

You can't blame some guys if they're downright terrified to flirt with women—especially at work. Nobody in his right mind wants to be accused of sexual harassment. Legalities aside, most of us don't relish rejection, either. Particularly by someone we're going to have to keep bumping into and interacting with. In their book Guy Knowledge, *writers Larry Keller and Christian Millman provide pointers on flirting fearlessly—and wisely.*

In the sometimes-barren landscape of workplace drudgery, crowded bars, and frenetic gyms, the smile from a comely female often breathes life back into a gray day. No wonder we flirt with them.

And though it may lead to a relationship, that's not always the aim. "No matter how happily a woman may be married," wrote the eminent U.S. journalist H. L. Mencken, "it always pleases her to discover that there is a nice man who wishes that she were not."

In order to flirt well, it's essential to know exactly what flirting is. "It's a charming and honest expression of interest in others," says Susan G. Rabin, a New York City relationship therapist, director of The School of Flirting, and author of *101 Ways to Flirt*. "Good flirts pay attention to other people; they make other people feel important and appreciated. It's a wonderful art."

Take note—flirting does not mean getting that head-turner down in purchasing alone in the file room. Nor does it mean sidling up to Sally Sloegin in a bar and trying to convince her to inspect the back seat of your Buick. "You can have sex on your mind, but keep it off your lips," Rabin says. "Women are so used to being sex objects and touched and pawed and called at. They're tired of that."

Is She Interested?

You should consider flirting a form of social badminton. It takes two active participants, both volleying and returning. Without a willing partner, you may as well fire your birdie into the wall. So, the first thing you need to consider is whether she's up to a bit of court time with you. If she's not, back off and respect that decision.

● **Check for a green light.**

It's not too difficult to determine if a woman is interested in flirting with you, says Rabin. The problems begin when a man doesn't bother to stop and see.

Uninvited advances are not flirtation, she stresses. Not only does that show poor taste on the part of the man but it may also constitute sexual harassment.

● Pay attention.
Look for telltale signs like a ready smile when she sees you approaching, suggests Rabin. If she buries her head in a file folder, it's best to move on. You may also notice her giving you short, sidelong glances during the course of the day. Another good sign. And she may actively seek you out for a chance to chat over the coffee machine. If you're honest with yourself, you'll know if she's intrigued by your wily charms.

Is She Not Interested?

Since the 1970s, Monica Moore, Ph.D., professor of psychology at Webster University in St. Louis, has spent countless hours studying the nonverbal signals women give off when they're interested in a man. And the ones when they're not.

Remember that you can't count on nonverbal communications to be a dictionary in which all behaviors mean the same thing for the same person. Think about the context, Dr. Moore says. But generally, she says, these are some of the more frequent warning signs that you should back off.

● She'll orient her body away from you.

● She'll nod less or not at all to your conversation.

● She'll stop looking you in the eye.

● She may cross her arms over her chest or cross her legs.

● She'll move her chair back from you.

● She'll stop smiling and may even frown.

Why can't she just say outright that she's uncomfortable? She's trying to spare your feelings, bud. "Women aren't little victims who can't say no," Dr. Moore says. "But it is very much the case that women in our culture have often been socialized to be more passive than men and to care for the feelings of others."

Making Your Move

Once you have established that the attraction is mutual, where do you begin?

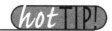

Get to know a woman better before you compliment her. Then, compliment her attire or performance, not physical qualities. Try "That's a nice dress" or "Great job on that report," rather than "Nice bod."

● Raise your sights.

Remember that 1979 Bellamy Brothers hit, "If I Said You Had a Beautiful Body, Would You Hold It against Me?" Well, forget it. Those kind of pickup lines can get you slapped in a bar, and in trouble at work. "Keep the comments and compliments above the neck," says Rabin.

● Question, but don't interrogate.

Don't go barging into her personal life, asking things like her age, her marital status, her cup size. She'll let you know the things she wants you to know. Asking appropriate questions is the hallmark of any good flirt, adds Rabin. It shows her that you find her truly interesting.

● Don't lurk.

Remember, no matter how interesting you may find her, you don't want to camp out next to her workstation or follow her from one exercise machine to the next at the gym. Flirting is a dance, says Rabin, but the dancers still need a rest from time to time. "If you don't push it and you don't go overboard, women will open up to you," she says.

● Have fun.

Flirting is more about enjoying a woman's company than a means to getting lucky, Rabin says. Sure, there's a subterranean sexual charge there. But it's not the focus of good flirting. "To let the joyful banter, the mystery, the wooing pass you by and go right for the kill is such a shame," she says. "It takes all the fun out of it."

Don't Cross the Line

It's no longer merely a matter of good manners for a guy to back off when a woman he's trying to flirt with sends out negative vibes. It's the law.

"Flirting is fun when both people want to participate," says Monica Moore, Ph.D., professor of psychology at Webster University in St. Louis. "But when someone is flirting with someone who is giving very definite signals that this is not acceptable, then we're talking about sexual harassment."

Workplace sexual harassment claims are on the rise. In 1991, the U.S. Equal Employment Opportunities Commission (EEOC) reported 6,883 cases filed across the country. Just 6 years later, that number more than doubled to 15,889. These days, what you say and do *can* be held against you in a court of law.

So when does innocent flirting cross the line into sexual harassment? According to the EEOC, if a woman's response to "unwelcome sexual advances, requests for sexual favors, and other verbal or physical conduct of a sexual nature . . . affects (her) employment, unreasonably interferes with (her) work performance, or creates an intimidating, hostile, or offensive work environment," *that's* sexual harassment.

The Office Romance

There is so much fear and downright hysteria about sexual harassment in the workplace nowadays that some so-called experts are warning men not to become involved with anybody they meet at work. That seems unrealistic and foolish to us, and that's why we like The Office Romance *by Dennis M. Powers, associate professor of business law at Southern Oregon University in Ashland. Powers says men need to be smart, but sexual harassment lawsuits at the office are uncommon and companies are increasingly recognizing that employees will have romances. The following excerpt comes from the chapter The Law of Romance.*

The law of romance is not the law of sexual harassment. It is separate but complementary. There are no statutes, codes, or specific regulations in this area. It is created by what sexual harassment is not and was never intended to be. Many academic researchers clearly believe that sexual harassment and romance are two distinct areas, not related, and this law simply reflects this commonsense division.

For example, a coworker asks for a date and is turned down. He or she accepts the response and doesn't ask again. Whether that coworker is the boss or a subordinate, clearly this isn't sexual harassment. If that person asks again later, discreetly and politely—again being refused and accepting it—it still isn't sexual harassment. Even if the recipient didn't like being asked out. Technically, you can ask, send a nice note, even give flowers, receiving a no response to all without committing illegal sexual harassment—up to the point where the recipient is reasonably made uncomfortable by these acts.

An insurance account executive said, "I've been asked out by men at work, some more than once, and I've later gone out with them. A friend of mine feels 'no means no' and that means no more asking out. I've asked her back, 'Does that mean forever and ever?' . . . Of course not. Asking for a date and dating isn't a 'one strike and you're out' ballgame. Take a look at how many relationships develop: people, feelings, and situations change. It's *how* a man, or a woman, asks someone out that's important, along with how they react to the response." The law agrees, provided the approach is relationship-oriented, not sexual or with innuendoes, and any subsequent approach is reasonable after receiving a refusal. Taking time before making another request makes sense, as obviously badgering someone to go out isn't going to meet with success. It's all in the approach, although this can depend on the personality of whomever's being asked.

As part of this law of romance, men and women should relate to each other respectfully and politely—whether at work or not. You don't say to one another "Nice, tight body," or "Sexy, sexy, sexy. . . ." You don't call each other "girls," "macho man," "sweetie," "hot stuff," or any other slang words, regardless of the sex of the recipient. Nor is this romance.

Reading *Playboy* in the company cafeteria isn't sexual harassment, no matter what some want you to believe. But if someone complains, this shouldn't become a cause célèbre because workers shouldn't be reading personal material (at least if controversial) at work anyway—not to mention that this isn't romance either.

perfect figures

One in every five working women in a poll commissioned by NBC News said they had an experience at their job in the previous 2 years that they felt was sexual harassment. The ratio rose to two in five among women under the age of 35.

One in five men and women admitted having made a comment within the previous 5 years about a coworker of the opposite sex that "crossed the line of appropriate behavior."

• • • • • • • • •

A man or woman can take the risk and compliment someone on their dress. If the person objects, then simply don't compliment them again and go on to someone more approachable. You can compliment men and women, no matter where they are (even at board meetings) and not be guilty of harassment under even the most conservative of policies. A person might be offended, but that's a different consideration.

Buying a valentine for someone, then writing "Best" and your name isn't unlawful. Even if you sign it "Love," this by itself doesn't meet the tests. Nor is buying a gift for someone who returns it.

It is true that what's on- and off-limits can depend entirely on how close a working relationship you've developed. For example, if you've known each other for years, then the other person will be more understanding or flexible. If you've met someone only once, then compliments, gifts, and the like may not be welcome. They aren't harassment either, but you'll be taking your chances.

A consensual affair even between a boss and a subordinate isn't sexual harassment by itself, although it could be portrayed this way after the fact. As part of this, firms are applying a *standard of reasonableness* to the conduct of supervisors involved romantically in reporting relationships. If supervisors violate this standard, then the companies discipline them. Otherwise, companies will work with the supervisors (such as facilitating a transfer or eliminating review responsibilities), given that there are no indications of bad motives or control. This is an important concept, as these firms are recognizing that reporting relationships by themselves aren't the problem—it's the conduct, motives, and actions of the participants.

"One-night stands" aren't sexual harassment either, provided both participants are willing. A 35-year-old marketing manager in New Jersey said, "I had a one-night stand with my boss when I was leaving the company. I had accepted a position with another firm, and they threw me a 'going-away' party. He drove me home afterward, and I was drunk . . . dead drunk. We made love in the parking lot of my condominium complex, and I don't remember much of that. It was just one of those nights." With that, she started laughing to herself.

Then there are the just plain "physical relationships" with nothing more at stake. A paralegal at a prestigious New York City law firm had an affair with her supervising paralegal. She didn't care whether either one loved the other or where it was going. "It was just a physical thing," she said. "It only lasted a few months, and that's all I wanted at the time." A friend of hers said, "When she's interested in someone, she makes it known." Not exactly romance, but not sexual harassment either. Would it be harassment if the man were the actor? To embrace true equality, it shouldn't be.

perfect figures

About three of four workers say it's okay to date a coworker, a survey by the American Management Association found. Nearly 40 percent of workplace romances lead to marriage or a long-term relationship, the study concluded.

The Courts

Court decisions don't address the law of romance—the cases rely on whether elements of the legal tests for harassment are missing or the fact patterns don't constitute it. The following cases illustrate aspects of the law of romance, all involving decisions where sexual harassment was not proved.

- A male employee testified that none of the female president's actions made him feel harassed, except for thank-you notes from her signed "Love" or "Much love." The man said he felt uncomfortable, rather than harassed. There was no evidence that the man communicated his feelings to the woman, and he gave her an expensive, personal Christmas gift during the same time period.

● A white supervisor asked a black employee how she would feel about dating a white person, stared at her during the elevator ride, and said that he had a crush on her and would "kiss her face" (although he didn't make any attempt to do so). He never touched her. Although this made the employee feel uncomfortable, the supervisor's actions didn't establish a hostile work environment.

perfect figures

More than 70 percent of companies have no written office romance policies, a recent study found.

● A supervisor and his subordinate had a romantic relationship. The court held that this relationship did not, without more being present, give rise to a sexual discrimination or sexual harassment claim.

● A supervisor's flattering remarks about a coworker, his favoritism toward her, and the kiss that she blew back at him weren't sufficiently pervasive conduct to create a hostile working environment for a coworker. The court held that favoritism by itself, absent evidence proving a sexual relationship existed between the two, didn't meet the test.

● Female coworkers told other female workers that they looked "hot" and one woman's dress and buttocks were complimented by those workers on several occasions. The former employees said that they never interpreted the comments as indicating that their coworkers wanted to have sex with them. There was also no proof that the alleged harassers were lesbians.

● The female plaintiff needed to prove that she neither solicited nor incited the harassment and that she considered the conduct undesirable and offensive. The court held that she didn't prove this.

● A former female employee admitted that she was never threatened or disciplined by her supervisor, nor did the supervisor use his position to affect adversely any of the terms and conditions of her employment. His motivation for touching her was held to be solely personal.

● Another case revolved around trying to decide whether the alleged harasser's invitation to the plaintiff was to go out on a date or to have sex with him. The court held that if it was to go on a date, then there couldn't be any harassment, regardless of what her response was.

Some companies argue that they don't want any lawsuits brought that could put them in an unfavorable light—whether the alleged behavior is illegal sexual harassment or not. They don't want the expense and therefore take strong actions to guard against any hint of "unwelcome" conduct. The problem with this approach is that they can't insulate themselves from lawsuits, even spurious ones. In return, restrictive companies buy wrongful termination lawsuits and bad morale for their heavy-handed policies. Having a nonrestrictive working environment, open communication channels, and clear but reasonable policies is a better defense. Pro-interactive companies don't have the same numbers of these problems.

The Stages of a Relationship

There are relatively few problems in the beginning or middle of work affairs, provided the participants don't bring their personal arguments into work with them. Although the vast majority of ended relationships don't end up as sexual harassment complaints, it's the breakup that creates the potential for legal trouble. Management must step in and work out the problems when difficulties occur. As one human resources executive said, "Usually, all we say is that your staying employed here depends on the two of you working out your problems, or deciding who transfers or leaves. If you can't decide, then both of you must leave. Our experience is that the parties fairly quickly work out their difficulties."

It isn't unreasonable for an employee to begin a discreet quest to win over another person's heart, provided the actions don't interfere with either's work performance. A company shouldn't be surprised if those efforts continue in the face of rejection. However, it isn't easy to decide when a pursuit taken delicately, in good taste, but persistently falls into the gray area of sexual harassment.

perfect figures

Percentage of people who are offended by dirty jokes at work: 77

When one person has had it with the other's pursuit, the company has to decide what to do about it. The same human resources executive observed, "We've had little problems here, as well. We will tell the one pursuing that he or she needs to stop and reconsider their actions. We'll say, 'You can apply for a transfer, stop and work out a truce, or leave. If you don't, then you leave.' We may recommend that they see a therapist or go into counseling, because we aren't interested in buying lawsuits." What's important is that companies are managing these personal, human relationship issues, just as they do any other human resources area.

There's Much More Love Than Hate

The overwhelming number of broken workplace romances, whether involving boss-subordinate relationships or not, don't wind up in the hands of the lawyers. Companies counsel, mediate, transfer, and separate responsibilities to solve the problems. The ex-lovers work out their difficulties, leave, or change departments: they put the broken romance behind them and go on to better things. The U.S. Equal Employment Opportunities Commission's (EEOC's) response to charges in most cases doesn't get too far; historically, the commission has turned down three-fourths of the harassment complaints it receives (due to lack of proof, facts that don't meet the legal tests, and other reasons).

SEX TRENDS

CYBER-HARASSMENT

Sexual harassment and other forms of on-the-job discrimination have gone electronic as workers use office technology to exchange off-color jokes and comments. About 20 percent of employers have gotten complaints about the appropriateness of e-mail, a survey found.

And a study by a software company found that more than half of employees with access to the Internet at work have received adult-oriented, racist, sexist, or inappropriate e-mail at work.

Firm upon firm, survey upon survey, all report there are many more office romances than sexual harassment cases. This shouldn't be too surprising when you look at the overall statistics. Given that the workforce is 135 million strong (nearly one-half women) and climbing, there are millions of workplace romances occurring every year. The EEOC had nearly 16,000 sexual harassment cases filed last year, of which the great majority involved sexual innuendoes, sleazy comments, and tasteless conduct— not broken relationships.

A total of 54,000 cases involving sexual harassment were filed with the EEOC over the past 6 years, of which only 5 percent (or some 3,000) dealt with quid pro quo (boss-subordinate and sex for services) harassment filings. In fact, the American Management Association's survey reported that 84 percent of those managers profiling an office romance said there was no official action taken against the participants (not even an "informal" talk by the boss)—only 7 percent reported "other action" taken, ranging from an "informal" talk with the boss to voluntary transfers or resignation by one partner (another 3 percent received a warning; 3 percent reported an involuntary transfer; and 3 percent gave no response).

perfect figures

Percentage of people who think that calling someone "honey" or "babe" at work is offensive: 68

Few firms need to take even official action against one or both romantic partners, and this includes when romances break up.

Any continuing connection between romance and harassment is wildly exaggerated. Cupid must somehow find a better press agent.

SEX WARS

" DOREEN, WOULD YOU...... PLEASE, PUT AWAY THE PEPPER SPRAY ····· MARRY ME? "

HELP ONLINE

ACLU

The American Civil Liberties Union (ACLU) has challenged
certain sex laws in several states and Puerto Rico.
You can search their Web site for more information.
www.aclu.org/sitesearch.html

LAWS, LAWS, AND MORE LAWS

To learn about every sort of law imaginable,
check out the Internet Law Library.
www.nsulaw.nova.edu/library/ushouse

STATE BY STATE STATUTES

To find out about laws—including sex laws—in the state where you live,
take a look at legal.online's listing of state laws on the Internet.
www.legalonline.com/statute2.htm

MAN'S GUIDE INTERVIEW

Fornicating for Justice

An Interview with Howard Fletcher

In many parts of the country, laws still exist that prohibit sexual acts that most of us take for granted. Engage in foreplay in the wrong state, and you could be bucking for a misdemeanor or felony charge.

Thinking about sucking your girlfriend's nipple? Think again. That's only for a baby to use.

Want your wife to wrap her lips around your penis? Could be a bad idea. If you think she is reluctant to swallow now, see how she swallows doing time in jail for going down on you.

In all honesty, there is virtually no risk of arrest or prosecution for the vast majority of Americans. But sex laws do exist, and they are used against otherwise guiltless citizens from time to time.

That's something that activist Howard Fletcher just refuses to accept. He is the co-founder of the National Sexual Rights Council, and he wants these laws stricken from every book in the land.

In November 1997, funded in part by a grant from Playboy *magazine founder Hugh Hefner, Fletcher, of Alaska, took a female friend down to Florida to break all three of the state's archaic sex laws—the first step in a long-term, complex plan to get the laws overturned.*

And if Fletcher can win in Florida, perhaps all other such laws can be put into their long-overdue graves. Fletcher is willing to go to court to fight this fight, and he's willing to risk going to jail for making whoopee.

How many other men in their late sixties would be willing to do that for you?

MAN'S GUIDE: I hear that you went down to Florida to break a few laws.

FLETCHER: As a matter of fact, we did.

MAN'S GUIDE: Well, what did you do; and why did you do it?

FLETCHER: Well, the reason why we did it is because our organization, the National Sexual Rights Council, feels that one of the most dangerous things in the United States today is the disproportionate influence that extremists on the religious right exert on our lawmakers and our society regarding sexual activity.

A very small group of wackos has a great deal of control over public policy. We decided to try to change that by going on the offensive and directly challenging some of these laws and getting them stricken down.

The problem is that when you want to get laws declared unconstitutional or get them changed and the lawmakers won't make the effort to do so, you have to get arrested for the crime so that you have standing in the court. You cannot just say a law is silly and get the courts to hear you. You have to actually be in a position where you are charged with breaking the law in question.

What we did in Florida was break three sex laws so that I could get legal standing in the Florida courts. One of those laws says that adultery is a crime, so I committed adultery with the friend whom I took with me.

One of the other laws I broke with her was an anti-fornication law. Actually, Florida doesn't have a law against fornication specifically. In their case, it is a law against lewd and lascivious cohabitation, which we were taking part in at the hotel room.

I find this law really interesting because there are probably thousands of elderly men and women on fixed incomes in Florida who are living together to reduce their expenses and so both can retain their Social Security benefits. Florida state law potentially makes them criminals.

The third law was a law against sodomy. In Florida, sodomy is any kind of sexual activity that is not for the purposes of procreation, such as oral sex and anal sex. Interestingly, the law specifically indicates that when a baby is suckling a mother's breast, that is not a violation of the law.

MAN'S GUIDE: So basically, the baby using the breast is okay, but if a man is using the breast . . .

FLETCHER: . . . or woman or anybody else . . .

MAN'S GUIDE: . . . they are committing a crime.

FLETCHER: They're committing a crime in Florida. Some of these kinds of laws are left over from 200 years ago when women were considered to be a form of property. And laws were deemed necessary for fathers and husbands to protect their property.

MAN'S GUIDE: So you went down to Florida with—who was it? A wife or a girlfriend?

FLETCHER: It was an old friend of mine. My wife knows her. To do this right and break all three laws, I needed somebody to commit these acts with.

MAN'S GUIDE: And it couldn't be your wife because you wanted to attack the adultery law as well. I see.

FLETCHER: Yes. But my wife and I may go down to Florida someday to break the sodomy law together.

MAN'S GUIDE: So you and your friend broke the laws. What did you do after that?

FLETCHER: First, we held a press conference. Everybody and his brother was there.

Then we marched over to the Boca Raton Police Department, admitted our crime, and tried to get arrested. Of course, they initially laughed us off and said that we had to be kidding. But ultimately, they treated it with all due respect, and they did a very professional job. They took down all the information and did the paperwork.

But they said that in the case of a misdemeanor offense like this, when they have not personally witnessed the activity, all they can do is file a report and leave it up to the prosecutors as to where the case will go from there.

MAN'S GUIDE: So to get arrested immediately for breaking these laws, you pretty much would have had to have sex in the police department.

FLETCHER: In the police department, after inviting somebody over to watch.

MAN'S GUIDE: So what is the status right now? Is the case active? Are you on your way to the pokey? What?

FLETCHER: The state did exactly what we thought they would. Nothing. They wanted to wait 30 days and then say, "We're not prosecuting this." That would have effectively nullified our case and rendered all our efforts meaningless.

So before they could say that they were not going to prosecute us, we went down to Miami to the federal courts and filed what is called a 1331 suit. It's called a federal question. And when you do this, you ask the court not to rule on whether you actually violated the law, but whether the law that you are alleged to have violated is constitutional.

I added an interesting clause in there, too. We decided to claim that the laws were not only unconstitutional and a violation of my first- and fourth-amendment rights, but that they violated my rights under the Americans with Disabilities Act.

> " If you believe there is a God, a God that made your body, and yet you think that you can do anything with that body that's dirty, then the fault lies with the manufacturer. "
>
> —Lenny Bruce
> in John Cohen's collection,
> *The Essential Lenny Bruce*,
> 1967

MAN'S GUIDE: Do tell.

FLETCHER: Well, being 65 or 66 years old at the time, I could not get it up one night during my visit. And because I clearly wanted to satisfy my friend, I had to rely heavily on oral sex, which is forbidden under Florida's sodomy law.

MAN'S GUIDE: You are tricky.

FLETCHER: Very tricky. But of course, the state of Florida is trying to make this go away. They spent 14 months throwing motions and appeals at us, making the statement that I have no standing and there is no reason for the federal courts to hear this case because there is no chance that I will be arrested for either adultery, sodomy, or lewd and lascivious cohabitation.

And that is true. They won't arrest me or charge me. They almost never arrest heterosexual people for violating these kinds of laws.

Many states do, however, use these laws against homosexuals from time to time.

So this whole thing has gone around and around, and one of my people missed a response deadline. So the judge threw the case out, and I had to go back and appeal, and so on.

The latest thing is that I finally got a judge to rule in favor of allowing the court case to proceed. What will happen now is anyone's guess.

MAN'S GUIDE: What is your wife's reaction to all of this?

FLETCHER: Well, if you are married, it is often implicit or assumed that the two of you have sexual exclusivity. My wife and I do not.

In a situation where the spouses expect each other not to have sex with anyone else, I can see some logic in allowing for one spouse to take the other to court.

But I do not think that adultery should be criminal, as it is in Florida. However, if you have sexual exclusivity and you cheat on your spouse, it could be construed as a violation of a contract, and there could be some civil damages there.

But you shouldn't put one of them in jail for committing adultery. It's the born-again Christians who seem to think that jail is an appropriate place for people who do these kinds of things.

MAN'S GUIDE: To be honest, my wife and I are born-again Christians, and we don't go for these laws any more than you do.

FLETCHER: Actually, that's always been one of my big points. The whole problem with this situation is that a few people at one extreme are speaking for a whole group and setting policies that many other members of that group would never advocate.

Are you familiar with what Walter Cronkite has done in this area?

MAN'S GUIDE: No.

FLETCHER: Walter Cronkite had some involvement with getting together some really top-notch religious leaders from many different faiths—Christians, Muslims, Jews, and so on.

They have put together an organization called the Interfaith Alliance. And what they are saying to various religious extremists is, "Stay out of our business. You do not speak for all Christians. Or all Muslims. Or all Jews. This is not the way we feel."

MAN'S GUIDE: So now that things are back on track and your case in Florida can go forward, what sort of time line are you looking at?

FLETCHER: God knows.

MAN'S GUIDE: So it could be in limbo for a while yet?

FLETCHER: Oh, yeah.

MAN'S GUIDE: Let's assume that you actually see a courtroom sometime before the second coming of Christ, you make your arguments, and you achieve your goal to get these laws axed. What then? Do you have to move on to another state and do the same thing you did in Florida?

FLETCHER: Well, once it is finally handled appropriately at the federal level, that's it. The problem is if it continues to be left to the states.

One of the most infamous sexual privacy decisions was handed down in 1986 in a case called *Bowers v. Harwick*. It all started when a police officer was serving a warrant at the back of a house, and saw this guy Harwick doing it with another guy. And Harwick was convicted on sodomy charges. The case went all the way up to the U.S. Supreme Court, where a five-to-four decision said that it was okay for states to criminalize homosexual behavior.

But the same year, the Supreme Court refused to hear a case like mine, which involved heterosexual activity.

Just recently, there was another sodomy case in Georgia, but this time the Georgia Supreme Court voted six to one that their own state's sodomy law was unconstitutional. (*Note:* Georgia state lawmakers have said they will introduce a new sodomy law.)

But the only way these laws will get tossed nationally is if we work through the federal court system.

One of our plans right now is to get everybody who is on our side organized and focused on specific issues. And the nice thing is that we do have some allies in the government. For example, I am really pleased with both of our U.S. senators up here in Alaska. They like our position.

But in general, the Republican party is being ruined from the inside out by this small group of extreme Christians who put so much pressure on them. It's ridiculous. And I think the people who are responsible for impeaching President Clinton because he lied about having sex with an intern were not acting in good faith. They were acting in political faith. I think we ought to get rid of all of those people, whether they are Democrats or Republicans.

Most Christians, or anyone else for that matter, do not want their preachers, their politicians, or their policemen in their bedrooms. None of us do. So I want to have all the organizations that are working on these kinds of issues get together to figure out a long-range political action plan. We're going to be out there trying to get coalitions together everywhere.

MAN'S GUIDE: Why do these laws persist? Most lawmakers in most states must realize these are stupid laws. Why doesn't somebody just bite the bullet, address the issue, and in a quick vote just undo these goofy laws?

FLETCHER: Well, they would, but there's so much pressure on them from this small minority of extremists. There are organizations with a lot of members and money whose entire purpose is to reclaim this country for Jesus.

> " Most Christians, or anyone else for that matter, do not want their preachers, their politicians, or their policemen in their bedrooms. None of us do. "

These people really believe that this should be a Christian country. But the problem is, which kind of Christians? Many people don't think Catholics are the right kind of Christians. And as far as most Christians are concerned, the Seventh-Day Adventists will have to go down the tube.

The last thing we should want in this country is a theocracy. Anytime you have a theocracy—and there are a couple of governments in the world where the religious leaders run the country directly—you have major problems.

The whole mess in Yugoslavia is a religious war. The Christian Serbians want the Muslim Albanians out of their country. Whenever you get religion involved in government, it's all going to go to hell.

And these politically minded extreme Christians focus on sex as one of their major issues because they know they can get people riled up about it.

It's not like I'm for sex just for sex's sake. I'm not Mr. Stud Muffin here. I'm a gray-haired great-grandfather. But it's just that these anti-sex laws are so ridiculous and potentially dangerous that we need to do something about them.

> **" Is sex dirty? Only if it's done right. "**
>
> —Woody Allen,
> *Everything You Always Wanted to Know about Sex,*
> 1972

MAN'S GUIDE: Any parting shots?

FLETCHER: Just that I would encourage everyone to get together to support sexual privacy issues.

I was so pleased to see five Republicans lose seats in the U.S. Congress after the impeachment mess. I was so happy to see that the public is not being swayed by the rhetoric. Questions were being asked of our president that no one should have been asking.

I don't approve of what President Clinton did, but it wasn't anyone's business except maybe his wife's.

QUICKIES

IT'S THE LAW

There was a time when all 50 states and Puerto Rico had sodomy laws, but in 32 states, those laws have been repealed by state legislatures or by courts, according to the American Civil Liberties Union (ACLU), which has challenged some sodomy laws.

Such laws generally outlaw anal and oral sex, even between consenting adults. Five states—Arkansas, Kansas, Missouri, Oklahoma, and Texas—ban these sexual acts exclusively between people of the same gender. Another 13 states and Puerto Rico prohibit these sexual acts between gays and heterosexuals alike. Those states are Alabama, Arizona, Florida, Idaho, Louisiana, Michigan, Massachusetts, Minnesota, Mississippi, North Carolina, South Carolina, Utah, and Virginia. The Puerto Rico statute is being challenged by the ACLU.

AND YOU THOUGHT CLINTON WAS FRISKY

The former deputy prime minister of Malaysia was arrested and charged with sexual misconduct for supposedly sodomizing a man 15 times and having sex with both Malaysian and foreign women. Two men were convicted of allegedly allowing the former government official and government reformer, Anwar Ibrahim, to sodomize them.

Ibrahim insisted the allegations were phony and an attempt to prevent him from exposing corruption in the government of his former boss. His supporters accused police of planning to inject Ibrahim with the AIDS virus after his arrest.

Sort of makes the Starr investigation seem pretty benign, doesn't it?

LADIES, START YOUR VIBRATORS

A federal judge struck down an Alabama law that banned the sale of vibrators, saying the state failed to prove the devices were obscene.

The Alabama legislature had barred the sale of items designed to enhance sexual pleasure, including vibrators and certain types of condoms. It also banned strip clubs.

The federal court ruling came in a lawsuit filed by the American Civil Liberties Union on behalf of six women who said they either sold vibrators or got from them and other sex toys sexual pleasure that they could not otherwise achieve.

PING-PONG DIPLOMACY

A stripper who shoots Ping-Pong balls and water from her vagina was declared a health hazard to spectators.

Stephanie Evans bills herself as "the human super soaker" and appears at the Ice House in Albuquerque, New Mexico, for a week every year. In 1997, the city forbade the club from serving pizza or drinks during her performances, saying that water was getting into drinks and onto food and that patrons were catching in their mouths objects that were expelled by Evans.

The club now warns customers to cover their plates and glassware when Evans performs.

> " An 8-year-old boy was suspended from school for composing a poem in which he rhymed 'Venus' with 'penis.' "

POETIC LICENSE DENIED

An 8-year-old boy was suspended for 3 days from his Salt Lake City elementary school after he composed a verse that rhymed "Venus" with "penis." A female classmate overheard the poem and told her parents. They in turn complained.

The school principal said she suspended the boy for sexual harassment because the word penis made the girl uncomfortable.

SEX BROUHAHA ELICITS FUNDS

A couple anonymously gave $350,000 to the State University of New York at New Paltz in support of free speech after the school and its president were attacked because the school sponsored a conference on sexuality. The women's studies department organized the confab, which included panels on sadomasochism, lesbianism, and safe sex. The governor ordered a probe of the university, and two university trustees called on the school's president to resign.

HOOKER DEFENSE DENIED

A Florida woman who claimed that antiprostitution laws violate the Constitution by discriminating against women as well as people who are unmarried, handicapped, mutilated, ugly, or elderly failed to persuade the U.S. Supreme Court. Without comment, the justices rejected her appeal.

DEAR DR. MANLY

Q: *After several months of unhelpful therapy for prostatitis, I went to the local medical library and dug through articles about current research, then took my doctor an article about a new treatment. He was furious. Should I have kept quiet?*

—P. R., SCHNECKSVILLE, PENNSYLVANIA

A: I'm furious, too. Furious that some doctors act this way. A patient has every right to be fully informed about all treatment options and to make educated treatment decisions. This is what patients' bills of rights are all about. They are law in some states. You have me worked up enough that I think I'll devote the whole column to this.

Sad to say, but many physicians are offended by patients who do their own homework. If doctors are unaware of a new treatment or don't know the answer to a question, some will dismiss it with a brush-off, rather than admit their own ignorance.

We do expect our physicians to have a wide and deep medical knowledge, and we do expect them to know things we don't. But we also know that they are mere mortals and can't know everything. I wish more of my colleagues would realize that and say things like, "I'm not sure I've seen that study; which journal was cited?" Or, "I've heard something of that treatment, but I haven't worked with it and will need to look into it a little more before I can address it authoritatively." And then make a note in the chart to look into it. And really do look into it and let the patient know what they think about it.

I asked Myron I. Murdock, M.D., clinical instructor of urology at George Washington University in Washington, D.C., for his suggestions for taking new treatment options to your doctor. These, he says, are the best strategies for getting what you want.

● Ask for his opinion.
"Presenting your information in a way that doesn't make the doctor feel threatened is key. I would say, 'Gee, I just read about a new therapy, but I know lots of physicians are leery of it. How do you feel about it?'" suggests Dr. Murdock. This approach works because it communicates first and foremost that you value his opinion.

● **Leave the research at home.**

"Ninety-nine percent of doctors absolutely hate it when their patients bring in materials of their own," says Dr. Murdock, who once had a mathematician patient send him a logarithmic graph of his prostate-cancer blood work.

Instead of handing your doctor a study, mention the fact that you were reading a relevant article and tell him what it's about. Then causally offer to send it to him later. He'll have time to look it over at his own convenience. You can ask him about it at your next appointment.

● **Know when to walk away.**

"If it gets to the point where he's not willing to talk about a question that you have—whatever that question may be—there's something wrong with that doctor," says Dr. Murdock. Remember, you're paying him for his time and his opinions. If you're not getting your questions answered, find someone else.

Amen.

Dr. Manly is a fictional character.
The actual advice was provided by a variety of
medical doctors and other qualified experts.

8

SPOT-CHECK
CYBERSEX

 Never has propositioning a woman—and succeeding—been so easy. According to a solicitation sent to Internet users, you can now have your very own virtual girlfriends via a computer program. They will pop up right on your screen and adapt to your likes and dislikes.

"You can actually have simple conversations," the come-on claimed. Well, that's realistic. We've had many simple conversations with real women—especially after our third Jack Daniel's.

"Their attitudes change with the different things you say, so you can say things that will upset them, and then say things that will please them," the solicitation continued. Like we don't get enough grief when we tick off real women?

But here's the "good" part: "Watch them as you ask them to take off different clothes and guide them through many different activities . . . including several sexual positions, using many unique toys, even bringing in multiple partners."

Cowabunga! No more having to talk nicey nice and drop $120 on theater tickets a couple of times before she decides she likes you. You can just say, "Off with the blouse, girl."

In truth, if the future of sex involves developing an intimate relationship with a computer screen, things are pretty grim. We don't think that's the future.

TOP TEN

Great Sex-Help Web Sites

Throughout this section of the book, you will find URLs for helpful and tastefully entertaining sex-related sites. (Of course, when deciding matters of taste, it depends who is tasting. We wouldn't recommend that you send your 10-year-old to any of these sites without first checking them out yourself. You don't want your kids knowing more than you, do you?) Here are 10 sites that are especially worth a look.

1 Try the Position Master, check your skills on the Orgazmatron, or just Ask the Sex Doc at the *Men's Health* magazine site, www.menshealth.com. Click on the "Sex" button on the home page.

2 The Guide to Love and Sex at www.loveandsex.com features fun stuff— quizzes on sex knowledge, advice on safer sex and family planning, and more

3 Sex Therapy Online at www.sexology.org lets you ask therapists for answers and advice concerning your sexuality questions

4 Emmaus Pastoral Counselling Services at www.emmaus.on.ca has a primer on what sex therapy is and who seeks it

5 Ask-a-Chick at www.ask-a-chick.com is a site staffed by women who are not professional counselors. You ask questions; the women give their perspectives

6 The Kinsey Institute Web site at www.indiana.edu/~kinsey is the official site of the famous sex research facility. It has research data, publications, and cyberlinks to clinics and other sexology sites

7 Tantra.com at www.tantra.com has information about tantra, the Kama Sutra, and other esoteric sex practices, plus discussion groups, gift ideas, and more

8 The InterNational Council on Infertility Information Dissemination site at www.inciid.org provides information pertaining to infertility, including adoption issues, infertility treatments, and professional and nonprofit organizations

9 The Sinclair Intimacy Institute at www.intimacyinstitute.com features a sexuality database, answers to frequently asked questions, and more

10 The home page of the Grey Clinic, an Indianapolis sexual health clinic, at www.greyclinic.com has information on a wide range of sexual topics

MUST READS

Cybersex

Just when you thought you had developed a certain sophistication about dating and sex etiquette, along comes all this dizzying computer technology that changes all the rules. Forget about drinks at your place if you're starting an online relationship. Writers Brian Chichester and Kenton Robinson help you negotiate the ins and outs of this electronic universe in this chapter from Sex Secrets.

When you bought that home computer, you probably figured the most fun you would have with it was playing a quick round of Solitaire in between balancing the family checkbook or working late on that spreadsheet. Terms like hard drive, software, or log off had no sexual connotations for you.

It's time for some new programming.

If you've been watching the news, you already know there's sex in cyberspace—the vast electronic frontier of computer networks and services that you can tap into using a home computer and a modem. Cybersex takes many forms, including photos, drawings, lurid storytelling, marketplaces, and, yes, venues where you can "meet" other sexual cybernauts and conduct "virtual" sexual encounters, all at the click of a mouse. Leave it to mankind to turn the most powerful tool of the Information Age into a toy for cheap thrills.

And leave it to lawyers and lawmakers to wrangle with the question of whether it's immoral and illegal. For years, the government has tried to rein in the amount of sexually explicit material on the Internet. The main reason— and it's a good one—is that they don't want children being exposed to the sort of truly graphic material that's available for any computer-savvy 8-year-old to discover. But because the Internet is so hard to regulate, many of the laws under debate are of the sweeping variety, making it illegal for anyone to upload, distribute, or download most sexually explicit material.

"This could go on for a while. Laws will be proposed, enacted, then watered down or shot down as unconstitutional," says Nancy Tamosaitis, author of *net.talk* and *The Penthouse Guide to Cybersex*. But from one day to the next, it's hard to know which way the wind blows. What could be perfectly legal titillation one day may be criminal the next. "Anyone who is interested in pursuing sex on the Net should keep up-to-date on the current climate and cybersex laws being discussed. It's for your own protection," says Tamosaitis. Think of it as electronic safe sex, and this chapter is your guide to practicing it.

How to Be Cybernaughty

It seems many people are quick to condemn sex via computer as "bad." Merely consider this image—a lonely, unsocial guy alone in his basement at 3:00 A.M., breathing heavily over a dirty conversation he's monitoring between two other strangers. Strikes you as pathetic, no?

Well, we suggest you be less judgmental about the whole thing. A compelling argument can be made for the many *advantages* to tapping into the vast online compendium of cybersex options.

"You could argue that cybersex is the ultimate form of safe sex. Whether you're downloading data for yourself or participating in an online encounter, you're in a very anonymous situation; there are fewer inhibitions. And it's not like you can catch a disease," Tamosaitis says.

perfect figures

Men are six times more likely than women to peruse sexually explicit material on the Internet.

More important, by taking advantage of the information online and interacting with some of the denizens there, you can come away with knowledge that can help your relationships off-line.

"It can be healthy if you're using your experiences online to expand your knowledge and understanding of women and what they want," says Phyllis Phlegar, a computer journalist in Colorado Springs and author of *Love Online*. "Some men say they get frank information online that they'd never get from women face-to-face. The barriers can come down online because you can be anonymous—you're usually using an online handle, not your real name."

We won't judge whether online sex is healthy. If it's for you, fine—journey well, be careful out there, and be respectful to yourself and others. Here's some advice on the different approaches available to you.

● Look up the law.
Before you go trolling for cybersex, stop in at the Internet site of the Electronic Frontier Foundation (EFF). EFF is a public interest organization that posts up-to-the-minute news and information about current and pending Internet laws. "It's the safest way to determine what's legal and what's not," says Tamosaitis. You can find EFF at www.eff.org or by doing an Internet search using the keywords "EFF" or "Electronic Frontier."

● Take pictures.
One of the most basic and passive forms of cybersexual activity is to download racy image files from any one of a number of resources—computer bulletin

boards; commercial online services, like Compuserve, Prodigy, or America On-line; and the Internet, the vast international network of computer systems. On the Internet you can find these image banks in a place called Usenet or in sites on the World Wide Web, an image-based version of the Internet. If you're on the Web, you can do a simple search using terms such as "sex" or "photos." You'll find a real smorgasbord, too, from sexy shots of supermodels in swim-suits to serious porn. These days, the racier photo banks may be available only on a subscriber basis. Read the terms of service for each site carefully before deciding to subscribe.

Online Adultery?

She's asleep in the next room. You're not tired—in fact, you're horny as hell. You fire up the computer, make your way to the "singles" chat room, and pretty soon find yourself engaged in heated conversation with "Bunny44D" or "DonnaMatrix" or some other sultry online babe.

Before you step into that computerized parlor, ask yourself one question: Are you being unfaithful?

Online affairs are a kind of gray area—you could make the argument that comparing online sex to adultery is like comparing the "killing" of an opponent in a computer game to murder. After all, it's not like you're actually meeting anyone; it's not like you're exchanging bodily fluids—heck, you're not doing anything wrong. You're just typing, right?

Well . . . that depends.

"It's a question of mindset," says Arlene Goldman, Ph.D., coordinator for the Jefferson Sexual Function Center at Thomas Jefferson University in Philadel-phia. "If you're doing something that you are deliberately concealing from your partner, then you need to rethink what you're doing."

An online affair can be just as dam-aging as flesh-and-blood infidelity, argues Phyllis Phlegar, a computer journalist in Colorado Springs and author of *Love Online*. "What's so injurious about an affair is not that you're having sex with someone else, it's the deception, it's the understanding that you are carrying on something secret and illicit outside of the marriage or relationship."

If you're single, of course, you're a free digital agent; go forth and sow your electronic oats, if that's your choice. But if you're in a relationship and want to

● Get advice.

The Internet and most online services have discussion areas devoted to sex and relationships. On the Internet look for "newsgroups" in the Usenet area. Tamosaitis says you can read questions and answers from hundreds of other people around the world at these newsgroup sites. And if you have a particular query, you can post your own question and get answers from around the world.

"Be sure to read the Frequently Asked Questions or FAQ file for any group first," Tamosaitis says. "If you have a question, chances are someone else has already asked it, and you'll find it there." Posting a question that's readily available in a FAQ is a serious breach of netiquette, and you could incur the wrath of veteran Netsurfers.

Tamosaitis recommends reading a newsgroup for a few weeks before you chip in your own 2 cents. When you think you've figured it out—and don't feel stupid, it can take people months—then you can start interacting.

● Don't catch a virus.

Even though you can't catch a disease from online sex, there's a chance your partner—the computer—could catch a virus. If you don't already own a virus detection program for your home computer, go out and buy one right now. Although many online services routinely check files for viruses, some can slip by. That sweet-looking snapshot of the supermodel you downloaded last night? She could be crawling with software bugs that will make your hard drive sag faster than you can say, "Byte me."

When downloading images, software, or other computer files, always run a virus check on them before you open them. If your program clears them, you're probably okay. But be aware that virus programs can only detect viruses they know about, and new viruses are being created all the time. Always pay attention to any glitches

perform some single-minded experiments in cyberspace, talk to your partner about it—see what her attitude is.

"If she has no problem with it, then explore away," says Nancy Tamosaitis, author of *net.talk* and *The Penthouse Guide to Cybersex*. "But consider that you're taking the first step down a slippery slope. Online affairs are a form of acting out. There's always the possibility that what starts out as a virtual relationship could lead to a real face-to-face meeting. And then you're really over the line."

your computer exhibits—slowing down, crashing, odd characters popping up in files. If you suspect you've downloaded an infected computer file, contact the online service or Internet site administrator you got the image from.

Having Cybersex

Yes, you can have sex from the comfort of your own keyboard. Using an online service and a computer bulletin board or Internet Relay Chat on the Internet, you can communicate with other online folks from around the world by typing messages back and forth to one another. If you find a willing partner, the two of you can go off to a private chat area and have your virtual way with one another.

Here's where you'll need a vital piece of equipment that's hardwired into any human computer—your imagination. Currently, cybersex is pretty low-tech; you simply exchange carnal knowledge with one another until one or both of you is satisfied. Some tech experts say that in the future you'll be able to use "teledildonics," devices that you hook to your erogenous zones and plug into the computer. An online lover would have a similar plug-and-play interface. Instead of typing back and forth, you'd actually be able to "touch" one another by sending signals through the ether that the computer systems and the dildonic devices would convert to tiny electric impulses that would simulate a touch or caress. This would be the safest sex of all—unless, say, a lightning bolt hits your power line while you're hooked up.

perfect figures

Almost half of the people visiting Internet sex sites are married, while another 17 percent are in committed relationships.

Meanwhile, it's all up to your creative verbal skills and your busy little fingers. Heed the following caveats—they'll help keep your adventures online from becoming too frustrating or dangerous.

● Take it slow.

As with any real relationship, if you find someone online who floats your electronic boat and you'd like to pursue her, don't push too hard to get personal too soon.

"Don't ask for or give out phone numbers too soon—and certainly take your time with F2Fs—face-to-face meetings," cautions Phlegar. Remember, you're total strangers—you've never even seen one another. "Take it slow. If you've spent several weeks messaging back and forth, then you might want to move to phone conversations or exchanging pictures. Once you've done that, you may want to meet face-to-face. If you take your time and use common sense, it can really be worth it, though." Phlegar ought to know—she met her husband online.

● Be a voyeur.

If you're a newbie—an online virgin who still doesn't quite understand what he's doing—then don't do anything. Watch and learn.

"Be a lurker," Tamosaitis says. If you're in a chat room, see how other people interact with one another, and figure out the rules of engagement before you start typing.

● Be mysterious.

Some of us get so carried away with the wonder of technology, we forget ourselves.

"It's easy in the heat of discussion to give away bits and pieces of information that people can use against you if they really want to," warns Phlegar. Like a serial killer in a crowded bar, there are nefarious sorts in cyberspace, looking for their next victim. "Before you know it, they can find out where you hide the key to your house, what's in your house, or when you're going on vacation. And you've told them because your defenses are down. Be coy," Phlegar says.

● Be a skeptic.

Take everything you see online with a grain of salt. "There's a classic *New Yorker* cartoon of a dog sitting at a computer. The caption reads: 'On the Internet no one knows you're a dog.' When someone's telling you something online, you have no way of knowing whether it's true," Tamosaitis says.

That can be an asset for you if, for example, you want people to think you're tall, dark, and handsome when you're actually not. But it can be a real downer when you consider that the person you've been chatting to for days could be, despite a feminine online handle, another horny guy like you. "It happens all the time," says Tamosaitis.

SEX TRENDS

PORN IS PROFITABLE

Estimates of total revenues from electronic porn for 1998 are estimated at between $750 million and $1 billion. That figure was expected to be higher for 1999 and 2000.

Let's Talk about Sex

Internet sex sites offer more than smutty photos and prurient products. You can actually get good sex-related advice there. In this article from Computer Life, *writer Jessica Shattuck explains why some people prefer getting sex advice online rather than in a face-to-face meeting with an expert. She also provides a primer on what sites are out there.*

There are many online sites that dispense advice and information about sex in response to user inquiries, such as Dr. Ruth Online, Go Ask Alice, and Swoon. Due to its anonymous nature, the Internet is peculiarly suited to such exchanges, wherein people ask questions too embarrassing to ask face-to-face. Such online sites usually offer a variety of services, such as Q&A, chat rooms, and message boards. Some services are big and professionally run; others, small and eccentric. To insure accountability, some sites require chat and message-board participants to include their e-mail addresses. Most online sex-advice sites are not pornographic; however, some carry online pornography company advertisements that are hot-linked to pornographic sites.

Online advice sites have given rise to a fast, frank, and often funny conversation about the hottest topic on the World Wide Web.

Americans have a strange relationship with sex. We are both obsessively fascinated by and prudishly discreet about everything from lingerie to love letters. While news of Marv Albert's snack habits and the president's late-night liaisons plaster the front pages of even the most respectable newspapers, sex advice columns are relegated to the alternative weeklies. Robert Mapplethorpe's nudes are banned from prominent museums, but photos of nude models sell Calvin Klein fragrances on bus billboards and in magazines everywhere. With paradoxes like these defining the place of sex in our society, it's not surprising that the hot, corporeal topic of sex on the cold, disembodied medium of the Internet has turned into a successful business enterprise and significant force in pop culture.

But while much has been made about the vast amount of server space devoted to pornog-

Before meeting face-to-face with an online acquaintance, exchange photos first. If she resists sending you one, ask why. If you don't find her attractive, end the cyber-romance sooner rather than later.

raphy (from hokey home pages of self-proclaimed porn stars to the slickest offerings of sex industry mainstays), the flip side of sex online has been largely overlooked. In the comfortably anonymous setting of sex advice site chat rooms, Q&As, and message boards, people are taking part in an open, informative, and often racy dialogue about sex—not just the smooth pop-culture fantasy that we see in movies, TV, and advertisements, but the nitty-gritty ins and outs of the real thing.

Lay of the Land

In 1991, Deb Levine, a sex educator at Columbia University, started a simple, text-based health advice site called Go Ask Alice, which quickly evolved into one of the first, if not the first, sex advice site online. "After getting more questions in one week over the Internet than I did in a month of face-to-face workshops, I could see sex and the Internet were a match made in heaven," Levine says.

Never mind that the two are an unlikely pair to say the least. "Sex happens behind closed doors," Levine points out. "We don't really talk about it even with friends and family. The anonymity of being behind a computer screen reduces the embarrassment that surrounds the subject and encourages honest communication."

Since the pioneering days of Go Ask Alice, sex advice sites of all shapes and sizes—from large, professionally run forums to wacky independent rants and raves—have sprung up all over cyberspace. Interactive versions of print advice columns and subsections of online magazines and content providers attract thousands of visitors a day with questions that range from "What's the tantric method?" to "Can Kellogg's corn flakes help me stop masturbating?"

With lots of well-organized material, expansive message boards, chats, and reputable "sexologists" or relationship counselors as hosts, sites like Thrive (which features Ask Delilah, a Q&A column by Deb Levine of Go Ask Alice fame) are homes for raging debates about topics as generally hush-hush as bent penises. As Dr. Ruth Westheimer says, "No Internet will ever replace a good human relationship with face-to-face interaction, but the skill of talking about sex can spill over into real-life relationships."

Online versions of print sex advice columns are also hot spots for the Internet's sex-talk coffee klatches. They tend to be more comprehensive, not to mention immediate, than their paper counterparts. The good ones offer all the extras—archives, message boards, cross-references, and chats—that the Internet can provide. Swoon, for example, a Conde Nast site affiliated with *Details*, *Glamour*, *GQ*, and *Mademoiselle* magazines, features mostly relationship

Everything You Ever Wanted to Know about Sex . . . and Then Some

If you'd like to put your own 2 cents about sex into cyberspace, these sites should get the conversation going.

GO ASK ALICE

**www.columbia.edu/cu/healthwise/
alice.html**

Run by Columbia University, this all-Q&A site is smart, frank, and informative. The Sexual Health section is probably its strongest resource; it offers valuable information (and links) about AIDS, sexually transmitted diseases, and birth control, among other things.

THRIVE

www.thriveonline.com/sex/

The information you'll find here is authoritative, straightforward, and extremely well-organized. Featuring a mix of message boards, links, Q&A columns, and chats, it's one of the most accessible and broadly focused advice sites online. For straightforward talk on topics like penis size and e-mail sex, this is the place.

DR. RUTH ONLINE

www.drruth.com

Real meat-and-potatoes sex advice delivered through Q&A (including a vast archive of past questions asked), a set of suggested links, and daily sex tips complete with videos—of Dr. Ruth speaking, that is. No message boards. If you're looking for kinky or outlandish—don't stop here.

ISADORA ALMAN'S SEXUALITY FORUM

www.askisadora.com

A sprawling site with the same flavor as her open-minded print column, the Sexuality Forum has it all—chat rooms, message board forums, and Q&A. Organization of the site is less than intuitive and the design is downright dull, but for answers to questions like "Do vegans swallow?" this is the place to go.

SWOON

www.swoon.com

Tag-lined the "Dating, Mating, Relating" site, Swoon caters to a younger, more frivolous crowd than Thrive or Dr. Ruth Online. Advice departments include Ian's Makeout Music (recommendations of tunes that'll put you and your date in the mood), Mademoiselle's Sex Q&A, and an ongoing forum titled "Let's Talk about Sex, Baby."

and sex-related advice presented in various creative venues. It logs in around five million page requests a month.

Despite the fact that print advice columns are almost always totally anonymous, people seem to feel a greater sense of security in divulging information online. Isadora Alman, of the popular, nationally syndicated Ask Isadora print sex-advice column, also has a lively online advice site. She remarks, "In the 13 years of my print column, I had maybe three letters on the subject of incest. When I started my bulletin board, I had three the first week! People perceive the online forum as more anonymous and somehow safer than writing letters." That said, a degree of accountability has been built into some advice sites to filter out troublemakers. Isadora, for example, has instituted a system in which you have to enter your e-mail address to participate in many of her chats and message boards.

The Little Guys

Big-name, professional sites and print column alter egos aren't the only places where people are letting it all hang out. Hundreds of amateur online entrepreneurs, chronic advice givers, and wanna-be Dr. Ruths have put up their own Web pages offering advice, chat, and general camaraderie of all flavors. These homespun sites are often more eccentric in approach—from down-home with a religious bent to no-holds-barred, tell it like it is. While they are not individually as heavily trafficked

---

THE COUCH

www.askthecouch.com

Entertaining Q&A with attitude, a rather desolate chat room, and a great set of oft-updated links to titles like "Bent Penis Got You Down?"

SEÑOR SEX

www.senorsex.com

One hundred percent adult content (the ads of Señor Sex's recent sponsors are for over-18-eyes only), this site offers answers to some of the more inspired—if not authentic—questions out there. Chat is nothing short of steamy, and the links are all to porn. This is an "advice" site that walks the line.

AMERICA'S FAVORITE MODERN SEXOLOGIST: DR. AVA CADELL

www.sexpert.com

Citing her background as scullery maid, glamor model, and movie sex symbol (a real Cinderella story), this "doctor" offers the been-there, done-that breed of expertise. Her site includes Q&A, seminars (like How to Turn a Man to Putty in Your Hands), and "sextainment."

(or, in some cases, as well-informed) as the larger sites, looser organization and often negligible supervision end up bringing less mainstream topics to the fore. Q&As at a popular homespun advice site called The Couch involved, for example, topics as disparate as foot fetishism and the possibility of getting pregnant through oral sex(!).

perfect figures

Nearly one in five people who visit Web sex sites say they do so at least some of the time from an office computer.

Most amateur advice sites have no more devious (or explicable) raison d'être than, say, the Jones family home page or the umpteenth Michael Bolton fan site. But there are, of course, plenty of manipulative sites out there that lure potential customers in with promises of advice and then hit them with product solicitations or further "counseling" for a charge. Equally questionable are sites that get advertising dollars from online porn companies—hot links and raunchy ad banners render some of them gateways to pornography rather than a real advice site. Dr. Ava Cadell's site, for example, features some Q&A but, more importantly, "sextainment" and a slew of products, such as an audiotape called "The Soundz of Sex," performed, of course, by the doctor herself.

The Dialogue

The online scene isn't just about asking questions and getting answers. As Isadora Alman puts it, "Many people like giving advice more than taking it." Since the most frequently asked questions tend to be what experts like Deb Levine, Isadora, and Dr. Ruth call the "Am I normal?" type, getting feedback from fellow surfers can be even more reassuring than getting a virtual pat on the shoulder from a professional. Dr. Ruth might not come out and tell you that prancing around your apartment in nothing but a fanny pack and goggles is peculiar, but pose that question on an Internet message board, and the feedback will most likely provide a better litmus test for what potential dates might think.

Of course, the line between looking for sex advice and looking for sex can be a fuzzy one on the Net. Chat room and message board conversation often strays from intellectual discussion of the topic at hand to more amorous dialogue, which can be informative in its own way. One of Thrive's message boards on breast size, for example, had plenty of theorizing on the pros and cons of plastic surgery—peppered with sexy descriptions and the occasional offer to "judge" the pair in question via an e-mailed snapshot or two.

But as Dr. Ruth, the first lady of sex talk, insists, "The Internet can help people become sexually literate. The questions they're asking and conversations they're having with each other online should become stepping stones for carrying this dialogue out in real life." This may be a tall order. But whether or not the open discussion of sex online leads to the face-to-face conversations Americans have traditionally avoided, there's no question that the Internet's cold web of wires has given a surprisingly full voice to the favorite taboo topic of all time.

SEX WARS

"I VISITED YOUR WEBSITE. IS THAT REALLY YOUR PENIS?"

HELP ONLINE

LITERATE SMUT

The online magazine Nerve offers a free
collection of essays, erotic fiction, views of books
and films, and links to other sex sites.
www.nerve.com

THE POOP ON PORN STARS

For answers to such probing questions as how much money porn actors
make or what porn stars have died, check out the Adult Movie FAQ.
www.rame.net

GOOEY GIRLS

If your idea of a sexy woman is one dipped in mud, chocolate,
or other gooey toppings, take a look at Messy Fun.
www.messyfun.com

AERIAL SEX

For stories on sex acts in the sky, visit the Mile-High Club.
www.milehighclub.com/tales

Love, Lust, and the Internet

An Interview with Deb Levine

Your eyes lock across the steamy atmosphere of a busy nightclub, the music throbbing in your veins. You press forward through the throngs of dancing couples until you are face-to-face, her perfume and your cologne intermingling with the scents of desire and sweat. The tension hangs in the air between you, but finally, you cross the interminable last inches separating your lips and hers, and you melt into a kiss made molten with passion and urgency. . . .

Except you won't have to worry about lipstick stains because your encounter was strictly electronic, an erotic meeting between two horny souls on the Internet.

It's called cybersex. And just like in the real world, sex is often preceded by dating. It may seem odd to imagine meeting someone and forming the start of a romance online, but it is possible. In fact, in some respects, it can even be advantageous to meeting anonymous people in bars or calling up women who advertise in the personal ads of newspapers.

Deb Levine knows all about the topics of cyberdating and cybersex. She is the author of The Joy of Cybersex: A Guide for Creative Lovers. *Also, for 5 years before she wrote the book, she was answering questions about sex and relationships on the World Wide Web, starting with a site that she developed at Columbia University called Go Ask Alice. More recently, she has built and maintained two Web sites at Thrive, an online health magazine, while creating her online personality of sex advice columnist Delilah. She is also the sexuality expert at Planned Parenthood's Teenwire Web site.*

MAN'S GUIDE: I guess the first question to ask here is, what is the fundamental difference between cyberdating and cybersex aside from the fact that you only use one hand to type when you are performing the latter?

LEVINE: Personally, I actually hate the "one-handed typing" line because it is not true. It is not what you do.

MAN'S GUIDE: Okay, so explain to me what cybersex really is about.

LEVINE: It is a variety of different things. But most commonly, people will enter into private chat rooms, and they will take turns typing to each other what they would like to do to the other person sexually and how they are feeling. But one person types for a while and the other person reads, and then the other person types.

Another form of cybersex is on the bulletin boards, where various individuals take turns telling erotic stories, but to a larger group of people than in the first type of cybersex. And what happens is, one person may start an erotic story, and someone else may come in later and write another component of the story, and many people are reading this ongoing tale.

Personally, I like to expand the definition of cybersex beyond just those two things, to include all of the sexual and erotic information you can find on the Internet.

> **"When men are pretending to be women . . . , you can pick up on that very quickly because their language is highly sexualized. And that is just not the way most women talk."**

MAN'S GUIDE: Everything from practical sex advice sites to pornographic sites, and anything in between?

LEVINE: Exactly.

MAN'S GUIDE: Is the primary purpose of cybersex just to achieve titillation, or to achieve sexual gratification?

LEVINE: Most people are masturbating.

MAN'S GUIDE: Okay. Let me play devil's advocate here. Certainly, I have partaken of my share of visits to porno sites. But if going online is your major way of meeting people or getting sexual gratification, what does that say about you? Why go online when there are women out there in the real world?

LEVINE: Well, the first thing we would have to do is to separate out cybersex from cyberdating, which I have not really talked about yet.

People go online for cyberdating for a variety of reasons. One reason might be that you want to meet someone, but you live in an isolated place, or you are very busy and you don't have time to go out and socialize very much. The Internet provides an easy way to get to know new people. It is simple. It is quick. I actually encourage people to use the dating services online because they can meet people online and then, in a month or so, take it off-line to carry on a real-time relationship.

When it comes to cybersex, I think of that more as sexual exploration. It is just another tool, like pornographic magazines, adult videos, topless bars, and so on. It is another place to explore your sexuality.

But the great advantage of sex on the Internet is that you have complete anonymity. You are in your own home, and your name and face are never attached to what you do unless you choose to disclose them. If you go into a video store and rent a porno movie or you buy a nudie magazine, your face is attached to the purchase.

MAN'S GUIDE: Is there a downside to cybersex and cyberdating?

LEVINE: There is definitely a downside. It would be naive to think there is not.

The way that I think about the whole phenomenon is to compare it to television. In the 1940s, not everyone had TVs in their homes. Now, almost everyone has them, and a lot of people have more than one in the house. But you make a choice about how much you are going to watch TV. As more and more people buy home computers, it will be commonplace for people to spend time on the Internet. You have to decide whether you are going to use the Internet as a tool to enhance your life or whether you are going to use it as an escape from life.

In my book, I talk about turning off the computer to bring what you learned on the Internet into your real life. I see the Internet as a tool to engage. If it becomes a substitute for interaction with human beings, it is a problem.

MAN'S GUIDE: When you are cyberdating, how do you break the ice online? Isn't it in some ways harder to distinguish yourself electronically? After all, no one can see your smile online.

LEVINE: Actually, I think the Internet is a great place to practice your dating skills. You can try out your lines on the Internet before you take a chance on them in the real world. Maybe you go into a chat room and see what seems to be a feminine screen name, and you say,

"Hey, haven't I seen you here before?" If she types, "Bug off," maybe you need to work on some new lines.

The Internet can be a sort of testing ground. You can even exit the chat room and come back on with another screen name to try again with the same woman but a different line. It is a great practice arena for shy people.

MAN'S GUIDE: But aren't there way too many shy guys and not enough shy girls? Isn't it like the personal ads in newspapers, where there is a serious dearth of women? Isn't it true that the ladies can pick and choose among the many available men, but the men have few opportunities to connect with someone?

LEVINE: Yes, it definitely is a woman's world out there in cyber-dating and personal ads. That may change significantly over the years, and it is changing in little ways now, but it is a problem. The best on-line dating services have a ratio of four men to one woman. Most services have ratios that are more like 10 to 1 or 15 to 1.

For this very reason, I give men different advice than I do women for using online dating services. For example, men can put an ad online, but that is not as important a factor as it is for women. For men, the most important thing is perfecting responses to ads from women who seem attractive or interesting. You cannot just craft a formulaic response to all ads, because that will show through very clearly. You have to respond to something very specific that the woman wrote in her ad. You have to put your personality into the response so it is not just "This is who I am." You really need to write with your heart and mind. In a sense, the Internet has brought back courtship.

> **" You have to decide whether you are going to use the Internet as a tool to enhance your life or whether you are going to use it as an escape from life. "**

A lot of people who say that they have trouble when they meet someone face-to-face are able to go online and really express themselves without any judgments about what they look like, what job they have, and how they fit into society. They have the chance to express their inner selves through words.

MAN'S GUIDE: So we're bringing back the nearly lost art of love letters.

> **LEVINE:** Exactly. That is another comparison I make. And I feel there is a certain sweetness in that.

MAN'S GUIDE: Whether in cybersex or cyberdating, how do you weed out people who aren't who they say they are, whether it is men pretending to be women, women who give utterly fabricated descriptions, or other situations along those lines?

> **LEVINE:** It is usually very obvious. When men are pretending to be women, for example, you can pick up on that very quickly because their language is highly sexualized. And that is just not the way most women talk.
>
> My advice is that if you are not sure whether or not people are who they say they are, trust your instincts. If you are going out to interact with other people on the Net, take your common sense with you. If you have an inkling that the person you are chatting with online is hugely overweight and hasn't left the couch in 20 years, you are probably right.

MAN'S GUIDE: That would certainly be a critical issue in cyberdating. But if you are going the cybersex route, does it even matter if it is a dude on the other end of the connection?

> **LEVINE:** Perfect question. Because that is the difference between cyberdating and cybersex. If you are going online for cyberdating and you are looking for a relationship, then you use the Internet more like any other form of personal ad. And to be honest, the Internet versions tend to be higher-end personal ads because most of the people who are online tend to be highly educated, they make enough money to afford a home computer, and they are often in professional careers. So you are getting a pretty sophisticated group of people out there for dating.
>
> As far as cybersex, the truth is that if you are going out there for sexual exploration, it does not really matter who is on the other end. Because what it is all about is getting turned on by the person in your imagination.

Remember that your imagination is the greatest asset that you bring to the Internet. When you are using videos or magazines, you are, in a sense, being told what to get turned on by. But on the Internet, it is more like erotic storytelling, where you create a lot of the images and action in your head. You could imagine Raquel Welch at the other end even though it really might be a wrinkly old woman who is typing away. But it doesn't matter because you are getting turned on in your own mind.

MAN'S GUIDE: So you meet someone you like online. Maybe you've even gotten intimate in a virtual sense. Do you have any advice on how to arrange for a nice, safe, pressure-free meeting face-to-face?

LEVINE: Behave as if you are going on any other blind date. First off, that means you want to pick a public place to meet. Don't meet at your home or her home.

When you go into that public place, I would suggest telling the staff that you are on a blind date, because usually they will watch out for you. They will often take care to be a little more sensitive to what is going on.

Also, do tell somebody where you are going just in case, for any reason, you need someone to provide you with an excuse or an escape route.

One other thing for the first meeting: Plan something casual, like having a drink or getting some coffee. Don't necessarily plan dinner, coffee, movie, and everything else. Plan something short in which you meet for maybe 45 minutes to an hour to get to know each other.

MAN'S GUIDE: Is it feasible or, for that matter, desirable to keep the relationship perpetually online?

LEVINE: There are people who have regular cybersex with the same person online, kind of like a casual affair. I don't think that is necessarily a problem.

On the other hand, if you are looking for a partner in life, having an online relationship is not going to get you to that goal. Relationships develop differently online then they do in real life. Online, they tend to develop much faster because people share more personal information about themselves much more quickly then they do face-to-face. That is partly due to the anonymity of the medium. So the relationship can ante up very quickly, and you can get emotionally involved with this person online. If you are never going to take it offline, I think it puts you too much in fantasy and it takes away from your being able to develop face-to-face relationships.

MAN'S GUIDE: How does the track record of cyberspace stack up against real-world activities such as answering traditional personal ads or letting friends fix you up on blind dates?

LEVINE: That is a great question, but I really don't think we know yet. And this is the reason why: Most people right now are still too embarrassed to say that they met online. I know many couples who have met online who are together right now; and when people ask how they met, they always talk about their first face-to-face meeting. They do not usually tell you about their courtship on the Internet, and they do not admit to using online dating services. It just isn't socially acceptable yet.

> **" The Internet is dangerous because (married) people don't have a sense of shame that they are doing something wrong to their partner. "**
>
> —John Gray, author of *Men Are from Mars, Women Are from Venus*

MAN'S GUIDE: Maybe this next question is a bit on the technical side, but one of the purported benefits of cybersex is its safety, because you cannot get an STD—a sexually transmitted disease. While you may not be worrying about your private parts, what about your computer parts?

LEVINE: (Long pause)You are not going to believe where my mind just went. And I won't tell you.

MAN'S GUIDE: I can imagine.

LEVINE: So you are talking about computer viruses?

MAN'S GUIDE: Yeah. Computer viruses as opposed to STDs. Can a malicious cybersex hacker-type person turn your hard drive into a limp one?

LEVINE: That's an interesting question. No one has asked me that one yet. Well, it is true that cybersex is definitely safe sex as far as STDs go.

MAN'S GUIDE: No argument there.

LEVINE: As far as computer viruses, there is some very standard advice on that front. First of all, never download a file that has ".exe" in the file name, unless it is coming from somebody you know well and trust. If it is some fun little item that a person you met online is sending to you, and it has a ".exe" extension, you should not download it. Those tend to be the files that execute the big viruses that make you have to rebuild your whole hard drive.

In general, it is mostly about downloading files wisely. Also, take the time to make sure you have up-to-date virus-protection software on your computer.

> " Statistically, the odds of really connecting with a suitable person online are slightly better than if you're just out meeting people in public. "
>
> —Esther Gwinnell, M.D., author of *Online Seductions: Falling in Love with Strangers on the Internet*

MAN'S GUIDE: So, much like with real-time sex, make sure you have protection with you.

LEVINE: You got it.

MAN'S GUIDE: I know that one of the great advantages of the Internet, sexually speaking, is that if you have one or more kinks or fetishes, it is so much easier to find people who share your interests and to find sites that cater to your predilections.

LEVINE: That's definitely true.

MAN'S GUIDE: Is that the primary sexual benefit of the Internet, or is the Net a place where "vanilla sex" can coexist with the exotic, the kinky, and maybe even the downright repulsive?

LEVINE: It is the latter. "Vanilla sex" definitely coexists with some of the wilder and kinkier stuff. But if you are interested in a kink, or there is someone you know who is into something different and you don't really understand it, the Internet is a great resource. It is a great place to find out about fetishes without experiencing any pressure to do something you are not comfortable with. If you have a fetish, it is a great place to find others who have the same fetish.

MAN'S GUIDE: Any parting advice?

LEVINE: Yes. My theme song is "Do not use a computer as a substitute for real-life love and intimacy." Computers and the Internet are tools to enhance real-life intimacy, but they are not substitutes. Nothing can substitute for physical touch and being close to a person.

QUICKIES

TOO MUCH OF A GOOD THING

Eight percent of people perusing sex sites on the Internet were found to be at risk for sexual compulsion problems, a 7-week study concluded. The results were published in *Professional Psychology: Research and Practice*, a journal published by the American Psychological Association. By contrast, an estimated 5 percent of the general population has sexual compulsivity problems.

In a questionnaire completed by 9,177 Internet users, 92 percent said they spend less than 11 hours a week in online sexual pursuits. It's the other 8 percent who could develop problems, according to the study's authors.

Most people said they use sexual material on the Internet as a source of entertainment more than for sexual release and reported that online experiences were satisfying, but not all that arousing, according to the study.

NOOKIE ON THE NET

A mobile brothel in Austria is using the Internet to boost business. Vienna Erotik Taxi and the Sweet Dreams escort and modeling agency lets clients choose from 40 women (and a handful of men) ages 19 to 40, who are pictured on its Web site. Customers can then reserve a woman via the Internet, or the old-fashioned way—by telephone. For $250 an hour, you get a 26-foot stretch limo complete with darkened windows, TV, beer and wine, porn videos, condoms—and of course, a woman.

The company's manager said most clients are businessmen who use the service to pick them up at the airport or transport them around the city between appointments.

DANNI'S HARD DRIVE THRIVES

One of the most successful operators of a sex online site is nude model and dancer Danni Ashe. Her all-woman-operated Danni's Hard Drive has been serving up nude photos, video sex channels, and sex e-zines since 1995. The site—which costs $14.95 a month for full access—has 25,000 paying members and five million hits a month. That averages to six hits per paying member each day. Now that's hardcore.

YOU'VE GOT ... A DATE

The Tom Hanks/Meg Ryan flick *You've Got Mail* inspired a weeks-long contest in a Singapore shopping center in which 60 contestants had to try to convince local celebrities—online—to go out with them. The winner's prize was fitting: a gala Valentine's Day screening of the movie with the celebrity date.

MOST POPULAR PORN

The most popular Internet porn site that costs you money to look at is Kara's Adult Playground, www.karasxxx.com. The most popular free site is PornCity, www.porncity.net. We're not recommending or endorsing either—just reporting facts.

FAVORITE THREE-LETTER WORD

"Sex" is the most popular search topic in search engines, with as many as 30 percent of online users visiting sex-oriented Web sites.

DEAR DR. MANLY

Q: *Okay. So I have an Internet connection. How do I lose my virtual virginity?* *How do I engage in cybersex?*
—H. T. R., Woody Creek, Colorado

A: First thing I want to suggest is that you wear a condom. That way, you can avoid catching any computer viruses.

Sorry. I was just taking advantage of your newbie status. You don't have to wear a condom, of course—at least not for protection from viruses. May not be a bad idea if you intend to go all the way while at the keyboard.

Some folks find cruising in sexual virtual reality boring. Others find cybersex a safe, healthy way to try out risqué fantasies. Cybersex, quite simply, is anonymous mutual masturbation via the Internet. I'm not going to advise it or discourage it. Is it healthy?

"Although it can't replace the intimacy of real sex, Internet sex can be a gratifying source of stimulation and a safe way to experience pleasure without risk or anxiety," says Michael Seiler, Ph.D., a certified sex therapist and codirector of the Phoenix Institute in Chicago.

I, personally, have never done the deed, or at least I won't admit it here if I have, so I turned to some more knowledgeable folks to answer your query.

"What would be a good first step?" my staff asked Cleo Odzer, Ph.D., author of *Virtual Spaces: Sex and the Cyber Citizen*. She suggested skipping the fancy sounds and graphics and starting with an old-fashioned, text-based virtual world called a MOO (short for *Multi-user-domain Object Orientation*). To reach Lambda MOO, one of the largest of these free-standing spots, point your little browser to www.moo.mud.org and follow the directions.

MOOs can be a little confusing at first. Hell, what isn't, besides ice cream? If you're patient enough to read the help screens, you'll be meeting people in about 30 minutes. That's pretty quick for a first date, huh? With cybersex, you can have a dozen one-night stands in one night. I'd say, "Don't try that at home, kids," except it seems that's probably about the only place you should try it. I wouldn't be engaging virtual vixens on the office computer system or at the library if I were you.

You ready to boogie? Want to mix and mingle? It's as easy as one, two, three. Take Dr. Odzer's advice.

❶ Be yourself.

The same things that make you charming and irresistible during happy hour work likewise online. "Show interest in the people you meet, ask questions, and give them plenty of attention and you'll do fine."

❷ Spin a fantasy.

Because Internet sex is anonymous, it provides the perfect opportunity to experiment with role-playing and fantasies that you'd never seriously consider in real life. Just keep in mind that others may be playing games, too: That hot-to-trot miniskirt-clad waitress you meet online may actually be a beer-bellied truck driver with tube socks. I don't know about you, but I hate waking up next to beer-bellied truck drivers in tube socks.

❸ Use cyberactions instead of words.

As you'll discover, there are two ways to communicate with your online partner. You can say things to her, or you can "do" things to her by issuing a special command called *emote* that makes your words appear as an action. "The key to rich cybersex is lots of actions. Instead of reading your statement 'I'm taking off your shirt,' her screen will show, 'Your partner removes your shirt.'"

When you're ready to move on to other MOOs, you can find a whole list by pointing your browser to www.chaco.com/lists/type/moo.html.

Dr. Manly is a fictional character.
The actual advice was provided by a variety of
medical doctors and other qualified experts.

---

credits

index

•T